ENGLISH PROSE STYLE

HERBERT READ

☆

ENGLISH
PROSE
STYLE

PANTHEON BOOKS

NEW YORK

The Library of Congress cataloged the first printing of this title as follows:

Read, Herbert Edward, 1893–1968

    English prose style. [New Ed.] New York, Pantheon Books [°1952]
         216 p. 22 cm.

    [1. English language—Style. I. Title.]
    PE1421.R35   1952a   808   52–9671

HISTORICAL NOTE

ORIGINALLY PUBLISHED IN 1928, this book has been in continuous demand ever since, and only minor revisions were made in the successive reprints. In the summer of 1947 I was invited to give a course of lectures at the School of English, Kenyon College, Ohio, and this provided an opportunity for a complete reconsideration of a subject I had first treated twenty years earlier. Though I did not find it necessary to alter the general plan of the book, several of the chapters have been recast, and additional specimens, generally of a more recent date, have been inserted either in the body of the text, or in a special Appendix.

H. R.

1952

CONTENTS

PAGE

INTRODUCTION ix
Prose and Poetry – pure prose – interest.

PART I

COMPOSITION

CHAPTER

I WORDS 3
Quality – sound – echo – onomatopoeia – alliteration – association – congruity – suggestion – use and
disuse – jargon – affectation.

II EPITHETS 15
Appropriateness – necessity – complexity – metaphorical overtones.

III METAPHOR AND OTHER FIGURES OF SPEECH . . 23
Limited function in prose – simple comparison –
simile – analogy – illumination and decoration –
riddles – kennings – other types of periphrasis –
personification.

IV THE SENTENCE 33
Its unity – construction – order of words – the
period – balance – punctuation – rhythm – the
aphorism.

V THE PARAGRAPH 52
Unity – liveliness – dignity – rhythm – configuration.

VI ARRANGEMENT 66
Instinctive: the essay – required effect – exordium.
Constructional: scaffolding – the novel.

PART II

RHETORIC

VII EXPOSITION 87
Reasoning – arrangement of ideas – emotional bias
– system

CHAPTER PAGE

VIII NARRATIVE 97
Active and passive – visual actuality – speed – concreteness – trimness – history – biography – travel.

IX FANTASY (FANCY) 125
Imagination and Fancy – objectivity and abritrariness – the fairy tale – utopias – possibilities of fantasy.

X IMAGINATION OR INVENTION – – – – – 136
Primary and secondary imagination – romanticism and classicism – decoration – duration – density.

XI IMPRESSIONISM 145
Sensation or emotion plus thought – intuition – emotion and rhythm – simulated moods – mysticism – sincerity – empathy – the interior monologue.

XII EXPRESSIONISM 158
Idiosyncrasy – sensibility – sentimentality – humours – fluidity.

XIII ELOQUENCE 167
Elegance – wit – irony – words and ideas – the theme – false eloquence – persuasion – character.

XIV UNITY 180
Unity and predominating passion – the strain of address – taste – corporate sense – pattern – discipline – uniformity – universality.

APPENDIX. 195
Additional passages for comparison and analysis.

CHRONOLOGICAL LIST OF THE PRINCIPAL AUTHORS QUOTED 211

INDEX 213

INTRODUCTION

. . . the other harmony of prose.

Dryden

Before beginning an enquiry into the nature of English prose style there are two very general questions which the reader might ask and which I must answer: what, in the abstract, is meant by Prose? and, what, in the abstract, is meant by Style? 'In the abstract'—that is to say, *a priori*, without the prejudice of particular examples, and as a preliminary to a more minute analysis.

There are two ways of distinguishing Prose from Poetry. One is merely external or mechanical: it defines Poetry as a mode of expression which is strictly related to a regular measure or metre; Prose as a mode of expression which avoids regularity of measure and seeks the utmost variety of rhythm. But as to the poetic half of this distinction it is obvious that it only accounts for Verse, and every reader knows that Verse is not necessarily Poetry—that Verse, indeed, is merely an outward *form* which may, or may not, be inspired with poetic feeling. Verse, therefore, is not an essential thing; it is merely a species of rhythm, and, in the abstract, a static, academic 'norm'. No such 'norm' is ever postulated for Prose; there is therefore no exact opposition between Prose and Verse. We are compelled to take into account the more essential sense of the word Poetry.

The distinction between Poetry and Prose is not and never can be a formal one. No minute analysis and definition of 'feet', no classification of metre, no theory of cadence or quantity, has ever resolved the multiple rhythms of Poetry and the multiple rhythms of Prose into two distinct and separable camps. The most that can be said is that Prose never assumes a regular, even beat, but this is a negative criterion of no practical value. That there is a surface distinction between Poetry and Prose must, I think, be admitted; but it is like the surface distinction between sea and land—one is liquid and wavy, the other solid and indented; but why distinguish the surfaces of things when the things themselves are so palpably different?

The distinction between Poetry and Prose is a material distinction; that is to say, since we are dealing with mental things, it is a psychological distinction. Poetry is the expression of one form of mental activity, Prose the expression of another form.

Poetry is creative expression: prose is constructive expression. That is perhaps a summary way of expressing a distinction we may hope to establish as we proceed. But 'creative' is a word to be used with discretion in a critical vocabulary, and it is certainly not the antithesis of 'constructive'. There is, however, a valuable distinction to be made between mental activities that take in impressions to condense and concentrate them; and mental activities that merely disperse impressions from the store of memory—the activities of *condensation* and *dispersion*. Poetry seems to be generated in the process of condensation; prose in the process of dispersion. Ezra Pound has pointed out that the German word for poetry (*Dichtung*) expresses this characteristic of poetry (*dichten* means 'to condense' in the chemical sense, as well as 'to compose' a poem).[1]

Condensation leads to transformation. The mental processes at work in imagination (a latent activity) are obscure, but in poetic experience the words are not merely drawn from the store of memory, as from a dictionary: they are born or re-born at the moment of expression.

The words are, in Bergsonian phraseology, a becoming; they develop in the mind *pari passu* with the development of the thought. There is no time interval between the words and the thought. The thought is the word and the word is thought, and both the thought and the word are Poetry.[2]

[1] *The ABC of Reading* (New Directions).

[2] Compare generally the ideas of Leone Vivante on this subject, in his works *Intelligence in Expression* (Eng. trans. 1925) and *Notes on the Originality of Thought* (Eng. trans. 1927); note particularly this paragraph from the first-named work:

'Constructive' implies ready-made materials; words stacked round the builder, ready for use. Prose is a structure of ready-made words. Its 'creative' function is confined to plan and elevation—functions these, too, of Poetry, but in Poetry subsidiary to the creative function.

Does it follow that Poetry is solely an affair of words? Words have their resonances and associations, and it is difficult to deny poetic significance to a single word, like Shakespeare's 'incarnadine', much less to a cluster of two or three words, like 'shady sadness', 'incense-breathing Morn', 'a peak in Darien', 'soft Lydian airs', 'Mount Abora' or 'star-inwrought'.[1]

Prose, too, is an affair of words, but not of words in themselves, but only of words as so much dead material given life, *which life is rhythm.* Paradoxical as it may seem, we now see that Poetry may inhere in a single word, in a single syllable, and may therefore in an .extreme case be without rhythm; Prose, however, does not exist except in the phrase, and the phrase always has rhythm of some kind.

This distinction between Poetry and Prose may seem a subtle matter; it may seem to be one difficult of application. It may be asked: how are we to recognize originality when we see it? I frankly resort to a personal doctrine. Observation convinces me that in Poetry, as in every other art, the people who recognize the art are few, and that these few recognize it intuitively. Just as the ear in some natural and innate way reacts to melody, and the eye to colour, so the intelligence reacts to poetry. I do not profess to explain these instinctive

'In prose the period is more subject to rules, whether in the collocation of words, in the structure of the phrase, or in the use of words; i.e. it is subject to conventional usage. Uncommon words can hardly be introduced; it seems wayward and arbitrary to use them, and in general we cannot depart from common usage—while in poetry a like "transgression", a like inversion or the uncommon use of a word passes, as such, unobserved. And this is due to the boldness which words have in poetry—because their meaning is entirely present, their every reason or value is present and active in them, in every moment of expression; and because, on the other hand, the very material, as it were, calls forth activity to form itself according to all its intrinsic values and forms and, being one with activity, is itself concept.'

[1] The linguistic aspects of poetry have been brilliantly discussed by Elizabeth Sewell in *The Structure of Poetry* (London, Routledge and Kegan Paul, 1951). Cf. especially I, 4 ('Words as Individuals') and I, 5 ('Words as Individuals in Ordinary Life and Poetry').

reactions; they are probably constitutional, but I see no reason to suppose that because words, rather than musical scales, are the medium of normal communication between men, therefore the art of words, whether poetry or prose, is in any degree made more accessible to ordinary men than the art of music. All art is difficult, remote, subtle; and though in the process of catharsis it may act as a release for emotions that are common to all men, yet in this process art is to many of us an unknown quantity. That is why the artist among us is so dangerous; he is always playing with social dynamite and is therefore banished from any ideal Republic. Only realistic philosophers, such as Aristotle, see that he has his uses.

The answer to the first question therefore is: that the difference between Poetry and Prose is a qualitative difference that has its effects in expression, but that these effects cannot be measured quantitatively, but only by the exercise of an intuitive judgment.

The second question is simpler. To define the varieties of English prose style is the purpose of the chapters that follow. But is there an abstract entity, an absolute or 'pure' prose style, to which all styles approximate, or against which all styles are judged? I think there probably is, but it follows from my definition of prose that such a style can never be exactly defined. But there are many negative restrictions—such as the one I have mentioned, that the rhythm of prose is never regular, and such as the rules against archaisms, metaphor, affectation, sentimentality, confusion, and inappropriate accent—and if all these restrictions are borne in mind at one and the same time we do arrive at a negative definition of perfection. But it remains a negative definition, with all the defects and uncertainties consequent on such definitions. Nevertheless, we can ask ourselves, if only for amusement, which among our prose writers come nearest to this indefinite ideal. We perceive immediately that of very few authors can it be said that they had no insidious faults. Take this test only: of how many writers, in the search for an appropriate and representative passage, could we trust to the offering of any page we opened at? Obviously, only of the consistently good and the consistently bad. But which writer can we claim to be consistently himself and consistently good? I have had some experience in the 'dipping audit' which I have applied to English prose writers during the preparation of this work, and only about three or four names occur to me as possible. There is Berkeley, there is Swift, there is Sterne, there is Southey, and, if modern examples must be quoted, there is W. H. Hudson and Bernard Shaw. Yet in Berkeley I know there are terrible wastes, as in the *Querist* and in *Siris* (where, too, there are the greatest delights); in Swift there are occasional lapses, due to anger or weariness; in Sterne the conversational ease is, after all, an instrument of limited range (it avoids what it cannot compass); in Southey there are forlorn failures of interest—an objection I would also hold against W. H. Hudson and Bernard Shaw. Swift is the only one of these prose writers in whom we may confidently expect no organic and inevitable lapses. The prose style of Swift is unique, an irrefrangible instrument of clear, animated, animating and effective thought. English prose has perhaps attained here and there a nobler profundity, and here and there a subtler complexity; but never has it maintained such a constant level of inspired expression.

The continued vitality of Swift's style is a great consolation to the theorist. It is true that this vitality is maintained largely in the nursery, but there is comfort in that thought too; the unsophisticated child is often a touchstone for falsity of any kind. Nor need we be dismayed by the fact that Swift shares his popularity with Bunyan and Defoe; the same qualities contribute to the same result. And yet the honest critic must recognize that in all these cases there is the added element of *interest*. It is curiosity that takes the average reader to a book; it is interest that sustains the effort of reading. A book is a mirror which the weak-kneed and nose-led part of humanity pick up in order to see their own reflections; the stalwarts read only when they are tired or sick, and so for the moment reduced to the commoner level. Looking into a book, the common reader expects to find other people, other environments, imaginary events; but always he is among these others, one of them, sharing their adventures. Does he stop to consider the style in which the book is written? Does he realize that there is such a thing as style? Is he aware of the hopes and fears of that unknown entity, the author? These are rhetorical questions, and need no answer. The common reader is a passive recipient of pleasures for which he pays a fair market price, when other pleasures are exhausted. It is not for the critic to adopt a lofty attitude about such a state. The question of values must be left to the moralist; and otherwise there is only literature, which is also the satisfaction of some form of appetite.

This book is therefore not concerned with the criticism of literature, which would involve not only style, but also this element of interest.[1] It is not primarily concerned with the reader's point of view, but with the writer's. I take the need for self-expression as granted, and seek only to formulate the means. In the historical fate of that expression I am only concerned to find a confirmation of my diagnosis.

I have been greatly guided by the classics of my subject, Aristotle's *Rhetoric* and his *Poetics*; and to two modern works of reference, Sir Henry Craik's *English Prose Selections* and Mr. H. W. Fowler's *Dictionary of Modern English Usage*, I have frequently had recourse, and freely acknowledge my indebtedness to their useful and suggestive pages. I also desire to express my gratitude to all those publishers who have concurred so readily in my making quotations, sometimes extensive, from works still copyright. Where such quotations occur, the name of the publisher is always given in a footnote.

---

[1] But cf. the quotation from Charles Maurras on p. xvi.

It is a natural, simple, and unaffected speech that I love, so written as it is spoken, and such upon the paper as it is in the mouth, a pithy, sinewy, full, strong, compendious and material speech, not so delicate and affected as vehement and piercing. Rather difficult than tedious, void of affection, free, loose, and bold, that every member of it seems to make a body; not pedantical, nor friar-like, nor lawyer-like, but rather downright, soldier-like.

FLORIO's *Montaigne*

No criticism can be instructive which descends not to particulars, and is not full of examples and illustrations.

DAVID HUME, *Of Simplicity and Refinement in Writing*

What does the mind enjoy in books? Either the style or nothing. But, someone says, what about the thought? The thought, that is the style, too.

CHARLES MAURRAS, *An Essay on Criticism*

It is hardly necessary to adduce proof that the identity of style and meaning is today firmly established.

W. K. WIMSATT, *The Prose Style of Samuel Johnson*

Un esprit médiocre croit écrire divinement; un bon esprit croit écrire raisonnablement.

LA BRUYÈRE, *Les Caractères*

The style of an author should be the image of his mind, but the choice and command of language is in the fruit of exercise.

EDWARD GIBBON, *Autobiography*

All styles are only means of subduing the reader.

T. E. HULME, *Notes on Language and Style*

Style consists in the order and the movement which we introduce into our thought.

BUFFON, *Discourse on Style*

In this way, being the response to man's organized and unceasing cravings for strength, clearness, order, dignity and sweetness, for a life intenser and more harmonious, what man writes comes to be greater than what man is.

VERNON LEE, *The Nature of the Writer*

PART I

COMPOSITION

The art of writing prose may be studied from two points of view. The first of these is concerned with the objective use of language and may properly be called COMPOSITION; *the second or subjective use of language is persuasive in intention and may properly be called* RHETORIC. *By the art of composition alone a certain negative style may be attained, which is remarkable only for its sustained avoidance of the pitfalls of common speech; but for a positive style it is necessary to infuse the composition with those personal elements belonging to the art of rhetoric.*

CHAPTER I

*

Words

WORDS ARE THE UNITS of composition, and the art of Prose must begin with a close attention to their quality. It may be said that most bad styles are to be traced to a neglect of this consideration; and certainly if style is reduced in the last analysis to a selective instinct, this instinct manifests itself most obviously in the use of words.

Words may be treated under various heads, but the first consideration must be given to their *Quality*.

The quality of a word is determined mainly by its vocal sounds, that is, the collocation of its vowels and consonants.

In Prose the primary function of the sound of the isolated word is its expressiveness. It must *mean* the thing it stands for, not only in the logical sense of accurately corresponding to the intention of the writer but also in the visual sense of conjuring up a reflection of the thing in its completest reality. The simplest type of such expressive words are those which still retain in their sound some echo of a sound associated with the thing they connote: for example, *murmur*, *clatter*, *cuckoo*, *grunt*, *hiss*. Such words are called *onomatopoeic*, from the Greek words meaning 'name-making'; and originate in the direct imitation of natural sounds, and of the sounds associated with things. But it would be rash to ascribe any particular virtue to such words on the assumption that they are of a remote origin and primitive vigour; rather, they seem to be comparatively late developments in language, due to a desire to add vitality to expression; that is to say, they are elements of style rather than of speech.[1]

[1] 'Though some echo words may be very old, the great majority are not; at any rate, on looking up the earliest ascertained date of a goodly number of such words in the *New English Dictionary*, I have been struck by the fact of so many of them being quite recent, not more than a few centuries old, and some not even that. To some extent their recent appearance in writing may be ascribed to the general character of the old literature as contrasted with our modern literature,

An extreme example of the use of onomatopoeic words is
found in the fourteenth century poem known as 'The
Harmonious Blacksmiths':

Swarte smekyd smethes smateryd wyth smoke
Dryve me to deth wyth den of here dyntes;
Swech noys on nyghtes he herd men never,
What knavene cry and clateryng of knockes!
The cammede kongons cryen after 'Col! col!'
And blowen here bellewys that al here brayn brestes.
Huf, puf, seith that on, Haf, paf, that other.
Thei spyttyn and spraulyn and spellyn many spelles,
Thei gnauen and gnacchen, thei gronys to-gydere,
And holdyn hem hote with here hard hamers.
Of a bole hyde ben here barm-fellys,
Here schankes ben schakled for the fere flunderys,
Hevy hamerys thei han that hard ben handled,
Stark strokes thei stryken on a stelyd stokke,
Lus! bus! las! das! rowtyn be rowe.
Swech dolful a dreme the devyl it to-dryve!
The mayster longith a lityl, and lascheth a lesse,
Twyneth hem tweyn and towchith a treble;
Tik! tak! hic! hac! tiket! taket! tyk! tak!
Lus! bus! las! das! swych lyf thei ledyn,
Alle clothe-merys, Cryst hem gyve sorwe!
May no man for brenwaterys on nyght han hys rest.

British Museum MS. Arundel, 292, f. 71 b.

A simpler example, showing the inventive occasions of such
words, may be quoted from White's *Selborne*:

The voice of the goose is trumpet-like, and *clanking*..

The marked use of onomatopoeic words is not generally
possible, for they stand only for a limited group of direct
sense perceptions, and do not reflect all the varieties of thought
and feeling involved in even the simplest forms of expression.
Yet the appropriate use of such a word will waken up from
drowsiness the whole of a sentence, as in this example:

which is less conventional, freer in many ways, more true to life in its infinite
variety and more true, too, to the spoken language of every day. . . . In all
languages the creation and use of echoic and symbolic words seems to have been
on the increase in historical times.   If to this we add the selective process through
which words which have only secondarily acquired symbolical value survive at
the cost of less adequate expressions, or less adequate forms of the same words,
and subsequently give rise to a host of derivatives, then we may say that languages
in course of time grow richer and richer in symbolic words.' Jespersen, *Language*,
pp. 410-11 (Macmillan).

But little do men perceive what Solitude is, and how far it extendeth. For a crowd is not company, and faces are but a gallery of pictures, and talk but a *tinkling* cymbal where there is no love.

FRANCIS BACON: *Of Friendship*

Far more important are those words, of which there are many thousands, which, while not formed from the sounds associated with the object named, yet by some subtle combination of vowel and consonant suggest by a seeming appropriateness the quality or kind of the object named.[1] This is perhaps the most important aspect of the problem of style as determined by the choice of words; for a good writer does not select his words by virtue of any pedantic leaning to this or that theory of their origin and proper use (as to whether, for example, they are of Latin or of Anglo-Saxon derivation), but within the limits of accepted meaning, is solely governed by the due measure of expressiveness implied in the syllables of a particular word.

This symbolism of sounds, the suggestive power of various combinations of vowels and consonants, has never been very carefully studied, but certain associations of suggestions may be briefly stated. It is obvious, for instance, that long vowels suggest a slower movement than the shorter vowels, and that vowels which we pronounce by opening the mouth convey the idea of more massive objects; while those which are formed by nearly closing the lips suggest more slight movements or more slender objects. . . . This suggestive power is due partly to direct imitation of natural sounds, but more to the movements of the vocal organs, and their analogy with the movements we wish to describe.

LOGAN PEARSALL SMITH, *The English Language*, pp. 102–3 and 104.[2]

We can perhaps make these distinctions more actual. There are at least three groups, differing in degree of subtlety:

(1) Mere onomatopoeia: *hiss, whirr, cluck, clap, bubble*, etc.
(2) Movement of lips, tongue and teeth to simulate the action described, plus suggestive sound: *blare, flare,*

[1] 'There is no denying . . . that there are words which we feel instinctively to be adequate to express the ideas they stand for, and others the sounds of which are felt to be more or less incongruous with their signification.' Jespersen, *op. cit.* p. 398.

[2] Home University Library (Oxford University Press).

peal, rustle, brittle, whistle, creep, patter, scrabble, puddle, shimmer, shiver, shudder, fiddle, sling, globe, etc.

(3) Sounds not imitative, but suggestive (musical equivalents): *glitter, swoon, mood, sheen, horror, smudge, still (tranquil), womb, jelly,* etc.

The words in the first group are obvious. Those of the second group are a degree more subtle; for example, *blare* and *flare*, where the opening consonants compel the lips to make movements suggestive of the actions implied. *Blare* is comparable with *blast* and *bleat*: the *bl* suggests forceful lipwork. *Flare* recalls *flame* and *flicker*: the *fl* suggests the *fl*apping action of tongues of flame. The vowels in all cases give the onomatopoeic sound. The third group is still subtler: the sound is not imitative, but analogous, or emotionally evocative; the movement merely appropriate.

The selection of the appropriate word from this point of view is a question of individual sensibility, and such sensibility, assuming that we are not born with it, is only to be acquired by attentive reading. To quote such words in a list would be an endless task: *death, flood, roof, torment, creep, ruin, horror, deluge, pomp, tinsel, weep, dark, maid,* are a few that I find on a single page of *Holy Dying*. But even among these few we discover two near synonyms, *flood* and *deluge*, the just and appropriate use of either in the context being a matter of nice discernment. 'The horror of an universal *deluge*' is right; and 'being like the poor sinners at Noah's *flood*' is right—the one, I think, because the epithet 'universal' requires a bed of soft sound on which to fall, and the other because the open sounds of 'Noah's' require a bank of firmness to contain them. But rhythm is also a determining factor in the selection of these and of all other words; and for this reason it is difficult to discern the exact quality of words in isolation. But consider the following passage:

Take away but the pomps of death, the disguises and solemn bugbears, the tinsel, and the actings by candle-light, and proper and fantastic ceremonies, the minstrels and the noise-makers, the women and the weepers, the swoonings and the shriekings, the nurses and the physicians, the dark room and the ministers, the kindred and the watchers; and then to die is easy, ready and quitted from its troublesome circumstances. It is the same harmless thing that a shepherd suffered yesterday, or a maidservant to-day; and at the same time in which you die, in that very night a thousand creatures die with you, some wise men, and many fools; and the wisdom of the first will not quit him, and the folly of the latter does not make him unable to die.

JEREMY TAYLOR: *The Rule and Exercises of Holy Dying*, ch. iii. sec. 7, 4.

Here the particular beauty of the style is achieved, not only by the use of many expressive words like *pomp, bugbear, tinsel, candle-light, fantastic,* but also by the marshalling in the first sentence of many elaborate and high-sounding words, and the sudden contrast of simple commonplace words in the second sentence. Here the rhythm is appropriate; but it is subsidiary in its effect to the right use of particular words.

The use of words is sometimes determined, as to their vocal quality, not singly but in a sequence, as in *Alliteration* and *Euphony.* Here the choice of a particular word will depend on its containing the same letter or sound as its neighbours.

The lingering day draws down to the sun-setting; the herdsmen, weary of the sun, come again with the cattle, to taste in their menzils the first sweetness of mirth and repose.—The day is done, and there rises the nightly freshness of this purest mountain air: and then to the cheerful song and the cup at the common fire. The moon rises ruddy from that solemn obscurity of jebel like a mighty beacon:—and the morrow will be as this day, days deadly drowned in the sun of the summer wilderness.

CHARLES M. DOUGHTY, *Travels in Arabia Deserta*, i.[1]

But the use of alliteration and euphony will be analysed more carefully when we come to discuss the Sentence (Chapter IV). Here we merely note that the word is not selected in perfect liberty, but is governed by the pattern of sound of which it is but a single member.

After sound, the quality of words is most determined by their *associations.* By their continued use in a certain connection words acquire an emotional surcharge of connotation which it is difficult to avoid in contexts where the simple use

[1] Random House.

is intended. Such words are usually descriptive of events or situations which give rise to an excess of emotion or enthusiasm. By their continued association with these excesses, the words are in danger of meaning the excessive state and not the original content, which was determined by an objective and dispassionate use. *Love, death, soul, god, heart, poetic, little, sweet, quaint, passionate, mystic, magic,* are all words which must be approached warily, if a vulgar or sentimental use of them is to be avoided. The words 'love' and 'hearts' in a passage like the following are not used with any definite connotation, but as hypnotic syllables which have only to be used 'lavishly' enough to evoke vague romantic sentiments in the minds for which they are designed:

On a morning like this, with a world full of flowers and singing birds, and a heart full of love (and yet, by a unique paradox, hungry as ever for the love of a slip of a boy with big black eyes and crow-black blackness of hair and skilful hands and a heart overflowing with tenderness, a heart that had given love lavishly as it had received it) Amaryllis stood studying the situation. She did not exactly see how she could be surfeited with love and hungry for love at the same time. She only knew that she was. For one minute she could not think of a thing more to do for the little house of John Guido. . . .
GENE STRATTON-PORTER, *The Magic Garden.*[1]

The surcharge of such words is not always base. There are words that have a magic ring of circumstance which no use can soil, as *honour, glory, courage, victory.* The difficulty in the use of these words is that they require a certain elevation of thought to give them their appropriate setting; and to attempt this elevation without the right equipment of mind and emotion is to risk bathos.

Apart from their sound and association, the choice of words is mainly governed by their *currency* and *congruity.* The state of a language is never constant, and almost every year words lose their life, and new words are born. To be aware of these subtle changes in the growth of a language requires the finest sensibility, and is perhaps peculiarly difficult for those who confine themselves to the reading of classical models.

[1] Doubleday, 1927.

The vitality of writing corresponds in some inexorable way to its contemporaneity, and is nourished not so much by the study of examples, as by the act of living, from which it takes an accent of reality. The history of a word is entirely irrelevant in prose style: its face-value in current usage is the only criterion.

In this sense the grossest form of misusage is due to a certain facetiousness of mood, and results in monstrous antiquarianisms like *howbeit, albeit, anent, anon, maugre, perchance, withal, divers, whit, fain, wot, betoken.* These are easily avoided by anyone of the least literary sensibility, but other words of the same type are due to pedantic opinions which are consciously held and openly defended; their use is determined not by their currency but by the writer's historical bias. This form of literary *Nationalism* leads to the substitution of obsolete or newly coined words of Saxon derivation for current words of Latin or Greek derivation. *Foreword* for *preface* is the typical example; but there are many others, of which *comely, folk, happenings, befall, clad,* are examples in frequent use. There is also a false idea of simplicity involved; the old Saxon words are so sturdy and uncouth, the new Latin words so sophisticated and elegant! An extreme predilection of this sort leads to what is known as 'Wardour Street' English, of which this is perhaps a fair example:

The day after, by the rede of the shepherd-folk, they turned up into the hills again, for they had no wish to raise the country against them; and to say sooth, Sir Godrick was somewhat pensive that he found enmity so far off his own land. So they rode the hills for five days, falling in with few folk, and going slowly because of the rough ways. Thereafter they needed victual, and had been fain of better lodging might they get it; and whereas they saw a fair plain well builded and tilled, with good roads through the same, and knew that this was the nighest way to the Wood Masterless, they turned down thither at all adventure, and found no evil haps there, but that the folk were well enough pleased to make their market of the riders, and had neither fear of them nor harboured enmity against them. Thus then they rode for two days, and at the end of the second day entered a good cheaping-town, unfenced save by timber pales. There they abode a whole day, yet warily, since, though there were no waged men-at-arms in the stead, there went about many stout carles, who all bore long whittles, and looked as if their bills and bows had not been far to seek. But no strife betid.

WILLIAM MORRIS, *The Sundering Flood*.[1]

But this Anglo-Saxon proclivity is not the only type of such error. There is an opposite tendency which takes the form of a *Latinization* of language, and of this style Johnson is perhaps the most outstanding example in our literature. Because our native language is barbarous in its origins it is felt that wherever possible a Latin word should be substituted for a Saxon one, and so we get *commencement* instead of *beginning*, and *termination* instead of *end*. This tendency, which is largely due to the influence of reading Latin authors, is not merely a question of words, but also of the *period* or *cadence* of the sentence, and in this light will be referred to in Chapter IV. Of *Gallicisms* and the introduction of current foreign words generally it is perhaps not necessary to say much: they are universally recognized as a sign of bad taste, especially if they presuppose the knowledge of a foreign language. A few foreign words, such as *cliché*, have no English equivalent and are in current use; and there may be others which are desirable. But except in technical works it will generally be found possible to avoid them. Translated foreign idioms, such as 'leap to the eyes', 'give furiously to think', are usually facetious in intention or vulgar in effect, and should therefore be avoided.

A more recent abuse of words comes under the heading of *jargon*. A pseudo-scientific profundity is given to simple or even obvious statements by translating them into technical phraseology, or merely by latinizing English words. The vulgarization of science, the limitations of technological education, and the practice of foreign-born American writers, are all influences that encourage this tendency. George Orwell once gave an effective parody of the process by translating a sentence from *Ecclesiastes* into modern jargon:

ECCLESIASTES: I returned, and saw under the sun, that the race is not to the swift, nor the battle to the strong, neither yet bread to the wise, nor yet riches to men of understanding, nor yet favour to men of skill; but time and chance happeneth to them all.

[1] Longman.

Objective consideration of contemporary phenomena compels the conclusion that success or failure in competitive activities exhibits no tendency to be commensurate with innate capacity, but that a considerable element of the unpredictable must invariably be taken into account.

Almost any standard work on pyschology or sociology will provide an example that is not a parody. E.g.:

Strength of Instigation to Aggression

The first step in elaborating the basic hypothesis is to restate it in the following quantitative form: the strength of instigation to aggression varies directly with the amount of frustration. The next step is to consider the factors which are responsible for the amount of frustration and therefore also responsible for the strength of instigation to aggression. It is assumed that there are three such factors: the strength of instigation to aggression should vary directly with (1) the strength of instigation to the frustrated response, (2) the degree of interference with the frustrated response, and (3) the number of frustrated response sequences. . . .

(1) *Strength of instigation to the frustrated response.* According to this principle, withdrawal of food from a hungry dog should produce more growling and baring of teeth than similar withdrawal from a satiated dog. . . .

An appeal to common experience gives this proposition an appearance of obvious validity which relevant experimental data are not yet completely adequate to check. Those that are cited here are regarded primarily as further illustrations and not as final proofs. An experiment by Sears and Sears was designed to utilise variations in the strength of a five-months-old baby's hunger instigation as the independent variable. During a three-week period, at two of the four daily feedings, the child's feeding was systematically interrupted by withdrawal of the bottle from the mouth after varying amounts of milk had been taken. With this method, frustration of sucking and eating occurred when the instigation to these acts was of several different strengths. The strength of the aggressive reaction was measured in terms of the immediacy of crying following the withdrawal. When the withdrawal occurred after only 0·5 oz. had been taken, crying began, on the average, after 5·0 seconds; after 2·5 oz. had been taken, the latency was 9·9 seconds; and after 4·5 oz. had been taken, it was 11·6 seconds. These figures indicate that as the child became more nearly satiated, i.e. as the strength of the instigation decreased, frustration induced a less and less immediate aggressive response.

JOHN DOLLARD and Others: *Frustration and Aggression*[1]

[1] Yale University Press.

I shall not consider the quality of words as determined by their individual history, for this is a separate study. It is concerned either with their origin and formation (philology) or with their varieties of meaning (semantics). But undoubtedly the ancient origin of certain words has some bearing on their expressive quality. *Ox, wolf, wheel, axle, night, star, snow, wind* and *thunder* are examples of such words, but rather than ascribe their expressiveness to their antiquity it would perhaps be more exact to explain their survival by their expressiveness. Their quality inheres, through all and after all, in their vocal appropriateness, and the writer had better be guided by the logic of poetic thought than by the romance of words.[1]

To use words with a too conscious knowledge of the time or the occasion of their origination is in bad taste; it is to use them in a sense that is not the currency of the writer's own time. It is a fault most often found in writers who affect a period, such as the eighteenth century, and varies from the occasional use of an affected word or phrase to a persistent and irritating allusiveness.

The use of *affected* words is generally associated with an

[1] Sean O'Faolain (*The Short Story*, Devin-Adair) quotes the following appropriate passage from Greenough and Kittredge, *Words and their Ways in English Speech* (Macmillan):

'By a succession of radiations the development of meaning may become almost infinitely complex. No dictionary can ever register a tithe of them, for, so long as language is alive, every speaker is constantly making new specialised amplifica-. tions of its words. . . . The limits of the definition must always be vague and even within these limits there is always scope for variety. If the speaker does not transgress these limits in a given instance we understand his meaning. . . . He has given us a conventional sign or symbol of his idea. Our interpretation of the sign will depend partly on the context, partly on what we know of the speaker, partly on the associations which we ourselves attach to the word. . . .' Cf. also Logan Pearsall Smith: 'Our modern knowledge of the antiquity of our Aryan words does much to open for us these vistas and vast avenues of time; and terms like *mother, father, brother, sister, night*, and *star* and *wind* [*Note*. This double use of 'and' is suspect. H.R.] are all the more beautiful and dear to us because we know that they belong to the innermost core of our race-experience, and are living sounds, conveyed to us by the uninterrupted speech of countless generations —ancient voices, echoing faintly out of the silence and darkness that lie far beyond the dawn of history.' *The English Language* (1912), pp. 134–5. This passage, from an excellent work on the philological quality of words, is an indication of the sentimental mood induced by an antiquarian attachment to words. To use words because of their age rather than because of their direct, current meaning, is to forego the clear expressiveness of language. All true expression is spontaneous. Style is spontaneity.

Compare Leone Vivante, *Notes on the Originality of Thought* (Eng. trans. 1926), *passim*.

affected personality.   The style is 'coloured' by the particular
affectation—for example, high falutin' (bombast), pomposity,
slang, jargon, euphuism; but these are questions which will
be more properly discussed under the heading of *Rhetoric*.
Not so obvious are *polite* words—words which by a large
volume of sound or syllables convey a false sense of superiority,
as, for example, *public convenience*. An old servant, on the
occasion of his retirement from service, was shown the
inscription which his colleagues proposed to have engraved
on a piece of silver they were giving him as a memento; he
asked that the word 'presented' might be substituted for
'given', since he thought it more appropriate to the occasion.
But though polite words are to be avoided in a pure style,
yet a studious avoidance of them may result in nothing but
flatness.[1]

It will be seen that it is difficult to judge words in isolation:
their use is in association, and then it will be found that the
unit of judgment or appeal is something more complex.

All these considerations are summarized in the word
congruity, and this is the quality that Hazlitt found so admirably
displayed by Burke:

Burke was so far from being a gaudy or flowery writer, that he
was one of the *severest* writers we have. His words are the most
like things; his style is the most strictly suited to the subject. He
unites every extreme and every variety of composition; the lowest
and the meanest words and descriptions with the highest. He
exults in the display of power, in shewing the extent, the force,
and intensity of his ideas; he is led on by the mere impulse and
vehemence of his fancy, not by the affectation of dazzling his
readers by gaudy conceits or pompous images. He was completely
carried away by his subject. He had no other object but to produce the strongest impression on his reader, by giving the truest,
the most characteristic, the fullest, and most forcible description
of things, trusting to the power of his own mind to mould them
into grace and beauty. He did not produce a splendid effect by
setting fire to the light vapours that float in the regions of fancy,
as the chemists make fine colours with phosphorus, but by the

---

[1] The substance of these last few paragraphs was well expressed by Montaigne:
'As in apparel it is a sign of pusillanimity for one to mark himself in some particular
and unusual fashion, so likewise in common speech, for one to hunt after new
phrases and unaccustomed quaint words, proceedeth from a scholastic and
childish ambition.   Let me use none other than are spoken in the halls (i.e. *halles*,
markets) of Paris' (*Of the Institution and Education of Children*, Florio's translation).

eagerness of his blows struck fire from the flint, and melted the hardest substances in the furnace of his imagination. The wheels of his imagination did not catch fire from the rottenness of the materials, but from the rapidity of their motion. One would suppose, to hear people talk of Burke, that his style was such as would have suited the *Lady's Magazine*; soft, smooth, showy, tender, insipid, full of fine words, without any meaning. The essence of the gaudy or glittering style consists in producing a momentary effect by fine words and images brought together without order or connection. Burke most frequently produced an effect by the remoteness and novelty of his combinations, by the force of contrast, by the striking manner in which the most opposite and unpromising materials were harmoniously blended together; not by laying his hands on all the fine things he could think of, but by bringing together those things which he knew would blaze out into glorious light by their collision. The florid style is a mixture of affectation and commonplace. Burke's was an union of untameable vigour and originality.

WILLIAM HAZLITT, *Essay on Edmund Burke.*

CHAPTER II

*

Epithets

A NOUN SUBSTANTIVE STANDS in an undivided empire of meaning, but it is an empire whose boundaries are undefined. Hardly a sentence passes but it is necessary to delimit or extend the meaning of a noun; and this we do by linking to it an epithet, that is, an adjectival word or phrase: *a man, many men, a good man, a black man,* are simple illustrations of various degrees of definition.

Man is no doubt an abstraction, built up of many particular events and acts of perception; but there is a limitation in this very abstraction; a vague but ready image is present in the mind, ready to be particularized by some concrete epithet. To say *a man* is merely to conjure up our own private idea of the typical man, perhaps a man in a black coat, striped trousers and a bowler hat, or perhaps the ideal athlete of Greek sculpture, or anything between these two extremes. To add an epithet implying an abstract quality like goodness scarcely makes any difference to our image; and this is the simple reason why such epithets are to be suspected of redundancy. To add a numerical epithet like *many* either multiplies the image in its indefiniteness, or creates another indefinite image of quantity, that is, *many men* is equivalent to *a crowd.* But to add an epithet of *quality* is to progress from the abstract and therefore unvisualized entity of *substance* to the definite entity of a *sense perception.* And since this is a progress from vagueness to vividness, it suggests that clear definition is an elementary need in prose style. But not all substantives are vague; and of epithets, not all that are appropriate are necessary. Indeed, we shall consider epithets under these two heads: namely, their Necessity and their Appropriateness.

A loose orotundity leads to the insertion of unnecessary attributes. It might seem to a novice that to introduce as many words as have a bearing on the subject must necessarily enlighten it. But as Congreve said (*Amendments of Mr. Collier's False and Imperfect Citations*), 'epithets are beautiful in poetry, but make prose languishing and cold'. *A man crossed the street* is a definite statement, vivid enough. To say *a man in black crossed the busy street* is to lose a certain immediateness of effect; for unless the context of the statement requires a man 'in black' and a 'busy' street, definitely for the furtherance of the narrative, then the understanding is merely delayed by the necessity of affixing these attributes to the general terms; for men are often enough in black, and streets busy. To say *a man in scarlet crossed the deserted street* is indeed to add to the vividness of the phrase; but these exceptional epithets, 'scarlet' and 'deserted', would never be used unless demanded by the context.

Another type of unnecessary epithet is not so much redundant, as presumptuous. It attributes to a thing a quality which cannot fairly belong to that thing, either carelessly, or merely for the sake of the empty resonance of a word. Such epithets are generally either loose personifications of inanimate objects, or dead or collapsed metaphors—in any case, unintended metaphors. 'The *wrathful* sea', the '*sleeping* ocean', 'the *slumberous* roll of the *silent* swell', '*unconscious* humour', '*beautiful* craft', are examples of this very prevalent form of inexactitude. The following verse shows a more sustained example:

My window, growing weary of the white
Of Winter's onslaughts, now rejoices in
The slow soft pulse of Spring that beats itself
Against the panes in cloudy tints of green.

L. G. BARNARD, *The Century Magazine*,
March, 1927.

If such epithets still retain the force of metaphors they may be justified; but more often they are the slipshod attributes of things not definitely seen, of vague imaginings and confused thoughts.

The general rule is: to omit all epithets that may be assumed, and to admit only those which definitely further action, interest or meaning.

The bad effect of unnecessary epithets can only be adequately illustrated by giving a passage of prose, and then repeating it with the unnecessary epithets omitted.

Shining serenely as some immeasurable mirror beneath the
smiling face of heaven, the solitary ocean lay in unrippled silence.
It was in those placid latitudes south of the line in the Pacific,
where weeks, aye months, often pass without the marginless blue
level being ruffled by any wandering keel.   Here, in almost perfect
security from molestation by man, the innumerable denizens of the
deep pursue their never-ending warfare, doubtless enjoying to the
full the brimming cup of life, without a weary moment, and with
no dreary anticipations of an unwanted old age.

Now it fell on a day that the calm surface of that bright sea was
broken by the sudden upheaval of a compact troop of sperm whales
from the inscrutable depths wherein they had been roaming and
recruiting their gigantic energies upon the abundant molluscs,
hideous of mien and insatiable of maw, that, like creations of a
diseased mind, lurked far below the sunshine.   The school consisted
of seven cows and one mighty bull, who was unique in appearance,
for instead of being in colour the unrelieved sepia common to his
kind, he was curiously mottled with creamy white, making the
immense oblong cube of his head look like a weather-worn monolith
of Siena marble.   Easeful as an Arabian khalif, he lolled supine
upon the glittering folds of his couch, the welcoming wavelets
caressing his vast form with gentlest touch, and murmuring softly
as by their united efforts they rocked him in rhythm with their
melodic lullaby.

FRANK T. BULLEN, A Sack of Shakings, pp. 1–2.[1]

If we analyse this passage we shall find many superfluous
epithets or phrases; for example:

serenely as is duplicated by *placid*

smiling is perhaps permissible, but facetious

solitary is implied in the following sentence

unrippled: a mirror is never rippled

weeks, aye: nothing is lost by saying simply *months*

marginless: not necessary after *immeasurable*

almost secure is better, because shorter, than *in almost perfect
    security*

by man: molestation here implies 'by man'

denizens of the deep: poetic *cliché*

never-ending: inexact, and therefore unnecessary, and even
    implied in *without a weary moment*.

---

[1] Collins. This inflationary style is not confined to minor writers. The
reader is recommended to make the same kind of analysis of a writer often, and
sometimes justly, praised for his style—Joseph Conrad. A passage for this
purpose is provided in the Appendix (p.196).

doubtless . . . *cup of life*: a presumptuous *cliché*, irrelevant, if not contradictory to the idea of warfare

dreary: prevented by the absence of weary moments

Now it fell on a day that: *One day* expresses the meaning

calm: already implied

compact: a troop implies compactness

inscrutable: to whom? Not to the whales, and there is no one else on the scene

abundant: perhaps permissible, but not strictly necessary

hideous . . . *maw*: a *cliché* phrase destroying the effect of the following simile

supine: a whale cannot loll in any other position

welcoming: this is objectionable as a ludicrous personification of inanimate forces, but it is also to some extent duplicated by *caressing*

softly: implied in *murmuring*, but perhaps permissible in the sense of *sweetly*.

melodic: implied in *lullaby*.

There are other stylistic defects in this passage, particularly an almost constant use of *clichés*, and, indeed, the whole passage is one distended *cliché*. But neglecting these, and omitting only the redundant epithets in the above list, with a few consequent modifications of syntax, the passage then gains greatly in force, directness and expressiveness.

Shining like some immeasurable mirror beneath the face of heaven, the ocean lay in silence. It was in those placid latitudes south of the line in the Pacific, where months often pass without the blue level being ruffled by any wandering keel. Here, almost secure from molestation, the innumerable inhabitants of the sea pursue their warfare without a weary moment and with no anticipations of an unwanted old age.

One day the surface of that bright sea was broken by the sudden upheaval of a troop of sperm whales from the depths wherein they had been roaming and recruiting their gigantic energies upon the molluscs that, like creations of a diseased mind, lurked far below the sunshine. The school consisted of seven cows and one mighty bull, who was unique in appearance, for instead of being in colour the unrelieved sepia common to his kind, he was curiously mottled with creamy white, making the immense oblong cube of his head look like a weather-worn monolith of Siena marble. Easeful as any Arabian khalif he lolled upon the glittering folds of his couch, the wavelets caressing his vast form and murmuring softly as by their united efforts they rocked him in rhythm with their lullaby.

Fifty words have been saved, but nothing essential has been taken from the meaning, whilst the force and 'activity' of the writing is all the greater for the lifting of this unnecessary burden of epithets.

The necessity of epithets can be determined by a nice judgment, but to use them *appropriately* is to employ a more intuitive faculty. In simple cases there is no choice: the meaning to be expressed demands one epithet and no other. But in other cases an unusual epithet must be sought to express a subtlety of meaning, or to convey a particular degree of feeling. To express the matter differently, appropriate epithets may be either *exact* or *happy*.

I remember, in the story of the Argonautics, when Jason set out to fetch the *golden* fleece, the poet saith, all the gods looked down from heaven that day to view the ship; and the nymphs stood upon the mountain tops to see the *noble* youth of Thessaly pulling at the oars; we may with more reason suppose the *good* angels to have looked down upon this ship of Noah's; and that not out of curiosity, as *idle* spectators, but with a PASSIONATE concern for its safety and deliverance. A ship, whose cargo was no less than a *whole* world; that carried the fortunes and hopes of all posterity, and if this had perished, the earth for anything we know had been nothing but a desert, a *great* ruin, a DEAD heap of rubbish, from the deluge to the conflagration. But death and hell, the grave and destruction, have their bounds. We may entertain ourselves with the consideration of the face of the deluge, and of the BROKEN AND DROWNED earth, in this scheme, with the *floating* ark, and the *guardian* angels.

THOMAS BURNET, *The Sacred Theory of the Earth.*

In a passage like this we may see clearly illustrated the various uses of epithets. The *golden* fleece is a necessary and exact epithet, for it distinguishes one particular fleece in history. *Noble* youth, *good* angels, *idle* spectators, *whole* world, *great* ruin, *floating* ark, *guardian* angels: these are all appropriate adjectives, and exact; they are not so strictly necessary. But 'a *passionate* concern', 'a *dead* heap of rubbish', 'the *broken and drowned* earth'—in these phrases the epithets are used not only appropriately, but also happily, since they strike us with a pleasant freshness and contribute largely to the animation of this particular style.

The free use of epithets is a characteristic of a mature literature, of highly developed civilizations and analytical minds. Apart from the considerations of necessity and appropriateness which have been illustrated, there is a problem which arises when epithets, justified in themselves by the nicety of judgment or subtlety of analysis, threaten merely by their frequency and aggregation to obscure the clarity of substantives, the speed of narrative, the *flow* of speech. If the two passages that follow are compared, and their general qualities placed in contrast, it will be difficult not to ascribe vitality to the first and enervation to the second; and historically these passages represent the full range of the development of English style.

(1) And on the morn they returned again to their ship, and sailed a long time in the sea after, ere they could find any land, till at last by the purveyance of God, they saw far from them a full fair island, full of green pasture, wherein were the whitest and greatest sheep that ever they saw. For every sheep was as great as an ox, and soon after came to them a goodly old man, which welcomed them and made them good cheer, and said: This is the island of sheep, and here is never cold weather, but ever summer, and that causeth the sheep to be so great and white; they eat of the best grass and herbs that is anywhere. And then this old man took his leave of them and bade them sail forth right east, and within short time by God's grace, they should come in to a place like Paradise, wherein they should keep their Eastertide.

And then they sailed forth, and came soon after to that land, but because of little depth in some places, and in some places were great rocks, but at the last they went upon an island weening to them that they had been safe, and made thereon a fire for to dress their dinner, but S. Brandon abode still in the ship, and when the fire was right hot and meat nigh sodden, then this island began to move, whereof the monks were afeard, and fled anon to ship and left the fire and meat behind them, and marvelled sore of the moving. And S. Brandon comforted them and said that it was a great fish named Jascoyne, which laboureth night and day to put his tail in his mouth, but for greatness he may not. And then anon they sailed west three days and nights ere they saw any land, wherefore they were right heavy, but soon after, as God would, they saw a fair island full of flowers, herbs, and trees, whereof they thanked God of his good grace, and anon they went on land, and when they had gone long in this they found a full fair well, and thereby stood a fair tree full of boughs, and on every bough sat a fair bird, and they sat so thick on the tree that unnethe any leaf of the tree might be seen. The number of them was so great, and they sang so merrily that it was a heavenly noise to hear, wherefore S. Brandon kneeled down on his knees and wept for joy, and made his prayers devoutly to our Lord God to know what these birds meant.

And then anon one of the birds fled from the tree to S. Brandon, and he with flickering of his wings made a full merry noise like a fiddle, that him seemed he heard never so joyful a melody. And then S. Brandon commanded the bird to tell him the cause why they sat so thick on the tree and sang so merrily; and then the bird said: Sometime we were angels in heaven, but when our master Lucifer fell down into hell for his high pride, we fell with him for our offences, some higher and some lower after the quality of the trespass, and because our trespass is but little, therefore our Lord hath set us here out of all pain, in full great joy and mirth after his pleasing, here to serve him on this tree in the best manner we can. The Sunday is a day of rest from all worldly occupation, and therefore that day all we be made as white as any snow for to praise our Lord in the best wise we may. And then this bird said to S. Brandon: That it is twelve months passed that ye departed from your abbey, and in the seventh year hereafter, ye shall see the place that ye desire to come to, and all these seven years ye shall keep your Easter here with us every year, and in the end of the seventh year ye shall come into the land of Behest. And this was on Easter day that the bird said these words to S. Brandon, and then this fowl flew again to his fellows that sat on the tree, and then all the birds began to sing evensong so merrily that it was a heavenly noise to hear. And after supper S. Brandon and his fellows went to bed and slept well, and on the morn they arose betimes, and then these birds began matins, prime, and hours, and all such service as christian men use to sing.

CAXTON's *Golden Legend:* 'The Life of S. Brandon'.

(2) I have remarked how, in the process of our brain-building, as the house of thought in which we live gets itself together, like some airy bird's-nest of floating thistle-down and chance straws, compact at last, little accidents have their consequence; and thus it happened that, as he walked one evening, a garden gate, usually closed, stood open; and lo! within, a great red hawthorn in full flower, embossing heavily the bleached and twisted trunk and branches, so aged that there were but few green leaves thereon—a plumage of tender, crimson fire out of the heart of the dry wood. The perfume of the tree had now and again reached him, in the currents of the wind, over the wall, and he had wondered what might be behind it, and was now allowed to fill his arms with the flowers—flowers enough for all the old blue-china pots along the

chimney-piece, making *fête* in the children's room. Was it some periodic moment in the expansion of soul within him, or mere trick of heat in the heavily-laden summer air? But the beauty of the thing struck home to him feverishly; and in dreams all night he loitered along a magic roadway of crimson flowers, which seemed to open ruddily in thick, fresh masses about his feet, and fill softly all the little hollows in the banks on either side. Always afterwards, summer by summer, as the flowers came on, the blossom of the red hawthorn still seemed to him absolutely the reddest of all things ; and the goodly crimson, still alive in the work of old Venetian masters or old Flemish tapestries, called out always from afar the recollection of the flame in those perishing little petals, as it pulsed gradually out of them, kept long in the drawers of an old cabinet. Also then, for the first time, he seemed to experience a passionateness in his relation to fair outward objects, an inexplicable excitement in their presence, which disturbed him, and from which he half longed to be free. A touch of regret or desire mingled all night with the remembered presence of the red flowers, and their perfume in the darkness about him; and the longing for some undivined, entire possession of them was the beginning of a revelation to him, growing ever clearer, with the coming of the gracious summer guise of fields and trees and persons in each succeeding year, of a certain, at times seemingly exclusive, predominance in his interests, of beautiful physical things, a kind of tyranny of the senses over him.

WALTER PATER, Miscellaneous Studies, '*The Child in the House*'.[1]

Pater, in his use of epithets, aims at the production of *metaphorical overtones* by the juxtaposition of particular words. The effect is more appropriate to poetry than to prose, as Fenollosa, who first used the phrase italicised, pointed out:

Poetry surpasses prose especially in that the poet selects for juxtaposition those words whose overtones blend into a delicate and lucid harmony. All arts follow the same law; refined harmony lies in the delicate balance of overtones. . . . How shall we determine the metaphorical overtones of neighbouring words?

The Chinese Written Character, ed. Ezra Pound, London, 1936.

Pater's unexpected use of the epithet 'bleached', applied to a tree, produces an authentic overtone; but the too-conscious cultivation of such effects brings us again to what Hazlitt called 'the gaudy and glittering style'. But we have now reached a point where it is necessary to investigate more closely the function of metaphor in prose style.

[1] Macmillan.

CHAPTER III

*

Metaphor and Other Figures of Speech

WE have seen that words used as epithets are words used to analyse a direct statement. We have in mind a complex image, and to express this image in its fullness we break it up into its constituent units:

> The hills stand snow-powdered, pale, bright.
> CARLYLE.

Metaphor is the opposite process: it is the synthesis of several units of observation into one commanding image; it is the expression of a complex idea, not by analysis, nor by abstract statement, but by a sudden perception of an objective relation. The complex idea is translated into a simple concrete equivalent.

The nature and importance of metaphors was clearly stated by Aristotle, in the *Poetics* (xxii. 16, 17):

... much the most important point is to be able to use metaphors, for this is the one thing that cannot be learned from others; and it is also a mark of genius, since a good metaphor implies an intuitive perception of the similarity in dissimilars.[1]

But in this passage Aristotle is writing of poetry. The ability to invent new metaphors is a sign of a poetic mind; and the main use of metaphors is always poetical. To say that a metaphor 'is the result of the search for a precise epithet'[2] is misleading. The precision sought for is one of equivalence, not of analytical description. And as prose is essentially the art of analytical description, it would seem that metaphor is

---

[1] 'The art of producing good metaphors is a token of the faculty for recognizing the universal and the common element underlying externally dissimilar objects.' Note to the translation of this passage of the *Poetics* by E. S. Bouchier (Oxford, 1907).

[2] J. Middleton Murry, *The Problem of Style*, p. 83. Fenollosa (*op. cit.*) gives a perfect definition of metaphor: 'the use of material images to suggest immaterial relations.'

of no particular relevance to it; for poetry it is perhaps a more necessary mode of expression.

We may say quite generally that the use of metaphor tends to obscure the essential nature of prose, because it substitutes a poetic equivalence for a direct statement. For this reason many of our best writers have been chary of this mode of writing—as Swift. 'The rogue never hazards a metaphor', said Johnson. 'Never' is perhaps an exaggeration, but it is true that we may read Swift for many pages without encountering imagery of any kind, except such as was at that time embodied in common speech.

On the fifth of November, which was the beginning of summer in those parts, the weather being very hazy, the seamen spied a rock, within half a cable's length of the ship; but the wind was so strong, that we were driven directly upon it, and immediately split. Six of the crew, of whom I was one, having let down the boat into the sea, made a shift to get clear of the ship and the rock. We rowed, by my computation, about three leagues, till we were able to work no longer, being already spent with labour while we were in the ship. We therefore trusted ourselves to the mercy of the waves, and in about half an hour the boat was overset by a sudden flurry from the north. What became of my companions in the boat, as well as of those who escaped on the rock, or were left in the vessel, I cannot tell; but conclude they were all lost. For my own part, I swam as fortune directed me, and was pushed forward by wind and tide. I often let my legs drop, and could feel no bottom: but when I was almost gone, and able to struggle no longer, I found myself within my depth; and by this time the storm was much abated. The declivity was so small, that I walked near a mile before I got to the shore, which I conjectured was about eight o'clock in the evening. I then advanced forward near half a mile, but could not discover any sign of houses or inhabitants; at least I was in so weak a condition that I did not observe them. I was extremely tired, and with that, and the heat of the weather, and about half a pint of brandy that I drank as I left the ship, I found myself much inclined to sleep. I lay down on the grass, which was very short and soft, where I slept sounder than ever I remember to have done in my life, and as I reckoned, about nine hours; for when I awaked it was just daylight. I attempted to rise, but was not able to stir: for as I happened to lie on my back, I found my arms and legs were strongly fastened on each side to the ground; and my hair, which was long and thick, tied down in the same manner. I likewise felt several slender ligatures across my body, from my armpits to my thighs. I could only look

upwards, the sun began to grow hot, and the light offended my
eyes. I heard a confused noise about me, but in the posture I lay,
could see nothing except the sky. In a little time I felt something
alive moving on my left leg, which advancing gently forward,
over my breast, came almost up to my chin; when bending my
eyes downward as much as I could, I perceived it to be a human
creature not six inches high, with a bow and arrow in his hands,
and a quiver at his back.

SWIFT, *Gulliver's Travels*, pt. i. ch. i.

In this passage there is not a single simile or metaphor;
there is not even a direct comparison, such as we find later
in the book. 'They climbed high trees as nimbly as a squirrel,
for they had strong extended claws before and behind,
terminating in sharp points, and hooked.' But a direct or
simple *comparison*, where the objects compared are of a common
nature, is not a figure of speech at all; to climb high trees
comes naturally to both Yahoos and squirrels. But if we say
of a man, or a horse, that he climbed high trees as nimbly as
a squirrel, then we compare the particular qualities of one
object to the general qualities of another, and this constitutes
a *simile*. If we go a step further, and in a manner *identify*
the man and the squirrel, as in 'This man, the squirrel of his
clan, climbed the high trees'—then we invent a metaphor.

Simile and Metaphor differ only in degree of stylistic
refinement. The Simile, in which a comparison is made
directly between two objects, belongs to an earlier stage of
literary expression: it is the deliberate elaboration of a
correspondence, often pursued for its own sake. But a
Metaphor is the swift illumination of an equivalence. Two
images, or an idea and an image, stand equal and opposite;
clash together and respond significantly, surprising the reader
with a sudden light.

This light may either illuminate or decorate the sentence in
which it is found; and perhaps we may divide all metaphors
into the *illuminative* and the *decorative*. By doing so we can
make more distinct the limited relevance of metaphor to
prose writing; for while both kinds are appropriate to poetry,
only the illuminative metaphor will be found appropriate in
pure prose style.

In narrative prose, such as the passage already quoted from Swift, there is no need for either illumination or decoration; metaphors would merely impede the action and are therefore properly discarded.

In exposition, whether of the descriptive kind or of the persuasive kind (see Chapter VII), it is again difficult to see any justification for decorative metaphors.   These are generally introduced either to display the poetic tendency of the writer's mind, and are therefore out of place; or to give an alternative expression to a thought which has already been expressed in direct language.   In this case they are redundant.

But it often happens in exposition that abstract language is inadequate to express a meaning clearly, and then metaphor may be introduced to illuminate the thought.   Paradoxically, it is in scientific prose that the illuminative metaphor is most effectively used.   The history of language and of early poetry, as well as the general results of modern psychology, according to a well-known logician, confirm the view that 'metaphors are not merely artificial devices for making discourse more vivid and poetical, but are also necessary for the apprehension and communication of new ideas'.   Metaphors 'are often the way in which creative minds perceive things, so that the explicit recognition that we are dealing with an analogy rather than a real identity comes later as a result of further reflection and analysis'.[1]

The language of scientific pioneers like Faraday, Darwin and Huxley abounds in illuminative metaphors.   Here, for example, is a paragraph from the work of a modern physicist:

I have said that all atoms are in motion, and that there is a constant struggle between some form of attractive force which would draw all the atoms together and this motion which would keep them independent.   The existence of an attractive force which we here take into account as something very important does not at first seem to be reconcilable with the atomic structure we have just considered, because in this we supposed that the outer shells of electrons would prevent the atoms from coming too close to each other.   It is a difficult point, because both views are entirely correct.   It is, no doubt, our present ignorance of the

[1] Morris R. Cohen: *A Preface to Logic* (Holt).

nature of these forces that prevents us from arriving at a clear understanding. We have seen how it can happen that when two atoms approach each other at great speeds they go through one another, while at moderate speeds they bound off each other like two billiard balls. We have to go a step further, and see how, at very slow speeds of approach, they may actually stick together. We have all seen those swinging gates which, when their swing is considerable, go to and fro without locking. When the swing has declined, however, the latch suddenly drops into its place, the gate is held and after a short rattle the motion is all over. We have to explain an effect something like that. When the two atoms meet, the repulsions of their electron shells usually cause them to recoil; but if the motion is small, and the atoms spend a longer time in each other's neighbourhood, there is time for something to happen in the internal arrangements of both atoms, like the drop of the latch-gate into its socket, and the atoms are held. It all depends on some structure of the atom which causes a want of uniformity over its surface, so that there is usually a repulsion; but the repulsion will be turned into attraction if the two atoms are allowed time to make the necessary arrangements, or even if at the outset they are presented to each other in the right way.

SIR WILLIAM BRAGG: *Concerning the Nature of Things.*[1]

The following passage shows the use of merely decorative metaphors:

The Oxford Movement may be a spent wave, but, before it broke on the shore, it reared, as its successor is now rearing, a brave and beautiful crest of liturgical and devotional life, the force of which certainly shifted the Anglican sands, though it failed to uncover any rock-bottom underlying them. It is enough if now and then a lone swimmer be borne by the tide, now at its full, to be dashed, more or less ungently, upon the Rock of Peter, to cling there in safety, while the impotent wave recedes and is lost in the restless sea.

M. A. CHAPMAN, in *Blackfriars*, April, 1921.
(Quoted by Stephen J. Brown, *The World of Imagery*, p. 308.)

By translating this passage into direct language the meaning could be preserved without any loss, and even clarified. Because of their vagueness, it is not always possible to be sure that exact equivalents have been found for the metaphors; but this only reveals the weakness of decorative metaphorical writing. The translation which follows may not be so emotive

[1] Bell.

as the original, but it is more definite, and to be definite is
the proper aim of expository writing:

The Oxford Movement may belong to the past, but before its
end it produced, like its successor of to-day, a fine sense of liturgical
devotional life, the force of which certainly had some effect on the
looser elements of the Anglican Church, though it failed to reach
any fundamental body of opinion. It is enough that the Movement, when at its height, led a few desperate individuals to become
converted to the Church of Rome, and there these remained in
security of mind when the Movement, losing its force, became a
merely historical phenomenon.

Hazlitt called such writers *hieroglyphical* writers. Here is his
description of them (itself not free from the vices it castigates):

. . . Such persons are in fact besotted with words, and their
brains are turned with the glittering but empty and sterile phantoms
of things. Personifications, capital letters, seas of sunbeams, visions
of glory, shining inscriptions, the figures of a transparency,
Britannia with her shield, or Hope leaning on an anchor, make up
their stock-in-trade. They may be considered as *hieroglyphical*
writers. Images stand out in their minds isolated and important
merely in themselves, without any ground-work of feeling—there
is no context in their imaginations. Words affect them in the
same way, by the mere sound, that is, by their possible, not by
their actual application to the subject in hand. They are fascinated
by first appearances, and have no sense of consequences. Nothing
more is meant by them than meets the ear: they understand or
feel nothing more than meets their eye. The web and texture of
the universe, and of the heart of man, is a mystery to them: they
have no faculty that strikes a chord in unison with it. They cannot
get beyond the daubings of fancy, the varnish of sentiment. Objects
are not linked to feelings, words to things, but images revolve in
splendid mockery, words represent themselves in their strange
rhapsodies. The categories of such a mind are pride and ignorance
—pride in outside show, to which they sacrifice everything, and
ignorance of the true worth and hidden structure both of words
and things. With a sovereign contempt for what is familiar and
natural, they are the slaves of vulgar affectation—of a routine of
high-flown phrases. Scorning to imitate realities, they are unable
to invent anything, to strike out one original idea. They are not
copyists of nature, it is true; but they are the poorest of all plagiarists,
the plagiarists of words. All is far-fetched, dear bought, artificial,
oriental in subject and allusion; all is mechanical, conventional,
vapid, formal, pedantic in style and execution. They startle and
confound the understanding of the reader by the remoteness and
obscurity of their illustrations; they soothe the ear by the monotony
of the same everlasting round of circuitous metaphors. They are

the *mock-school* in poetry and prose. They flounder about between fustian in expression and bathos in sentiment. They tantalise the fancy, but never reach the head nor touch the heart.

WILLIAM HAZLITT, Essay on *Familiar Style*.

In the following passage an idea is stated and is then followed by a metaphor (it is hardly a simile) which has the effect of illuminating and fixing the meaning in our minds. Incidentally this passage shows an example of a metaphor followed out in all its implications, extending and branching out and at each stage bringing fresh light to illuminate the idea:[1]

Heathenism, if we consider life at large, is the primal and universal religion. It has never been my good fortune to see wild beasts in the jungle, but I have sometimes watched a wild bull in the ring, and I can imagine no more striking, simple, and heroic example of animal faith; especially when the bull is what is technically called noble, that is, when he follows the lure again and again with eternal singleness of thought, eternal courage, and no suspicion of a hidden agency that is mocking him. What the red rag is to this brave creature, their passions, inclinations, and chance notions are to the heathen. What they will they will; and they would deem it weakness and disloyalty to ask whether it is worth willing or whether it is attainable. The bull, magnificently sniffing the air, surveys the arena with the cool contempt and disbelief of the idealist, as if he said: 'You seem, you are a seeming; I do not quarrel with you, I do not fear you. I am real, you are nothing.' Then suddenly, when his eye is caught by some bright cloak displayed before him, his whole soul changes. His will awakes, and he seems to say: 'You are my destiny; I want you, I hate you, you shall be mine, you shall not stand in my path. I will gore you. I will disprove you. I will pass beyond you. I shall be, you shall not have been.' Later, when sorely wounded and near his end, he grows blind to all these excitements. He smells the moist earth, and turns to the dungeon where an hour ago he was at peace. He remembers the herd, the pasture beyond, and he dreams, 'I shall not die, for I love life. I shall be young again, young always, for I love youth. All this outcry is nought to me, this strange suffering is nought. I will go to the fields again, to graze, to roam, to love.'

So exactly, with not one least concession to the unsuspected reality, the heathen soul stands bravely before a painted world, covets some bauble, and defies death. Heathenism is the religion

---

[1] A difficult feat, more often than not involving the author in runaway and mixed metaphors, and a general violence of statement. The greatest master of the branching metaphor is perhaps Henry James. Cf. the passage quoted in *The London Book of English Prose*, II, viii, 23.

of will, the faith which life has in itself because it is life, and in its
aims because it is pursuing them.

GEÓRGE SANTAYANA, *Egotism in German Philosophy*.[1]

The passage from Swift (p. 24) has shown us narrative prose
that is completely independent of the use of metaphor. The
following passage from a work of great clarity and precision,
will show the same independence in expository prose:

Physical Science is that department of knowledge which relates
to the order of nature, or, in other words, to the regular succession
of events.

The name of physical science, however, is often applied in a
more or less restricted manner to those branches of science in which
the phenomena considered are of the simplest and most abstract
kind, excluding the consideration of the more complex phenomena,
such as those observed in beings.

The simplest case of all is that in which an event or phenomenon
can be described as a change in the arrangement of certain bodies.
Thus the motion of the moon may be described by stating the
changes in her position relative to the earth in the order in which
they follow one another.

In other cases we may know that some change of arrangement
has taken place, but we may not be able to ascertain what that
change is.

Thus when water freezes we know that the molecules or smallest
parts of the substance must be arranged differently in ice and in
water. We also know that this arrangement in ice must have a
certain kind of symmetry, because the ice is in the form of symmetrical crystals, but we have as yet no precise knowledge of the
actual arrangement of the molecules in ice. But whenever we can
completely describe the change of arrangement we have a knowledge, perfect so far as it extends, of what has taken place, though
we may still have to learn the necessary conditions under which a
similar event will always take place.

Hence the first part of physical science relates to the relative
position and motion of bodies.

J. CLERK MAXWELL, *Matter and Motion*, pp. 9 and 10.[2]

The historical evolution of an art often runs from complexity
to simplicity, and Jespersen has suggested that this is true also
of the development of language. It would seem to be true
not only of language itself but also of the arts of language.
Early literature is characterized by the frequent use of *riddles*
and *periphrases* ('kennings'). Riddles are primitive metaphors,

roundabout descriptions or stories designed to convey their subject as a sudden and vivid revelation in the mind of the reader:[1]

My nose is downward; I go deep and dig into the ground; I move as the grey foe of the wood guides me, and my lord who goes stooping as guardian at my tail; he pushes me in the plain, bears and urges me, sows in my track. I hasten forth, brought from the grove, strongly bound, carried on the wagon, I have many wounds; on one side of me as I go there is green, and on the other my track is clear black. Driven through my back a cunning point hangs beneath; another on my head fixed and prone falls at the side, so that I tear with my teeth, if he who is my lord serves me rightly from behind.

'Plough'—from *Anglo-Saxon Poetry*
(Everyman Library), p. 327.

Kennings are very characteristic of Anglo-Saxon literature; for examples: 'world-candle' (sun), 'word-hoard' (mind or speech), 'battle-adders' (arrows), 'the head jewels' (eyes). They differ from later metaphors in that they have a deceptive intention, and may, indeed, have their origin in some form of taboo. Primitive man associated the thing and its name in an intimate fashion, and when the thing was an object of veneration or fear, he would seek for some form of periphrasis so as to avoid a direct reference. A kenning is a simple periphrasis of this kind.

Metonymy is a special form of periphrasis; something associated with an idea is made to serve for the expression of that idea. 'From the *cradle* to the *grave*', 'Loyalty to the *throne*', 'an officer of the *Crown*'.

Synecdoche is still another type of concise periphrasis; a part of a thing is made to serve for the expression of the whole. 'A fleet of fifty *sail*', 'All *hands* on deck', 'A force of a thousand *rifles*'.

The use of all these forms of periphrasis is a matter of discretion; they are better avoided unless they are fresh enough to add to the vividness or significance of a passage; or unless they have become so current as to pass without equivocation for the master word.

Personification or *Actualization* is another figure of speech related to metaphor, and has its origins in primitive modes,

[1] Cf. Aristotle, *Rhet.*, III, ii. 12.

such as the Anglo-Saxon riddle; but like metaphor, of which, indeed, it is a collapsed form (for one of the terms of comparison has been suppressed, or identified with the object to which it is compared), it is more appropriate to poetic expression. It consists in endowing inanimate things with animate (and generally human) action. A sustained process of personification or actualization may sometimes be used to give vitality to descriptive prose, but only with discretion.

It was a hot July afternoon, the world laid out open to the sun to admit its penetration. All nature seemed swollen to its fullest. The very air was half asleep, and the distant sounds carried so slowly that they died away before they could reach their destination; or perhaps the ear forgot to listen.

The house, too, had indulged itself, and had lost a little its melancholy air. The summer decked it with garlands, for the still newly-green creepers crept up the walls and on to the roof, almost high enough to gain the chimney-pots. But the house held them like hats, carefully out of reach, and the creepers, snubbed, pried into the open windows. The smooth lawns lay tantalizingly about, just out of the way of the blundering, clumsy house kept prisoner by the chain of gravel. The lawn, a green-clad monster, arched its back against the yew hedge, and put out emerald feelers all through the garden and turfed alley-ways.

VALENTINE DOBRÉE, *Your Cuckoo Sings by Kind*, pp. 51–2.[1]

The concision of personification, of metonymy and of synecdoche, was one way of escape from the complexity and unwieldiness of the periphrasis and the riddle. Comparison, simile and metaphor renounce the mere love of indirectness; they denote a growth in poetic sensibility, and in the use of metaphor we have, indeed, one of the main agents in the growth of intelligence. It has been a main agent, too, in the growth of language, most words and idioms being in the nature of dead metaphors. But whatever we may say of it, and however great and inclusive the function we assign to it, essentially it belongs to the sphere of poetry. But it is equally possible to say that science itself, in its formative stage, also belongs to the sphere of poetry[2]

[1] Knopf.

[2] Cf. Fenollosa: 'In diction and in grammatical form science is utterly opposed to logic. Primitive men who created language agreed with science and not with logic. Logic has abused the language which they left to her mercy. Poetry agrees with science and not with logic.' *Op. cit.*, p. 32.

CHAPTER IV

*

The Sentence

THE SENTENCE AS A UNIT in prose style is best approached from the evolutionary standpoint suggested by Jespersen. The further back we go in the history of known languages, the more we find that the sentence was one indissoluble whole in which those elements we are accustomed to think of as single words were not yet separated.[1] Jespersen says too, that we must think of primitive language 'as consisting (chiefly at least) of very long words, full of difficult sounds, and sung rather than spoke'.

This supports the view I wish to advance as to the function of the sentence in prose writing. The sentence is a single cry. It is a unit of expression, and its various qualities—length, rhythm and structure—are determined by a right sense of this unity.

The process by which the various parts of speech became differentiated is of great interest, but must not concern us here. We will only note that in all probability the sentence, as distinct from the primitive indissoluble sound suggested by Jespersen, arose when it first became possible to distinguish between action and objects—between things in themselves and the mobile properties of those things. For then the verb became distinct from the substantive, and these two parts of speech give us the essentials of a sentence.

A substantive may stand alone as a sentence, and sometimes does, effectively. But the verb is always understood, or some construction including a verb. When a verb stands alone it usually has the previous sentence, or the subject of the previous sentence, as a latent subject or predicate. Such isolation of a noun or a verb is merely a device of punctuation: to gain

[1] *Op. cit.* p. 421. Cf. Piaget, *Language and Thought of the Child* (Humanities Press): 'The line of development of language, as of perception, is from the whole to the part, from syncretism to analysis, and not vice versa.'

vividness (though the gain be only typographical) the word
in question is as it were framed between two full stops. The
following passages illustrate the deliberate use of this manner
of composition, and it is a mannerism less liable to abuse than
many since it tends to concision rather than verbosity. It has
the vitality of directly transmitted thought, of the 'interior
monologue' which takes place in each thinking mind. On
the other hand, it lends itself to false dramaticism and a sham
'poetic' atmosphere:

The day was beginning to break as they walked along together.
The light shot up from the east, filling the sky with a warm tinge
of soft half-light. And it grew and grew till suddenly the broad,
clear light fell upon them.

It was day. How quiet looked the town in the full, soft clearness.
The houses seemed to sleep in the middle of strange, soft, thrilling
sound. The wonderful first flush of the day. It fell on the outcasts
as they walked on. Through the quietness of the streets they could
hear the low, deep sound of the waters of the Gulf beating on the
beach.

Day. It had come after darkness. It was shining for these
nameless and homeless men just as it was shining for kings or for
those whose names rang greatly through the world.

Two straying passing figures coming from nowhere and going
nowhere.

Day had come for them.   BART KENNEDY, *A Sailor Tramp*.[1]

On the steps of the Paris Stock Exchange the gold-skinned men
quoting prices on their gemmed fingers. Gabble of geese. They
swarmed loud, uncouth about the temple, their heads thickplotting
under maladroit silk hats. Not theirs: these clothes, this speech,
these gestures. Their full slow eyes belied the words, the gestures
eager and unoffending, but knew the rancours massed about them
and knew their zeal was vain. Vain patience to heap and hoard.
Time surely would scatter all. A hoard heaped by the roadside:
plundered and passing on. Their eyes knew the years of wandering,
and, patient, knew the dishonours of their flesh.

JAMES JOYCE, *Ulysses*.[2]

Sometimes the verb is omitted from a sentence as unessential
to its meaning:

No matins here of birds; not a rock partridge-cock, calling with
blithesome chuckle over the extreme waterless desolation.

C. M. DOUGHTY, *Arabia Deserta*, i.[3]

[1] Grant Richards.   [2] Random House.   [3] Random House.

Again, the device suggests poetry rather than prose. 'The moment we use the copula, the moment we express subjective inclusions, poetry evaporates' (Fenollosa). But as Fenollosa makes clear, in prose it is not so much the presence or absence of the verb that matters, but the choice between a transitive and an intransitive verb. The great strength of the English language, he points out, 'lies in its splendid array of transitive verbs, drawn both from Anglo-Saxon and from Latin sources. . . . Their power lies in their recognition of nature as a vast storehouse of forces . . . I had to discover for myself why Shakespeare's English was so immeasurably superior to all others. I found that it was his persistent, natural, and magnificent use of hundreds of transitive verbs. Rarely will you find an "is" in his sentences. . . . A study of Shakespeare's verbs should underline all exercises in style.'

Sentences in their variety run from simplicity to complexity, a progress not necessarily reflected in length: a long sentence may be extremely simple in construction—indeed, *must be* simple if it is to convey its sense easily.

Other things being equal, a series of short sentences will convey an impression of speed, and are therefore suited to the narration of action or historical events; whilst longer sentences give an air of solemnity and deliberation to writing. In the first of the following passages, the great variety in the length of the sentences gives animation to a serious subject; whilst in the second passage a more trivial subject is, by the grandeur and dignity of the sentences, endowed with a fictitious seriousness:

France, by the perfidy of her leaders, has utterly disgraced the tone of lenient council in the cabinets of princes, and disarmed it of its most potent topics. She has sanctified the dark suspicious maxims of tyrannous distrust; and taught kings to tremble at (what will hereafter be called) the delusive plausibilities of moral politicians. Sovereigns will consider those who advise them to place an unlimited confidence in their people as subverters of their thrones; as traitors who aim at their destruction, by leading their easy good nature, under specious pretences, to admit combinations of bold and faithless men into a participation of their power. This alone, if there were nothing else, is an irreparable calamity to you and to mankind. Remember that your parliament of Paris told your king, that in calling the states together, he had nothing to fear but the prodigal excess of their zeal in providing for the support of the throne. It is right that these men should hide their heads. It is right that they should bear their part in the ruin which their counsel has brought on their sovereign and their country. Such sanguine declarations tend to lull authority asleep; to encourage it rashly to engage in perilous adventures of untried policy; to neglect those provisions, preparations and precautions, which distinguish benevolence from imbecility; and without which no man can answer for the salutary effect of any abstract plan of government or of freedom. For want of these, they have seen the medicine of the state corrupted into its poison. They have seen the French rebel against a mild and lawful monarch, with more fury, outrage and insult, than ever any people has been known to raise against the most illegal usurper, or the most sanguinary tyrant. Their resistance was made to concession; their revolt was from protection; their blow was aimed at a hand holding out graces, favours, and immunities.

This was unnatural. The rest is in order. They have found their punishment in their success. Laws overturned; tribunals subverted; industry without vigour; commerce expiring; the revenue unpaid, yet the people impoverished; a church pillaged, and a state not relieved; civil and military anarchy made the constitution of the kingdom; everything human and divine sacrificed to the idol of public credit, and national bankruptcy the consequence; and to crown all, the paper securities of new, precarious, tottering power, the discredited paper securities of impoverished fraud, and beggared rapine, held out as a currency for the support of an empire, in lieu of the two great recognised species that represent the lasting conventional credit of mankind, which disappeared and hid themselves in the earth from whence they came, when the principle of property, whose creatures and representatives they are, was systematically subverted.

Were all these dreadful things necessary? Were they the inevitable results of the desperate struggle of determined patriots, compelled to wade through blood and tumult, to the quiet shore of a tranquil and prosperous liberty? No! nothing like it. The fresh ruins of France, which shock our feelings wherever we can turn our eyes, are not the devastation of civil war; they are the sad, but instructive monuments of rash and ignorant counsel in time of profound peace. They are the display of inconsiderate and presumptuous, because unresisted and irresistible, authority.

The persons who have thus squandered away the precious treasure of their crimes, the persons who have made this prodigal and wild waste of public evils (the last stake reserved for the ultimate ransom of the state) have met in their progress with little, or rather with no opposition at all. Their whole march was more like a triumphal procession than the progress of a war. Their pioneers have gone before them, and demolished and laid everything level at their feet. Not one drop of their blood have they shed in the cause of the country they have ruined. They have made no sacrifices to their projects of greater consequence than their shoe-buckles, whilst they were imprisoning their king, murdering their fellow-citizens, and bathing in tears, and plunging in poverty and distress, thousands of worthy men and worthy families. Their cruelty has not even been the base result of fear. It has been the effect of their sense of perfect safety, in authorizing treasons, robberies, rapes, assassinations, slaughters and burnings throughout their harassed land. But the cause of all was plain from the beginning.

EDMUND BURKE, *Reflections on the Revolution in France.*

Nothing is more destructive, either in regard to the health, or the vigilance and industry of the poor than the infamous liquor, the name of which, derived from Juniper in *Dutch*, is now by frequent use and the laconick spirit of the nation, from a word of middling length shrunk into a monosyllable, intoxicating gin, that charms the unactive, the desperate and crazy of either sex, and makes the starving sot behold his rags and nakedness with stupid indolence, or banter both in senseless laughter, and more insipid jests; it is a fiery lake that sets the brain in flame, burns up the entrails, and scorches every part within; and at the same time a *Lethe* of oblivion, in which the wretch immersed drowns his most pinching cares, and, with his reason all anxious reflections on brats that cry for food, hard winter's frosts, and horrid empty home.

In hot and adust tempers it makes men quarrelsome, renders 'em brutes and savages, sets 'em on to fight for nothing, and has often been the cause of murder. It has broke and destroyed the strongest constitutions, thrown 'em into consumptions, and been the fatal and immediate occasion of apoplexies, phrensies, and sudden death. But as these latter mischiefs happen but seldom, they might be overlooked and connived at, but this cannot be said of the many diseases that are familiar to the liquor, and which are daily and hourly produced by it; such as loss of appetite, fevers, black and yellow jaundice, convulsions, stone and gravel, dropsies and leucophlegmacies.

Among the doating admirers of this liquid poison, many of the meanest rank, from a sincere affection to the commodity itself, become dealers in it, and take delight to help others to what they love themselves, as whores commence bawds to make the profits of one trade subservient to the pleasures of the other. But as these starvelings commonly drink more than their gains, they seldom by selling mend the wretchedness of condition they laboured under whilst they were only buyers. In the fag-end and out-skirts of the town, and all places of the vilest resort, it's sold in some part or other of almost every house, frequently in cellars and sometimes in the garret. The petty traders in this *Stygian* comfort are supplied by others in somewhat higher station, that keep professed brandy shops, and are as little to be envied as the former; and among the middling people, I know not a more miserable shift for a livelihood than their calling; whoever would thrive in it must in the first place be of a watchful and suspicious, as well as a bold and resolute temper, that he may not be imposed upon by cheats and sharpers, nor out-bully'd by the oaths and imprecations of hackney coachmen and foot-soldiers; in the second, he ought to be a dabster at gross jokes and loud laughter, and have all the winning ways to allure customers and draw out their money, and be well versed in the low jests and ralleries the mob make use of to banter prudence and frugality. He must be affable and obsequious to the most despicable; always ready and officious to help down a porter with his load, shake hands with a basket-woman, pull off his hat to an oyster wench, and be familiar with a beggar; with patience and good humour he must be able to endure the filthy actions and viler language of nasty drabs, and lewdest rake-hells, and without a frown or the least aversion bear with all the stench and squalor, noise and impertinence that the utmost indigence, laziness and ebriety can produce in the most shameless and abandoned vulgar.

The vast number of the shops I speak of throughout the city and suburbs, are an astonishing evidence of the many seducers that, in a lawful occupation are accessory to the introduction and increase of all the sloth, sottishness, want and misery which the abuse of strong waters is the immediate cause of, to lift above mediocrity perhaps half a dozen men that deal in the same commodity by wholesale; whilst among the retailers, though qualify'd as I required, a much greater number are broke and ruined, for not abstaining from the *Circean* cup they hold out to others; and the more fortunate are their whole lifetime obliged to take the uncommon pains, endure the hardships, and swallow all the ungrateful and shocking things I named, for little or nothing beyond a bare sustenance, and their daily bread.

BERNARD DE MANDEVILLE, *Fable of the Bees* (Remark G.).

The simple clause may be varied only in the order of its words: 'Cold was the night' for 'The night was cold'; and here all that is gained is an unusual emphasis on the word *cold*. But in compound sentences there is scope for much greater variety—words within clauses, and clauses within the sentence. Everything must depend on the required emphasis, and the emphasis is secured by the rhythm, and the rhythm by the

necessities of expression. Let us therefore proceed straight to
the examination of such sentences.

Pleasant, as the fiery heat of the desert daylight is done, is our
homely evening fire. The sun gone down upon a highland steppe
of Arabia, whose common altitude is above three thousand feet,
the thin dry air is presently refreshed, the sand is soon cold; wherein
yet at three fingers' depth is left a sunny warmth of the past day's
heat until the new sunrise. After a half hour it is the blue night,
and clear hoary starlight in which there shines the girdle of the
milky way, with a marvellous clarity. As the sun is setting, the
nomad housewife brings in a truss of sticks and dry bushes, which
she has pulled or hoed with a mattock (a tool they have seldom)
in the wilderness; she casts down this provision by our hearthside,
for the sweet-smelling evening fire. But to Hirfa, his sheykhly
young wife, Zeyd had given a little Beduin maid to help her.
The housewife has upon her woman's side an hearth apart, which
is the cooking-fire. Commonly Hirfa baked then, under the ashes,
a bread-cake for the stranger: Zeyd her husband, who is miserable,
or for other cause, eats not yet, but only near midnight, as he is
come again from the mejlis and would go in to sleep.

C. M. DOUGHTY, *Arabia Deserta*, i.[1]

In this passage the arrangement of clauses, and of words
within clauses, is, as always in Doughty's writing, very
deliberate. The paragraph begins with an inversion, to
bring into prominence the word 'pleasant', which word is the
keynote of the passage. The subject of the first sentence,
'our homely evening fire', is reserved to the end, not only to
suspend 'pleasant' in a still more marked isolation, but to
give the subject itself an emphasis, by placing it where we
should least expect it. In the next sentence clauses are
treated in much the same way as words in the first sentence.
The purpose is to describe the effect of the going down of
the sun, and the direct way would be to use adverbial phrases,
as, for example, '*when* the sun has gone down'. But direct
statements are more vivid, and in this particular case permit,
without confusion of syntax, the insertion of qualifying clauses
like 'whose common altitude is above three thousand feet'.
But the main object is the compact accretion of details of
observation. The third sentence is again remarkable for its
careful disposition of emphasis, and the rest of the paragraph

[1] Random House.

eases its rhythm to permit a relaxed observation; it is now not so much direct visualization, as comment. The retardation of the rhythm, towards the end of the paragraph, until it ends with a sense of inevitability on the word 'sleep', is also a deliberate effect.

When it is desired to contrast opposing ideas, this is most effectively done by confining them within a single sentence. The two ideas are placed in *antithesis*, which is a balance or opposition of sense:

> They went down to the camp in black, but they came back to the town in white; they went down to the camp in ropes, they came back in chains of gold; they went down to the camp with their feet in fetters, but came back with their steps enlarged under them; they went also to the camp looking for death, but they came back from thence with assurance of life; they went down to the camp with heavy hearts, but came back with pipe and tabor playing before them.
>
> JOHN BUNYAN: *Life and Death of Mr. Badman.*

Antithesis has been a very popular device with self-conscious writers, and particularly with the Eighteenth Century school, from Bolingbroke to Gibbon. Used with discretion it adds point and vivacity to expression; but when abused it becomes tedious and artificial.

> If by a more noble and more adequate conception, that be considered as wit which is at once natural and new, that which, though not obvious, is, upon its first production, acknowledged to be just; if it be that which he that never found it, wonders how he missed; to wit of this kind the metaphysical poets have seldom risen. Their thoughts are often new, but seldom natural; they are not obvious, but neither are they just; and the reader, far from wondering that he missed them, wonders more frequently by what perverseness of industry they were ever found.
>
> SAMUEL JOHNSON, *Life of Cowley.*

Mr. Wimsatt, in his book on Johnson's prose style, distinguishes three ways of binding groups of words, viz. (1) by the use of conjunctive or disjunctive words, (2) by the syntax of words, and (3) by the repetition of identical words. What he calls *parallelism* or *balance* is achieved by the simple pairing of words ('faults and follies'), by two elements in each member ('unnatural thoughts and rugged numbers'), by three elements

('Examples of national calamities and scenes of extensive misery'), and even by four elements ('the various forms of connubial felicity, the unexpected causes of lasting discord')— all examples from Johnson. There is in addition the device of antithetical parallels, e.g. 'a state too high for contempt and too low for envy'. Such antithetical clauses have been compared 'to the false handles and keyholes with which furniture is decorated'.[1]

But Hazlitt gave the most effective criticism of such mannerisms in his essay on 'Edmund Burke':

Burke was not a verbose writer. If he sometimes multiplies words, it is not for want of ideas, but because there are no words that fully express his ideas, and he tries to do it as well as he can by different ones. He had nothing of the *set* or formal style, the measured cadence, and stately phraseology of Johnson, and most of our modern writers. This style, which is what we understand by the *artificial*, is all in one key. It selects a certain set of words to represent all ideas whatever, as the most dignified and elegant, and excludes all others as low and vulgar. The words are not fitted to the things, but the things to the words. Everything is seen through a false medium. It is putting a mask on the face of nature, which may indeed hide some specks and blemishes, but takes away all beauty, delicacy, and variety. It destroys all dignity or elevation, because nothing can be raised where all is on a level, and completely destroys all force, expression, truth, and character, by arbitrarily confounding the differences of things, and reducing everything to the same insipid standard. To suppose that this stiff uniformity can add anything to real grace or dignity, is like supposing that the human body in order to be perfectly graceful, should never deviate from its upright posture. Another mischief of this method is, that it confounds all ranks in literature. Where there is no room for variety, no discrimination, no nicety to be shewn in matching the idea with its proper word, there can be no room for taste or elegance. A man must easily learn the art of writing, when every sentence is to be cast in the same mould: where he is only allowed the use of one word, he cannot choose wrong, nor will he be in much danger of making himself ridiculous by affectation or false glitter, when, whatever subject he treats of, he must treat of it in the same way. This indeed is to wear golden chains for the sake of ornament.

WILLIAM HAZLITT, Essay on *Edmund Burke*.

---

[1] Quoted by Wimsatt, *op. cit.*, p. 49, from Whately's *Elements of Rhetoric*, 1828, which does not give the source of the comparison.

Compare also Coleridge:

The style of Junius is a sort of metre, the law of which is a balance of thesis and antithesis. When he gets out of this aphorismic metre into a sentence of five or six lines long, nothing can exceed the slovenliness of the English. Horne Tooke and a long sentence seem the only two antagonists that were too much for him. Still the antithesis of Junius is a real antithesis of images or thought; but the antithesis of Johnson is rarely more than verbal.

Table Talk, July 3, 1833 (Oxford edn., 1917) p. 255.

Antithesis operates by a tension or suspense between two ideas; the sentence becomes a balance between equal but opposite forces. A similar kind of suspense is maintained in the *period* proper. A period is a complex sentence of which the meaning remains in suspense until the completion of the sentence. The main sentence of the following passage from Wordsworth's *Convention of Cintra* is an extreme example:

But it is a belief propagated in books, and which passes currently among talking men as part of their familiar wisdom, that the hearts of the many *are* constitutionally weak; that they *do* languish; and are slow to answer to the requisition of things. I entreat those who are in this delusion, to look behind them and about them for the evidence of experience. Now this, rightly understood, not only gives no support to any such belief; but proves that the truth is in direct opposition to it. The history of all ages; tumults after tumults; wars, foreign or civil, with short, or with no breathing-spaces, from generation to generation; wars—why and wherefore? yet with courage, with perseverance, with self-sacrifice, with enthusiasm—with cruelty driving forward the cruel man from its own terrible nakedness, and attracting the more benign by the accompaniment of some shadow which seems to sanctify it; the senseless weaving and interweaving of factions—vanishing and reviving and piercing each other like the Northern Lights; public commotions, and those in the bosom of the individual; the long calenture, to which the Lover is subject; the blast, like the blast of the desert, which sweeps perennially through a frightful solitude of its own making in the mind of the Gamester; the slow quickening but ever quickening descent of appetite down which the Miser is propelled; the agony and cleaving oppression of grief; the ghost-like hauntings of shame; the incubus of revenge; the life-distemper of ambition;—these inward existences, and the visible and familiar occurrences of daily life in every town and village; the patient curiosity and contagious acclamations of the multitude in the streets of the city and within the walls of the theatre; a procession, or a rural dance; a hunting, or a horse-race; a flood, or a fire;

rejoicing and ringing of bells for an unexpected gift of good fortune, or the coming of a foolish heir to his estate;—these demonstrate incontestably that the passions of men (I mean, the soul of sensibility in the heart of man)—in all quarrels, in all contests, in all quests, in all delights, in all employments which are either sought by men or thrust upon them—do immeasurably transcend their objects. The true sorrow of humanity consists in this;—not that the mind of man fails; but that the course and demands of action and of life so rarely correspond with the dignity and intensity of human desires; and hence that, which is slow to languish, is too easily turned aside and abused.

WILLIAM WORDSWORTH, *Convention of Cintra.*

Most periods can be analysed into subject, verb and predicate, the subject or verb being in the nature of an extensive catalogue. Wordsworth's sentence is really of this nature, though somewhat disguised by its eloquence. The following sentence of Burke's has a more obvious catalogue-subject:

To be bred in a place of estimation; to see nothing low and sordid from one's infancy; to be taught to respect one's self; to be habituated to the censorial inspection of the public eye; to look early to public opinion; to stand upon such elevated ground as to be enabled to take a large view of the widespread and infinitely diversified combinations of men and affairs in a large society; to have leisure to read, to reflect, to converse; to be enabled to draw the court and attention of the wise and learned wherever they are to be found;—to be habituated in armies to command and to obey; to be taught to despise danger in the pursuit of honour and duty; to be formed to the greatest degree of vigilance, foresight, and circumspection, in a state of things in which no fault is committed with impunity, and the slightest mistakes draw on the most ruinous consequences—to be led to a guarded and regulated conduct, from a sense that you are considered as an instructor of your fellow-citizens in their highest concerns, and that you act as a reconciler between God and man—to be employed as an administrator of law and justice, and to be thereby amongst the first benefactors of mankind—to be a professor of high science or of liberal and ingenuous art—to be amongst rich traders, who from their success are presumed to have sharp and vigorous under-standings, and to possess the virtues of diligence, order, constancy, and regularity, and to have cultivated an habitual regard to commutative justice—these are the circumstances of men, that form what I should call a *natural* aristocracy, without which there is no nation.

BURKE, *Appeal from the New to the Old Whigs.*

A truer period is one in which the suspense is created by a complexity of clauses, as in the following example:

Corruption could not spread with so much success, though reduced into a system, and though some ministers, with equal impudence and folly, avowed it by themselves and their advocates, to be the principal expedient by which they governed; if a long and almost unobserved progression of causes and effects did not prepare the conjuncture.

BOLINGBROKE, *Spirit of Patriotism.*

Not all long and complex sentences have the architectural harmony of the period. Many such sentences are often in the nature of an agglomeration of inconsistent and unrelated clauses, and should really be split up into several sentences. There is an extreme example in a letter of Swift's, which shows that Swift could on occasion write like a servant girl:

Last year a paper was brought here from England, called a Dialogue between the Archbishop of Canterbury and Mr. Higgins, which we ordered to be burnt by the common hangman, as it well deserved, though we have no more to do with his Grace of Canterbury, than you have with the Archbishop of Dublin, whom you suffer to be abused openly, and by name, by that paltry rascal of an observator; and lately upon an affair, wherein he had no concern; I mean, the business of the missionary of Drogheda, wherein our excellent primate was engaged, and did nothing but according to law and discretion.

JONATHAN SWIFT, *Letter concerning the Sacramental Test.*

Such a sentence betrays itself, if by nothing else, by its rhythm; it jerks along like a car in distress; and this is because we so often come to a point which completes the sense of a possible sentence within the sentence. There is no suspense from beginning to end, but only an inorganic aggregation of phrases.

The danger with all long and complex sentences is that they may lack *balance*. The sense may be logically clear, the rhythm may be easy, but still they try our patience or offend our sensibilities. There is a want of proportion between the subject and the predicate, or between either of these and the verb—not so much a proportion of sense, which would result in humour, but a proportion of structure, the simple against the complicated, the devious against the direct.

As sentences increase in complexity, the use of punctuation becomes more complicated and more worthy of attention. At least three methods of punctuation have been used in English prose writing, these being determined respectively by structure, respiration and rhythm.

Punctuation by structure is logical: it serves to indicate and help the sense of what is being said. It marks off the processes of thought, outlines the steps of the argument; in fact, orders and controls the expression in the interests of meaning:

Concerning faith, the principal object whereof is that eternal verity which hath discovered the treasures of hidden wisdom in Christ; concerning hope, the highest object whereof is that ever-lasting goodness which in Christ doth quicken the dead; concerning charity, the final object whereof is that incomprehensible beauty which shineth in the countenance of Christ the Son of the living God: concerning these virtues, the first of which beginning here with a weak apprehension of things not seen, endeth with the intuitive vision of God in the world to come; the second beginning here with a trembling expectation of things far removed and as yet but only heard of, endeth with real and actual fruition of that which no tongue can express; the third beginning here with a weak inclination of heart towards him unto whom we are not able to approach, endeth with endless union, the mystery whereof is higher than the reach of the thoughts of men; concerning that faith, hope, and charity, without which there can be no salvation, was there ever any mention made saving only in that law which God himself hath from heaven revealed?

RICHARD HOOKER, *Of the Laws of Ecclesiastical Polity*, I. xi. 6.

The logic of this passage is not entirely controlled by punctuation; there enter into its structure repetitions such as that of the word 'concerning', and enumeration, and rhythm. But the structure is perfectly reflected in the punctuation, and is determined by it.

Punctuation by 'respiration' is determined by physical ease; it is assumed that what is read is really spoken, however unconsciously; and that since our natural speech is punctuated by the physical limits of respiration, our silent or imaginary speech should conform to similar laws. Each stop—comma, semi-colon, colon, full-stop—represents a degree of pause; it has a certain time-value and is inserted to represent a proportionate duration. This type of punctuation is perhaps the one most commonly in use, and almost any passage of colloquial prose will illustrate it:

His loose entertainments in this stage were, as usual with gentlemen cadets of noble families in the country, sporting on horseback; for which there was opportunity enough at his grandfather's house (at Kirtling), where was a very large and well-stocked deer park: and at least twice a week in the season there was killing of deer. The method then was for the keeper with a large cross bow and arrow to wound the deer, and two or three disciplined park hounds pursued till he dropped. There was most of the country sports used there for diverting a large family, as setting, coursing, bowling; and he was in it all; and, within doors, backgammon and cards with his fraternity and others; wherein his parts did not fail him for he was an expert gamester. He used to please himself with raillery, as he found any that by minority of age or majority of folly and self-conceit were exposed to be so practised upon. I could give instances enough of this sort and not unpleasant, if such trifles were to be indulged in a design such as mine is. His most solemn entertainment was music, in which he was not only master, but doctor. This for the country; where, to make good his exhibition, he was contented (though in truth forced) to pass the greater part of his time. But in town, he had his select of friends and acquaintance; and with them he passed his time merrily and profitably for he was as brisk at every diversion as the best. Even after his purse flowed sufficiently a petit supper and a bottle always pleased him. But he fell into no course of excess or vice; and whenever he was a little overtaken it was a warning to him to take better care afterwards: and against women his modesty was an effectual guard, though he was as much inclined as any man which made him desirous to marry. And that made his continence a positive virtue; for who may not be good that is not inclined to evil? The virtue of goodness is where a contrary inclination is strove with and conquered. He was in town a noted hunter of music meetings; and very often the fancy prevailed to go about town and see trades work; which is a very diverting and instructive entertainment. There was not anything extraordinary which he did not, if he might visit, for his information as well as diversion; as engines, shows, lectures, and even so low as to hear Hugh Peters preach.

ROGER NORTH, *Life of the Rt. Hon. Francis North,*
Baron Guildford.

Punctuation, whether logical or mechanical, should always be subordinate to the general sense of rhythm but may also itself determine rhythm. But this use of punctuation is artificial and rare; it is the mark of the conscious artist, of Donne and Browne, of Milton and Ruskin, and of Pater. It is raised to great complexity and effectiveness by Doughty, to whom punctuation is almost a system of rhythmical notation, to be deliberately observed by the reader, and given due weight. This famous speech from Landor illustrates the more obvious qualities of such a mode of punctuation:

Laodameia died; Helen died; Leda, the beloved of Jupiter, went before. It is better to repose in the earth betimes than to sit up late; better, than to cling pertinaciously to what we feel crumbling under us, and to protract an inevitable fall. We may enjoy the present while we are insensible of infirmity and decay: but the present, like a note in music, is nothing but as it appertains to what is past and what is to come. There are no fields of amaranth on this side of the grave: there are no voices, O Rhodopé, that are not soon mute, however tuneful: there is no name, with whatever emphasis of passionate love repeated, of which the echo is not faint at last.

W. S. LANDOR, *Aesop and Rhodopé.*

The rhythm of this passage is controlled by the subtle distinction in value made between the colon and semi-colon. The semi-colon seems to mark a carrying over of an even beat; the colon, the recovery of an initial emphasis. In Doughty, however, the poor company of stops is made to serve a score of uses:

Here passing, in my former journeys, we saw Arab horsemen which approached us; we being too many for them, they came but to beg insolently a handful of tobacco. In their camps such would be kind hosts; but had we fallen into their hands in the desert we should have found them fiends, they would have stripped us, and perchance in a savage wantonness have cut some of our throats. These were three long-haired Beduins that bid us *salaam* (peace); and a fourth shock-haired cyclops of the desert, whom the fleetness of their mares had outstripped, trotted in after them, uncouthly seated upon the rawbone narrow withers of his dromedary, without saddle, without bridle, and only as an herdsman driving her with his voice and the camel-stick. His fellows rode with naked legs and unshod upon their beautiful mares' bare backs, the halter in one hand, and the long balanced lance, wavering upon the shoulder, in the other. We should think them sprawling riders; for a boast or war-like exercise, in the presence of our armed company, they let us view how fairly they could ride a career and turn: striking back heels and seated low, with pressed thighs, they parted at a hand-galop, made a tourney or two easily upon the plain; and now wheeling wide, they betook themselves down in the desert, every man bearing and handling his spear as at point to strike a foeman; so fetching a compass and we marching, they a little out of breath came gallantly again. Under the most ragged of these riders was a very perfect young and startling chestnut mare,—so shapely there are only few among them. Never combed by her rude master, but all shining beautiful and gentle of herself, she seemed a darling life upon that savage soil not worthy of her gracious pasterns: the strutting tail flowed down even to the ground, and the mane (*orfa*) was shed by the loving nurture of her mother Nature.

CHARLES M. DOUGHTY, Travels in Arabia
Deserta, i.[1]

Though the sentence is the unit of rhythm, it is not the whole of rhythm. Rhythm, as I shall attempt to show in the next chapter, is an affair of the paragraph, and rhythmically the sentence is subordinate to the paragraph. A sentence must be isolated to stand secure in its rhythm, and this is one of the requisites of an aphorism—that it is complete in its own rhythm.

The hours of folly are measur'd by the clock; but of wisdom, no clock can measure.

No bird soars too high, if he soars with his own wings.

The roaring of lions, the howling of wolves, the raging of the stormy sea, and the destructive sword, are portions of eternity, too great for the eye of man.

WILLIAM BLAKE, The Marriage of Heaven and Hell.

The following marginal note from the *Ancient Mariner* is a perfect example of the independent sentence:

In his loneliness and fixedness he yearneth towards the journeying Moon, and the stars that still sojourn, yet still move onward; and every where the blue sky belongs to them, and is their appointed rest, and their native country and their own natural homes, which they enter unannounced, as lords that are certainly expected and yet there is a silent joy at their arrival.

In a sentence the rhythm keeps close to the inner necessities of expression; it is determined in the act of creation. It is the natural modulation of the single cry. Only in the paragraph does it become modified in the interests of a larger

[1] Random House.

unity. We might, therefore, expect to find authors who though perfect in the formation of their sentences, neglect the paragraph and its wider, all-embracing sweep. And this indeed is the case, and may be the explanation of some stylistic defect which at first we find hard to analyse. Writers of foreign extraction, in whom the idiom of a language is not perfectly engrained, are particularly liable to this fault—as we find in Joseph Conrad and George Santayana. In the case of Santayana in particular the individual sentences may be rhythmical enough, but they do not form part of a more sustained rhythm; they follow in a series of minute percussions; they are like stepping-stones that finally weary the strained attention of the reader:

True love, it used to be said, is love at first sight. Manners have much to do with such incidents, and the race which happens to set at a given time the fashion in literature makes its temperament public and exercises a sort of contagion over all men's fancies. If women are rarely seen and ordinarily not to be spoken to; if all imagination has to build upon is a furtive glance or casual motion, people fall in love at first sight. For they must fall in love somehow, and any stimulus is enough if none more powerful is forthcoming. When society, on the contrary, allows constant and easy intercourse between the sexes, a first impression, if not reinforced, will soon be hidden and obliterated by others. Acquaintance becomes necessary for love when it is necessary for memory. But what makes true love is not the information conveyed by acquaintance, not any circumstantial charms that may be therein discovered: it is still a deep and dumb instinctive affinity, an inexplicable emotion seizing the heart, an influence organizing the world, like a luminous crystal, about one magic point. So that although love seldom springs up suddenly in these days into anything like a full-blown passion, it is sight, it is presence, that makes in time a conquest over the heart; for all virtues, sympathies, confidences will fail to move a man to tenderness and to worship unless a poignant effluence from the object envelops him, so that he begins to walk, as it were, in a dream.

Not to believe in love is a great sign of dulness. There are some people so indirect and lumbering that they think all real affection must rest on circumstantial evidence. But a finely constituted being is sensitive to its deepest affinities. This is precisely what refinement consists in, that we may feel in things immediate and infinitesimal a sure premonition of things ultimate and important. Fine senses vibrate at once to harmonies which it may take long to verify; so sight is finer than touch, and thought than sensation.

Well-bred instinct meets reason halfway, and is prepared for the consonances that may follow. Beautiful things, when taste is formed, are obviously and unaccountably beautiful. The grounds we may bring ourselves to assign for our preferences are discovered by analysing those preferences, and articulate judgments follow upon emotions which they ought to express, but which they sometimes sophisticate. So too the reasons we give for love either express what it feels or else are insincere, attempting to justify at the bar of reason and convention something which is far more primitive than they and underlies them both.

GEORGE SANTAYANA, *Reason in Society*.[1]

But foreigners are not the only writers who practise this fatal, lapidary style. Emerson may be quoted as an example of an author who was so concerned with the aphoristic quality of his sentences that he forgot the rhythmical life of his paragraphs:[2]

We have a great deal more kindness than is ever spoken. Maugre all the selfishness that chills like east winds the world, the whole human family is bathed with an element of love like a fine ether. How many persons we meet in houses, whom we scarcely speak to, whom yet we honour, and who honour us! How many we see in the street, or sit with in church, whom, though silently, we warmly rejoice to be with! Read the language of these wandering eye-beams. The heart knoweth.

RALPH WALDO EMERSON, *Essay on Friendship*.

In the passage from Santayana we feel in each sentence the force of the same even and impassive mood. The rhythms are consequently too uniform. In the case of Emerson the sentences do not seem to belong to each other; the transitions are mostly abrupt; there is no carrying-over of the rhythm from one sentence to another.

It is in such transitions of sense and rhythm that conjunctions play their part; and the appropriate use of conjunctions is, indeed, one of the marks of a good style. 'Of all the parts of speech', wrote George Campbell,[3] 'the conjunctions are the most unfriendly to vivacity.' And he quotes Exodus xv. 9, 10, as an example of vigour due to simplicity of phrasing:

[1] Scribner.
[2] His essays were actually composed by grouping together sentences which he had separately entered into a journal.
[3] *Philosophy of Rhetoric*, iii. 3.

The enemy said, I will pursue; I will overtake; I will divide the spoil; my revenge shall be satiated upon them: I will draw my sword; my hand shall destroy them: thou blewest with thy breath; the sea covered them; they sank as lead in the mighty waters.

But here, as Campbell notes, 'the natural connection of the particulars mentioned is both close and manifest; and it is this consideration which entirely supersedes the artificial signs of that connection, such as conjunctions and relatives'. The whole verse is actually suspended in one animation, in one breath, as it were. But where this natural connection is lacking, the result of dispensing with rhythmical transitions is exacting to the attention and ultimately wearying. Coleridge made the best comment on the use of conjunctions:

A close reasoner and a good writer in general may be known by his pertinent use of *connectives*. Read that page of Johnson (the Whig—author of *A humble and hearty Address to all English Protestants in the present Army*, 1686.); you cannot alter one conjunction without spoiling the sense. It is a linked strain throughout. In your modern books, for the most part, the sentences in a page have the same connexion with each other that marbles have with a bag; they touch without adhering.

Table Talk, May 15, 1833.

CHAPTER V

*

The Paragraph

THE PARAGRAPH IS A device of punctuation. The indentation by which it is marked implies no more than an additional breathing space. Like the other marks of punctuation which we have dealt with in the previous chapter it may be determined by logical, physical, or rhythmical needs. Logically it may be said to denote the full development of a single idea, and this indeed is the common definition of the paragraph. It is, however, in no way an adequate or helpful definition. A good deal depends on what is meant by an 'idea'; it is a vague term. But whether we mean an intellectual notion, or a playful fancy, or indeed any definite concept at all, this definition as such will be found of very little application to the paragraphs we find in literature. Take the following passage:

There can be no doubt that this remarkable man owed the vast influence which he exercised over his contemporaries at least as much to his gloomy egotism as to the real power of his poetry. We never could very clearly understand how it is that egotism, so unpopular in conversation, should be so popular in writing; or how it is that men who affect in their compositions qualities and feelings they have not, impose so much more easily on their contemporaries than on posterity. The interest which the loves of Petrarch excited in his own time, and the pitying fondness with which half Europe looked upon Rousseau are well known. To readers of our age, the love of Petrarch seems to have been love of that kind which breaks no hearts, and the sufferings of Rousseau to have deserved laughter rather than pity, to have been partly counterfeited, and partly the consequences of his own perverseness and vanity.

What our grandchildren may think of the character of Lord Byron, as exhibited in his poetry, we will not pretend to guess. It is certain that the interest which he excited during his life is without a parallel in literary history. The feeling with which young readers of poetry regarded him can be conceived only by those who have experienced it. To people who are unacquainted with real calamity, 'nothing is so dainty sweet as lovely melancholy'.

This faint image of sorrow has in all ages been considered by young gentlemen as agreeable excitement. Old gentlemen and middle-aged gentlemen have so many real causes of sadness that they are rarely inclined 'to be as sad as night only for wantonness'. Indeed they want the power almost as much as the inclination. We know very few persons engaged in active life who, even if they were to procure stools to be melancholy upon, and were to sit down with all the premeditation of Master Stephen, would be able to enjoy much of what somebody calls 'the ecstasy of woe'.

Among that large class of young persons whose reading is almost entirely confined to works of imagination, the popularity of Byron was unbounded   They bought pictures of him; they treasured up the smallest relics of him; they learned his poems by heart, and did their best to write like him, and to look like him.   Many of them practised at the glass in the hope of catching the curl of the upper lip, and the scowl of the brow, which appear in some of his portraits. A few discarded their neck-cloths in imitation of their great leader. For some years the Minerva press sent forth no novel without a mysterious, unhappy, Lara-like peer.   The number of hopeful undergraduates and medical students who became things of dark imaginings, on whom the freshness of the heart ceased to fall like dew, whose passions had consumed themselves to dust, and to whom the relief of tears was denied, passes all calculation.   This was not the worst.   There was created in the minds of many of these enthusiasts a pernicious and absurd association between intellectual power and moral depravity.   From the poetry of Lord Byron they drew a system of ethics, compounded of misanthropy and voluptuousness, a system in which the two great commandments were, to hate your neighbour, and to love your neighbour's wife.

This affectation has passed away; and a few more years will destroy whatever remains of that magical potency which once belonged to the name of Byron.   To us he is still a man, young, noble, and unhappy.   To our children he will be merely a writer; and their impartial judgment will appoint his place among writers; without regard to his rank or to his private history.   That his poetry will undergo a severe sifting, that much of what has been admired by his contemporaries will be rejected as worthless, we have little doubt.   But we have as little doubt that, after the closest scrutiny, there will still remain much that can only perish with the English language.

LORD MACAULAY, *Essays* (Moore's *Life of Lord Byron*).

In these four paragraphs there are several 'ideas', which may be analysed in this way:

Para. 1. The influence of Byron's egotism, as distinct from his poetry. The popularity of egotism in writing generally.

Para. 2. Byron's melancholy. Melancholy and youth.
Para. 3. The popularity of Byron. His bad influence.
Para. 4. Posterity will judge Byron by his writings alone.
It is certain that some of these are imperishable.

All four paragraphs have one subject in common—Lord Byron; and they are all concerned with the same argument—the relation between Byron's character and his poetry. Each paragraph is really a separate exploration of an aspect of this general theme, but there is no single 'idea' developed in each paragraph; there are, as a matter of fact, usually two—a particular observation and a general reflection; or we may get a general observation and particular instances, involving many separate 'ideas'.

It is nearer the truth to say that a writer seizes upon some particular aspect of his subject and holds that aspect in his mind until he has seen it in all profitable lights. This process may take two or it may take twenty paragraphs: there is no rule, and whatever unity may govern the paragraph, it is not the unity of the development of a single idea.

In logical writing there seems to be no good reason why the paragraph should end until the argument is over. When once you have started on a trend of close reasoning, even the break of a paragraph may be disconcerting. Thus in good scientific writing the paragraphs are often found to be long and compact, giving the page that forbidding appearance of solidity which is popularly associated with 'serious' books. In the following passage there is no sense of strain or of breathlessness, and its length is justified by the unity of its argument:

It remains for us now to deal with the other characteristic, hardness, which is popularly attributed to matter. There are certain persons who, when men's ignorance as to the nature of matter is suggested to them, are content to remark that one has only to knock one's head against a stone wall in order to have a valid demonstration of the existence and the nature of matter. Now if this statement be of any value, it can only mean that the sense-impression of hardness is the essential test of the presence of matter in these persons' opinion. But none of us doubt the existence of the sense-impression hardness associated with other sense-impressions in certain permanent groups; we have been

aware of it from childhood's days, and do not require its existence
to be experimentally demonstrated now. It is one of those muscular
sense-impressions which we shall see are conceived by science to
be describable in terms of the relative acceleration of certain parts
of our body and of external bodies. ¶ But it is difficult to grasp
how the sense-impression of hardness can tell us more of the nature
of matter than the sense-impression of softness might be supposed
to do. There are clearly many things which are popularly termed
matter and are certainly not hard. Further, there are things
which satisfy the definitions of matter as that which moves or as
that which fills space, but which are very far indeed from producing
any sense-impression of the nature of hardness or softness; nor
would they even satisfy our definition if we said that matter is
that which is heavy, heaviness being certainly a more widely-spread
factor of material groups of sense-impressions than hardness.
Between the sun and planets, between the atoms of bodies, physicists
conceive the ether to exist, a medium whose vibrations constitute
the channel by means of which electro-magnetic and optical energy
is transferred from one body to another. In the first place, the
ether is a pure conception by aid of which we correlate in conceptual
space various motions. These motions are the symbols by which
we briefly describe the sequences and relationships we perceive
between various groups of phenomena. The ether is thus a mode
of resuming our perceptual experience; but like a good many other
conceptions of which we have no direct perception, physicists
project it into the phenomenal world and assert its real existence.
There seems to be just as much, or little, logic in this assertion as in
the postulate that there is a real substratum, matter, at the back
of groups of sense-impressions; both at present are metaphysical
statements. ¶ Now there is no evidence forthcoming that the
ether must be conceived as either hard or heavy, and yet it can
be strained or its parts put in relative motion. Further, from
Professor Tait's standpoint, it occupies space. Hence those who
associate matter with hardness and weight must be prepared to
deny that the ether is matter, or be content to call it non-matter.
¶ It is worth noting, at the same time, that the metaphysicians—
whether they be materialists asserting the phenomenal existence
both of space and of a permanent substratum of sense-impression,
or 'common-sense' philosophers asking us to knock our heads
against stone walls—reach hopelessly divergent results when they
say that matter is that which moves, that matter occupies space,
and that matter is that which is heavy and hard.

KARL PEARSON, *The Grammar of Science*.[1]

A poorer writer might have been tempted to break this
paragraph up at the points I have indicated with a ¶. The

[1] Dutton.

sense would remain the same, and perhaps the cogency; but the persuasive flow would have suffered three checks.

But this general rule does not exclude the use of paragraphs as a schematic device, to give emphasis to the transitions of thought. In the following passage the logical structure is indicated by a system of paragraphing accompanied by an enumeration that indicates the relationship between the main point of the argument and the corollaries or inferences dependent on them. Such devices are, however, scientific rather than artistic: they analyse thought rather than compose a style.

6.4312   The solution of the riddle of life in space and time lies *outside* space and time.

6.432   *How* the world is, is completely indifferent for what is higher.   God does not reveal himself in the world.

6.4321   The facts all belong only to the task and not to its performance.

6.44   Not *how* the world is, is the mystical, but *that* it is.

6.45   The contemplation of the world *sub specie aeterni* is its contemplation as a limited whole.

The feeling of the world as a limited whole is the mystical feeling.

6.5   For an answer which cannot be expressed the question too cannot be expressed.

The riddle does not exist.

If a question can be put at all, then it *can* also be answered.

6.51   Scepticism is *not* irrefutable, but palpably senseless, if it would doubt where a question cannot be asked.

For doubt can only exist where there is a question; a question only where there is an answer, and this only where something *can* be *said*.

6.52   We feel that even if *all possible* scientific questions can be answered, the problems of life have still not been touched at all.   Of course there is then no question left, and just this is the answer.

6.521   The solution of the problem of life is seen in the vanishing of this problem.

6.522   There is indeed the inexpressible.   This *shows* itself; it is the mystical.

6.53   The right method of philosophy would be this: to say nothing except what can be said, i.e. something that has nothing to do with philosophy: and then always, when someone else wished to say something metaphysical, to demonstrate to him that he had given no meaning to

certain signs in his propositions. This method would be
unsatisfying to the other—he would not have the feeling
that we were teaching philosophy—but it would be the
only strictly correct method.

6.54   My propositions are elucidatory in this way: he who
understands me finally recognises them as senseless, when
he has climbed out through them, on them, over them.
(He must, so to speak, throw away the ladder, after he
has climbed up on it.)

He must surmount these propositions; then he sees the
world rightly.

Whereof one cannot speak, thereof one must be silent.

LUDWIG WITTGENSTEIN, Tractatus Logico-
Philosophicus.[1]

Comparable devices are used in military operation orders,
where absolute precision of meaning is a matter of life or death.[2]

In public speaking it is customary for the orator to make a
pause and indulge in various gestures of physical relaxation
when he has come to a point where he expects applause.
The moment, at least, is propitious for it. Or his reason may
be that he wishes to give special emphasis to his next sentence
by making it the first sentence of a peroration.

The paragraphing of many writers is of this kind. A writer
like Sterne, who always remembers that he is addressing an
invisible audience, inevitably breaks off one paragraph and
begins another at 'the psychological moment'. Almost any
page will illustrate this:

I had scarce uttered the words, when a poor monk of the order
of St. Francis came into the room to beg something for his convent.
No man cares to have his virtues the sport of contingencies—or one
man may be generous, as another man is puissant—*sed, non quo ad
hanc*—or be it as it may—for there is no regular reasoning upon the
ebbs and flows of our humours; they may depend upon the same
causes, for aught I know, which influences the tides themselves—
'twould oft be no discredit to us, to suppose it was so: I'm sure at
least for myself, that in many a case I should be more highly satisfied,
to have it said by the world, 'I had had an affair with the moon, in
which there was neither sin nor shame', than have it pass altogether
as my own act and deed, wherein there was so much of both.
—But be this as it may. The moment I cast my eyes upon him,

<hr>

1 Humanities Press.

2 Cf. *London Book of English Prose*, II, vi, 13—an operation order by General
Wavell.

I was predetermined not to give him a single sous; and accordingly I put my purse into my pocket—button'd it up—set myself a little more upon my center, and advanced up gravely to him: there was something, I fear, forbidding in my look: I have his figure this moment before my eyes, and think there was that in it which deserved better.

The monk, as I judged from the break in his tonsure, a few scattered white hairs upon his temples being all that remained of it, might be about seventy—but from his eyes, and that sort of fire which was in them, which seemed more temper'd by courtesy than years, could be no more than sixty—Truth might lie between— He was certainly sixty-five; and the general air of his countenance, notwithstanding something seem'd to have been planting wrinkles in it before their time, agreed to the account.

It was one of those heads which Guido has often painted—mild, pale—penetrating, free from all commonplace ideas of fat contented ignorance looking downwards upon the earth—it look'd forwards; but look'd, as if it look'd at something beyond this world. How one of his order came by it, heaven above, who let it fall upon a monk's shoulders, best knows; but it would have suited a Bramin, and had I met it upon the plains of Indostan, I had reverenced it.

The rest of his outline may be given in a few strokes; one might put it into the hands of any one to design, for 'twas neither elegant or otherwise, but as character and expression made it so: it was a thin, spare form, something above the common size, if it lost not the distinction by a bend forward in the figure—but it was the attitude of Entreaty; and as it now stands presented to my imagination, it gain'd more than it lost by it.

When he had entered the room three paces, he stood still; and laying his left hand upon his breast (a slender white staff with which he journeyed being in his right)—when I had got close up to him, he introduced himself with the little story of the wants of his convent, and the poverty of his order—and did it with so simple a grace—and such an air of deprecation was there in the whole cast of his look and figure—I was bewitch'd not to have been struck with it—

—A better reason was, I had predetermined not to give him a single sous.

LAURENCE STERNE, *A Sentimental Journey.*

This kind of paragraphing might be called *witty*. There is still another kind which is as nice in its determination, and that is the *rhythmical*.

The scientific study of English prose rhythm, despite the very complete and provocative history devoted to it by Professor Saintsbury,[1] is still very much in its infancy.

[1] *A History of English Prose Rhythm.* George Saintsbury. Second edition, 1922.

Professor Saintsbury has analysed the rhythms of most of our writers who have any pretence to any, but he resolutely, and perhaps rightly, refuses to classify these rhythms. Prose rhythm does not trip along in metrical feet, as verse does, but sweeps on in longer units. The paragraph is, indeed, the first complete and independent unit of prose rhythm. The sentence has rhythm, but as we have seen, a prose all sentences, even if these are in themselves perfectly rhythmical, is not perfect prose. The sentences must be dissolved in a wider movement and this wider movement is the rhythm of the paragraph—a rhythm that begins with the first syllable of the paragraph and is not complete without the last syllable. With the last syllable the rhythm ends and there is a rest.

The rhythmical unity of the paragraph may be a unity of actual composition: compare Gibbon's conscious practice (the conscious practice of many writers, but perhaps more often an unconscious instinct)—

'It has always been my practice to cast a long paragraph in a single mould, to try it by my ear, to deposit it in my memory, but to suspend the action of the pen till I had given the last polish to my work.'—*Autobiography*.

Rhythm in this sense may be no more than 'an instinct for the difference between what sounds right and what sounds wrong' (Fowler: *Modern English Usage*). This might be still a question of 'ear', but Wimsatt (*op. cit.*, p. 8) holds that 'prose rhythm is a matter of emphasis; it is putting the important words where they sound important. It is a matter of coherence; it is putting the right idea in the right place.' It would follow, as Wimsatt recognizes, that we should not properly speak of rhythm at all in relation to prose—' "Rhythm", when used literally, means "measure" or "regularity", and since the movement of good prose is precisely *not* regular but varied with the sense, the union of the terms "prose" and "rhythm" has been none of the happiest.'

Mr. Wimsatt's interpretation of rhythm is perhaps a little academic—modern verse has done a good deal to break down the notion of an essential regularity in rhythm—at the most it remains as a background 'ghost' to make us more aware of the irregular subtleties of verse rhythms. It would seem now that the whole subject of rhythm must be reconsidered in the light of gestalt psychology, for the rhythm, whether of a stanza of verse or of a paragraph of prose, is obviously one of those individual and characteristic entities, 'existing as something detached and *having* a shape or form as one of its attributes', which has been called a *gestalt*. If we compare the following definition of a *gestalt* with our conception of the paragraph, it will be seen how exactly they correspond:

A *gestalt* not only makes its own boundaries, but also within its boundaries rules and determines its parts in a sort of hierarchy giving this a central position, this the role of a mere decorative detail, that the function of contrast, and so forth. If then a part, by virtue of properties which belong to it quite independently of the role it plays in the whole, acquires a weight and thereby an effect that is greater than that accorded to it by the law of the whole, then to this extent the demand lodged in this part is extraneous, the effect impure.

It is characteristic of a good *gestalt* not only that it produces a hierarchical unity of its parts, but also that this unity is of a particular kind. A good *gestalt* cannot be changed without changing its quality, and must deteriorate if the changes introduced are of a minor order.

K. KOFFKA: 'Problems in the Psychology of Art.' Bryn Mawr, Monograph on *Art*, 1940.

The unity of the following paragraphs may be studied from this point of view:

To subsist in lasting Monuments, to live in their productions, to exist in their names and predicament of chimeras, was large satisfaction unto old expectations, and made one part of their Elysiums. But all this is nothing in the Metaphysics of true belief. To live indeed is to be again ourselves, which being not only an hope but an evidence in noble believers; 'tis all one to lie in St. Innocent's churchyard, as in the sands of Aegypt; Ready to be anything, in the ecstasy of being ever, and as content with six foot as the Moles of Adrianus.

SIR THOMAS BROWNE, *Urn Burial*.

Full day came quickly to show me the reality of one of my early visions, and I suppose I may not expect many more such minutes as I spent when watching from the 'Capella's' bridge the forest of the Amazon take shape. It was soon over. The morning light brimmed at the forest top, and spilled into the river. The channel filled with sunshine. There is was then. In the cliff to starboard

I could see even the boughs and trunks; they were veins of silver in a mass of solid chrysolite. This forest had not the rounded and dull verdure of our own woods in midsummer, with deep bays of shadow. It was a sheer front, uniform, shadowless, and astonishingly vivid. I thought then the appearance of the forest was but a local feature, and so gazed at it for what it would show next. It had nothing else to show me. Clumps of palms threw their fronds above the roof of the forest in some places, or a giant exogen raised a dome; but that was all. Those strong characters in the growth were seen only in passing. They did not change that outlook ahead of converging lines of level green heights rising directly from a brownish flood. Occasionally the river narrowed, or we passed close to one wall, and then we could see the texture of the forest surface, though we could never see into it for more than a few yards, except where, in some places, habitations were thrust into the base of the woods, as in lower caverns. An exuberant wealth of forms built up that forest which was so featureless from a little distance. The numerous palms gave grace and life to the façade, for their plumes flung in noble arcs from tall and slender columns, or sprayed directly from the ground in emerald fountains. The rest was inextricable confusion. Vines looped across the front of green, binding the forest with cordage, and the roots of epiphytes hung from upper boughs, like hanks of twine.

H. M. Tomlinson, *The Sea and the Jungle.*[1]

Rhythm is not an *a priori* construction. It is not an ideal form to which we fit our words. Above all it is not a musical notation to which our words submit.

Rhythm is more profound than this. It is born, not with the words, but with the thought, and with whatever confluence of instincts and emotions the thought is accompanied. As the thought takes shape in the mind, it takes *a* shape. It has always been recognized that clear thinking precedes good writing. There is about good writing a visual actuality. It exactly reproduces what we should metaphorically call the contour of our thought. The metaphor is for once exact: thought has a contour or shape. The paragraph is the perception of this contour or shape.

The writer has towards his materials, words, the same relation that an artist, say a modeller, has towards his material, clay. The paragraph is a plastic mass, and it takes its shape from the thought it has to express: its shape *is* the thought.

[1] Dutton.

This is the distinction between a dead paragraph and a living paragraph: in the first case a writer's words flow until either a phase of his logic is complete, or the simulated oratory of his periods demands a pause, or for no reason whatsoever; but in the second case the words rise like clay on the potter's wheel: the downward force of attention, or concentration, or intuition, and the driving force of emotion or feeling—between these forces the words rise up, take shape, become a complete pattern a 'good' *gestalt*.

Let us look at one or two longer passages of prose in which the articulation into paragraphs is determined by a rhythmical configuration:

O, sir, I do now feel myself inwrapped on the sudden into those mazes and labyrinths of dreadful and hideous thoughts, that which way to get out, or which way to end, I know not, unless I turn mine eyes, and with your help lift up my hands to that eternal and propitious throne, where nothing is readier than grace and refuge to the distresses of mortal suppliants: and it were a shame to leave these serious thoughts less piously than the heathen were wont to conclude their graver discourses.

Thou, therefore, that sittest in light and glory unapproachable, parent of angels and men! next, thee I implore, omnipotent King, Redeemer of that lost remnant whose nature thou didst assume, ineffable and everlasting Love! and thou, the third subsistence of divine infinitude, illumining Spirit, the joy and solace of created things! one Tripersonal godhead! look upon this thy poor and almost spent and expiring church, leave her not thus a prey to these importunate wolves, that wait and think long till they devour thy tender flock; these wild boars that have broke into thy vineyard, and left the print of their polluting hooves on the souls of thy servants.   O let them not bring about their damned designs, that stand now at the entrance of the bottomless pit, expecting the watchword to open and let out those dreadful locusts and scorpions, to reinvolve us in that pitchy cloud of infernal darkness, where we shall never more see the sun of thy truth again, never hope for the cheerful dawn, never more hear the bird of morning sing.   Be moved with pity at the afflicted state of this our shaken monarchy, that now lies labouring under her throes, and struggling against the grudges of more dreaded calamities.

O thou, that after the impetuous rage of five bloody inundations, and the succeeding sword of intestine war, soaking the land in her own gore, didst pity the sad and ceaseless revolution of our swift and thick-coming sorrows; when we were quite breathless, of thy free grace didst motion peace and terms of covenant with us; and having first well nigh freed us from antichristian thraldom, didst build up this Britannic empire to a glorious and enviable height, with all her daughter-islands about her; stay us in this felicity, let not the obstinacy of our half-obedience and will-worship bring forth that viper of sedition, that for these fourscore years hath been breeding to eat through the entrail of our peace; but let her cast her abortive spawn without the danger of this travailing and throbbing kingdom: that we may still remember in our solemn thanksgivings, how for us, the northern ocean even to the frozen Thule was scattered with the proud shipwrecks of the Spanish armada, and the very maw of hell ransacked, and made to give up her concealed destruction, ere she could vent it in that horrible and damned blast.

O how much more glorious will those former deliverances appear, when we shall know them not only to have saved us from greatest miseries past, but to have reserved us for greatest happiness to come! Hitherto thou hast freed but us, and that not fully, from the unjust and tyrannous claim of thy foes; now unite us entirely, and appropriate us to thyself, tie us everlastingly in willing homage to the prerogative of thy eternal throne.

And now we know, O thou our most certain hope and defence, that thine enemies have been consulting all the sorceries of the great whore, and have joined their plots with that sad intelligencing tyrant that mischiefs the world with his mines of Ophir, and lies thirsting to revenge his naval ruins that have larded our seas: but let them all take counsel together, and let it come to nought; let them decree, and do thou cancel it; let them gather themselves, and be scattered; let them embattle themselves, and be broken; let them embattle, and be broken, for thou art with us.

Then, amidst the hymns and hallelujahs of saints, some one may perhaps be heard offering at high strains in new and lofty measure to sing and celebrate thy divine mercies and marvellous judgments in this land throughout all ages; whereby this great and warlike nation, instructed and inured to the fervent and continual practice of truth and righteousness, and casting far from her the rags of her whole vices, may press on hard to that high and happy emulation to be found the soberest, wisest, and most Christian people at that day, when thou, the eternal and shortly expected King, shall open the clouds to judge the several kingdoms of the world, and distributing national honours and rewards to religious and just commonwealths, shalt put an end to all earthly tyrannies, proclaiming thy universal and mild monarchy through heaven and earth; where they undoubtedly, that by their labours, counsels, and prayers, have been earnest for the common good of religion and their country, shall receive above the inferior orders of the blessed, the regal addition of principalities, legions and thrones into their glorious titles, and in supereminence of beatific vision, progressing the dateless and irrevoluble circle of eternity, shall clasp inseparable hands with joy and bliss, in overmeasure for ever.

But they contrary, that by the impairing and diminution of the true faith, the distresses and servitude of their country, aspire to high dignity, rule, and promotion here, after a shameful end in this life (which God grant them), shall be thrown down eternally into the darkest and deepest gulf of hell, where, under the despiteful control, the trample and spurn of all the other damned, that in the anguish of their torture, shall have no other ease than to exercise a raving and bestial tyranny over them as their slaves and negroes, they shall remain in that plight for ever, the basest, the lowermost, the most dejected, most underfoot, and downtrodden vassals of perdition.

JOHN MILTON, *Of Reformation in England.*

She was talking to me of a sheep that had died, but I could not understand because of her dialect. It never occurred to her that I could not understand. She only thought me different, stupid. And she talked on. The ewes had lived under the house, and a part was divided off for the he-goat, because the other people brought their she-goats to be covered by the he-goat. But how the ewe came to die I could not make out.

Her fingers worked away all the time in a little, half-fretful movement, yet spontaneous as butterflies leaping here and there. She chattered rapidly on in her Italian that I could not understand, looking meanwhile into my face, because the story roused her somewhat. Yet not a feature moved. Her eyes remained candid and open and unconscious as the skies. Only a sharp will in them now and then seemed to gleam at me, as if to dominate me.

Her shuttle had caught in a dead chicory plant, and spun no more. She did not notice. I stooped and broke off the twigs. There was a glint of blue on them yet. Seeing what I was doing, she merely withdrew a few inches from the plant. Her bobbin hung free.

She went on with her tale, looking at me wonderfully. She seemed like the Creation, like the beginning of the world, the first morning. Her eyes were like the first morning of the world, so ageless.

Her thread broke. She seemed to take no notice, but mechanically picked up the shuttle, wound up a length of worsted, connected the ends from her wool strand, set the bobbin spinning again, and went on talking, in her half-intimate, half-unconscious fashion, as if she were talking to her own world in me.

So she stood in the sunshine on the little platform, old and yet like the morning, erect and solitary, sun-coloured, sun-discoloured, whilst I at her elbow, like a piece of night and moonshine, stood smiling into her eyes, afraid lest she should deny me existence.

Which she did. She had stopped talking, did not look at me any more, but went on with her spinning, the brown shuttle twisting gaily. So she stood, belonging to the sunshine and the weather, taking no more notice of me than of the dark-stained caper-bush which hung from the wall above her head, whilst I, waiting at her side, was like the moon in the daytime sky, over-shone, obliterated, in spite of my black clothes.

'How long has it taken you to do that much?' I asked.

She waited a minute, glanced at her bobbin.

'This much? I don't know. A day or two.'

'But you do it quickly.'

She looked at me, as if suspiciously and derisively. Then, quite suddenly, she started forward and went across the terrace to the great blue-and-white checked cloth that was drying on the wall. I hesitated. She had cut off her consciousness from me. So I turned and ran away, taking the steps two at a time, to get away from her. In a moment I was between the walls, climbing upwards, hidden.

D. H. LAWRENCE, *Twilight in Italy*, pp. 41–4.[1]

These two passages are entirely different in mood and construction, yet in both of them each paragraph has its indefeasible unity. In Milton each is dominated by a powerful rhythm: from the first syllable to the last there is no break in the mighty sweep of linked and modulated sounds. The rhythm is all-determining, and it would be no more defensible to alter one of these rhythms than it would be to meddle with a movement in one of Beethoven's sonatas.

In the passage from *Twilight in Italy* the unity of the paragraphs is no less intact, but it is more sophisticated. Each paragraph opens with an action of the old spinning-woman; almost as invariably it closes with a reflection of, or concerning, the narrator. That is to say, each paragraph is a complete action and reaction. The rhythm, like an accompaniment, passes from staccato emphasis to a falling cadence. But if every paragraph were in this rhythm, the effect would be monotonous. So we find one paragraph, the third in the passage, which exactly reverses the rhythm.

[1] Duckworth.

CHAPTER VI

*

Arrangement

THE ARRANGEMENT OF paragraphs within a larger unit of composition is mainly a question of rhetoric, and will be dealt with in Part II. But in rhetoric we consider arrangement as a means to secure a particular effect; from the point of view of composition we have to consider arrangement as an end in itself, as a pattern of aesthetic worth, a 'good' gestalt independent of the ideas expressed.

Such arrangement of material is either intuitive or constructional. Intuitively the writer feels that his theme has a certain broad rhythm, and that the rhythm of his paragraphs is subordinate to this broader effect. We speak of the *course* of exposition, the *speed* of narrative, the *flow* of eloquence, the *flight* of imagination, and all these dead metaphors originally expressed the qualities of different methods of composition. The analysis of these effects we leave to later chapters; here we are concerned with the compositional devices used to produce such effects.

Intuitive arrangement is appropriate to the short composition, such as the essay and short story. A logical exposition may, indeed, be short enough to have the outward appearance of an essay, but 'article', or 'treatise', or 'sketch', would be descriptive enough, whereas in the word 'essay' there is an original implication which conforms to the present idea of an intuitive arrangement. An essay is an 'attempt at'—an attempt at the expression of an idea or mood or feeling lurking unexpressed in the mind. It is an informal attempt to create a pattern in words which shall correspond with the idea, mood or feeling. It has some analogy to 'improvising' in music. It is the counterpart in prose of the lyric in poetry.

The essay is as old as any occasional writing; it is an impersonal form of letter writing—an open letter that need

not be addressed to anyone in particular. But in the modern
world, and especially in England, it has been cultivated for
its own sake, as a special form of literature, and though it
has never been hedged round by any precise rules of composition, yet the type has now for the last two or three hundred
years been fairly distinct. Bacon is in many ways the founder
of the self-conscious essay, and in an essay by him we find a
central theme round which are gathered a number of detached
observations and apothegms, linked together in an easy,
direct manner. The actual mode of composition is not known,
but if a man of genius, like Bacon, were to keep notebooks
of his daily thoughts and immediate observations, and then
draw together from these notebooks all that referred to a
common theme, he would have the substance of one of these
essays. The form would be determined by arranging the
separate notes in relevant groups, and then taking the groups
in the easiest order of transition. The method is the same as
Emerson's referred to on page 50, but Bacon, though not
guiltless of imperfect paragraphs, had more care than Emerson
for the transition between sentence and sentence.

The casual form of the essay, as initiated by Bacon, was
found particularly appropriate to the periodical literature
that developed in the early eighteenth century, and at the
hands of Addison, Steele and Goldsmith, the essay became
more varied, more distinctive, and less weighty. The skeleton
of a notebook is no longer visible, and the whole performance
is more airy, subtle and amusing. In a short but characteristic
example we shall see the general features of the form as it was
perfected in the eighteenth century.

It is usually said by grammarians, that the use of language is to
express our wants and desires; but men who know the world hold,
and I think with some show of reason, that he who best knows
how to keep his necessities private is the most likely person to have
them redressed; and that the true use of speech is not so much to
express our wants, as to conceal them.

When we reflect on the manner in which mankind generally
confer their favours, there appears something so attractive in riches,
that the large heap generally collects from the smaller; and the
poor find as much pleasure in increasing the enormous mass of
the rich, as the miser, who owns it, sees happiness in its increase.

Nor is there anything repugnant to the laws of morality. Seneca himself allows, that in conferring benefits, the present should always be suited to the dignity of the receiver. Thus the rich receive large presents, and are thanked for accepting them; men of middling stations are obliged to be content with presents something less; while the beggar, who may be truly said to want indeed, is well paid if a farthing rewards his warmest solicitations.

Every man who has seen the world, and has had his ups and downs in life, as the expression is, must have frequently experienced the truth of this doctrine, and must know, that to have much, or to seem to have it, is the only way to have more. Ovid finely compares a man of broken fortune to a falling column; the lower it sinks, the greater is that weight it is obliged to sustain. Thus, when a man's circumstances are such that he has no occasion to borrow, he finds numbers willing to lend him; but should his wants be such that he sues for a trifle, it is two to one whether he may be trusted with the smallest sum. A certain young fellow whom I knew, whenever he had occasion to ask his friend for a guinea, used to prelude his request as if he wanted two hundred; and talked so familiarly of large sums, that none could ever think he wanted a small one. The same gentleman, whenever he wanted credit for a suit of clothes, always made the proposal in a laced coat; for he found by experience, that if he appeared shabby on these occasions, his tailor had taken an oath against trusting; or what was every whit as bad, his foreman was out of the way, and should not be at home for some time.

There can be no inducements to reveal our wants, except to find pity, and by this means relief; but before a poor man opens his mind in such circumstances, he should first consider whether he is contented to lose the esteem of the person he solicits, and whether he is willing to give up friendship to excite compassion. Pity and friendship are passions incompatible with each other; and it is impossible that both can reside in any breast for the smallest space, without impairing each other. Friendship is made up of esteem and pleasure; pity is composed of sorrow and contempt: the mind may for some time fluctuate between them, but it never can entertain both at once.

In fact pity, though may it often relieve, is but at best a short-lived passion, and seldom affords distress more than transitory assistance; with some it scarce lasts from the first impulse till the hand can be put in the pocket; with others it may continue for twice that space; and on some of extraordinary sensibility I have seen it operate for half an hour together: but still, last as it may, it generally produces but beggarly effects; and where, from this motive, we give five farthings, from others we give pounds; whatever be our feelings from the first impulse of distress, when the same distress solicits a second time, we then feel with diminished sensibility; and, like the repetition of an echo, every stroke becomes weaker; till, at last, our sensations lose all mixture of sorrow, and degenerate into downright contempt. These speculations bring to my mind the fate of a very good-natured fellow who is now no more. He was bred in a counting-house, and his father dying just as he was out of his time, left him an handsome fortune, and many friends to advise with. The restraint in which my friend had been brought up had thrown a gloom upon his temper, which some regard as prudence, and, from such considerations, he had every day repeated offers of friendship. Such as had money, were ready to offer him their assistance that way; and they who had daughters, frequently, in the warmth of affection, advised him to marry. My friend, however, was in good circumstances; he wanted neither money, friends, nor a wife, and therefore modestly declined their proposals.

Some errors, however, in the management of his affairs, and several losses in trade, soon brought him to a different way of thinking; and he at last considered that it was his best way to let his friends know that their offers were at length acceptable. His first address was to a scrivener, who had formerly made him frequent offers of money and friendship, at a time when, perhaps, he knew those offers would have been refused. As a man, there-fore, confident of not being refused, he requested the use of a hundred guineas for a few days, as he just then had occasion for money. 'And pray, Sir', replied the scrivener, 'do you want all this money?'—'Want it, Sir', says the other, 'if I did not want it, I should not have asked it.'—'I am sorry for that', said the friend; 'for those who want money when they borrow, will always want money when they should come to pay. To say the truth, Sir, money is money now; and I believe it is all sunk in the bottom of the sea, for my part; and he that has got a little, is a fool if he does not keep what he has got.'

Not quite disconcerted by this refusal, our adventurer was resolved to apply to another, whom he knew was the very best friend he had in the world. The gentleman whom he now addressed, received his proposal with all the affability that could be expected from generous friendship. 'Let me see—you want a hundred guineas; and, pray, dear Jack, would not fifty answer?'—'If you have but fifty to spare, Sir, I must be contented.'—'Fifty to spare! I do not say that, for I believe I have but twenty about me.'—'Then I must borrow the other thirty from some other friend.'—'And pray,' replied the friend, 'would it not be the best way to borrow the whole money from that other friend, and then one note will serve for all, you know? You know, my dear Sir, that you need make no ceremony with me at any time; you know I'm your friend, when you choose a bit of dinner or so—You, Tom,

see the gentleman down. You won't forget to dine with us now
and then? Your very humble servant.'

Distressed, but not discouraged, at this treatment, he was at
last resolved to find that assistance from love, which he could not
have from friendship. A young lady, a distant relation by the
mother's side, had a fortune in her own hands; and, as she had
already made all the advances that her sex's modesty would permit,
he made his proposal with confidence. He soon, however, perceived, that *No bankrupt ever found the fair one kind.* She had lately
fallen deeply in love with another, who had more money, and the
whole neighbourhood thought it would be a match.

Every day now began to strip my poor friend of his former
finery: his clothes flew piece by piece to the pawnbroker's, and he
seemed at length equipped in the genuine livery of misfortune.
But still he thought himself secure from actual necessity; the
numberless invitations he had received to dine, even after his
losses, were yet unanswered; he was, therefore, now resolved to
accept of a dinner, because he wanted one; and in this manner he
actually lived among his friends a whole week without being openly
affronted. The last place I saw him in was at a reverend divine's.
He had, as he fancied, just nicked the time of dinner, for he came
in as the cloth was laying. He took a chair without being desired,
and talked for some time without being attended to. He assured
the company, that nothing procured so good an appetite as a walk
in the Park, where he had been that morning. He went on, and
praised the figure of the damask tablecloth; talked of a feast where
he had been the day before, but that the venison was overdone.
But all this procured him no invitation: finding, therefore, the
gentleman of the house insensible to all his fetches, he thought
proper, at last, to retire, and mend his appetite by a second walk
in the Park.

You then, O ye beggars of my acquaintance, whether in rags or
lace—whether in Kent Street, or the Mall—whether at the Smyrna
or St. Giles's,—might I be permitted to advise as a friend, never
seem to want the favour which you solicit. Apply to every passion
but human pity for redress. You may find permanent relief from
vanity, from self-interest, or from avarice but from compassion—
never. The very eloquence of a poor man is disgusting; and that
mouth which is opened even by wisdom, is seldom expected to
close without the horrors of a petition.

To ward off the gripe of poverty, you must pretend to be a
stranger to her, and she will at least use you with ceremony. If
you be caught dining upon a halfpenny porringer of pease-soup
and potatoes, praise the wholesomeness of your frugal repast.
You may observe that Dr. Cheyne has prescribed pease-broth for
the gravel; hint that you are not one of those who are always
making a deity of your belly. If, again, you are obliged to wear

flimsy stuff in the midst of winter, be the first to remark that stuffs
are very much worn at Paris; or, if there be found some irreparable
defects in any part of your equipage, which cannot be concealed
by all the arts of sitting cross-legged, coaxing, or darning, say that
neither you nor Samson Gideon were ever very fond of dress.
If you be a philosopher, hint that Plato or Seneca are the tailors
you choose to employ; assure the company, that man ought to be
content with a bare covering, since what is now so much his pride,
was formerly his shame.

In short, however caught, never give out; but ascribe to the
frugality of your disposition, what others might be apt to attribute
to the narrowness of your circumstances. To be poor, and to
seem poor, is a certain method never to rise: pride in the great is
hateful; in the wise it is ridiculous; but beggarly pride is a rational
vanity which I have been taught to applaud and excuse.

OLIVER GOLDSMITH, *On the Use of Language.*

This essay is a good example of the general characteristics
of this form of composition.   It may be analysed into:

1. A beginning on familiar ground.
2. Announcement of a paradoxical theme, which is to be
    the subject of the essay.
3. Development of the theme by appeal to common
    experience, etc.
4. Illustration of the theme by anecdote.
5. Deductions from the illustration.
6. Summary of theme and statement of moral.

This kind of structure will be found as the basis of all the more
or less didactic types of essay writing.   Sometimes the anecdote
occupies the greater part of the essay, and sometimes, when
the theme is more historical or descriptive, the anecdote may
disappear altogether.   But it must be confessed that in general
the essay does not readily yield to analysis: it is most successful
when least premeditated.   In two minor matters, however,
a general rule can be laid down: the first words should be
either familiar or arresting, and the last should be emphatic.
'The Victorian age was united on the question of port. . . .'[1]
—that is a good beginning because our interest is immediately
held.   According to our temperament we at once think:

[1] Introduction by Bonamy Dobrée to *The Bachelor of the Albany*, by Marmion
Savage.   Ed. 1927.

How odd that the Victorians should be united on such a trifling subject; or: What an excellent and mollifying thing to be united on; or: What acrimonies and discords such a unity forfends. And when the writer goes on to discuss the characteristics of Victorian fiction in general, and of the book he is writing about in particular, we follow because our interest has been aroused.

The end of a composition should be natural. There should be a sense that the end is due; that enough, and no more than enough, has been said on the subject; and this drawing to a conclusion should be emphasized by an appropriate rhythm, as in music. What this rhythm should be is perhaps a matter of individual taste; and different subjects demand a separate treatment. But most generally the last paragraph of a composition will be found to end on a slow but heavily accented movement, as in these examples:

I lingered round them, under that benign sky: watched the moths fluttering among the heath and hare-bells, listened to the soft wind breathing through the grass, and wondered how any one could ever imagine unquiet slumbers for the sleepers in that quiet earth.

EMILY BRONTË, *Wuthering Heights.*

Nor do we envy the man who can study either the life or the writings of the great poet and patriot, without aspiring to emulate, not indeed the sublime works with which his genius has enriched our literature, but the zeal with which he laboured for the public good, the fortitude with which he endured every private calamity, the lofty disdain with which he looked down on temptations and dangers, the deadly hatred which he bore to bigots and tyrants, and the faith which he so sternly kept with his country and with his fame.

MACAULAY, *Essay on Milton.*

. . . And with this his head dropped on her shoulder; she felt that in his weakness he had fainted. But alone with him in the dusky church a great dread was on her of what might still happen, for his face had the whiteness of death.

HENRY JAMES, *The Altar of the Dead,* p. 51.[1]

Whilst they are some ages ahead of the rest of the world in the art of living; whilst in some directions they do not represent the modern spirit, but constitute it—this vanguard of civility and

[1] Macmillan.

power they coldly hold, marching in phalanx, lock-step, foot after foot, file after file of heroes, ten thousand deep.

EMERSON, *English Traits*, chap. v.

But there are many ways of securing an emphatic conclusion, other than this of a retarded rhythm, and one of them is a sudden recovery, an airy surprise of rhythm, as in this example:

He was earnest and unwearied in the search of knowledge with which his vigorous soul is now satisfied, and employed in a continual praise of that God that first breathed it into his active body: that body, which once was a Temple of the Holy Ghost, and is now become a small quantity of Christian dust:—
But I shall see it re-animated.

IZAAK WALTON, *The Life of Dr. John Donne*.

A more common mode of clinching the conclusion of a composition is to end with some clue word, such as the very title of the composition:

He waited a moment, dropping again on the seat. So, while she still stood, he looked up at her; with the sense somehow that there were too many things and that they were all together, terribly, irresistibly, doubtless, blessedly, in her eyes and her whole person; which thus affected him for the moment as more than he could bear. He leaned forward, dropping his elbows to his knees and pressing his head on his hands. So he stayed, saying nothing; only, with the sense of her own sustained, renewed and wonderful action, knowing that an arm had passed round him and that he was held. She was beside him on the bench of desolation.

HENRY JAMES, 'The Bench of Desolation' (*The Finer Grain*, pp. 306–7).[1]

In these examples we have quoted indifferently from essays and short stories, and indeed it should be noted that there is close structural correspondence between the essay and the short story. What else is the short story but the illustrative anecdote grown until it has absorbed all the other elements in the structure of the occasional essay? Of course, other things have happened in the process: and particularly the quiet meditative humour of the essay has been quickened by an immediate dramatic interest; but essentially the short story, like the essay, is intuitively arranged. It is a complete unit of expression, seen in its entirety from beginning to end,

[1] Methuen.

a single coherent 'shape'—a lyrical and not a logical utterance.[1]

Constructional arrangement is either a logical arrangement of units of an intuitive character, such as may be required for the selection and ordering of a volume of essays or short stories; or it is an arrangement of logical thought in such a manner that the structure of the composition reflects the order and sequence of the thinking. The actual process of logical writing will be examined in Chapter VII, and here it is only necessary to point out that such a structure must be completed before the actual writing of the treatise is begun. It is a preliminary ordering of material, so as to make the most effective use of that material—to avoid repetitions and redundancies, to secure the presentation of arguments in their due sequence, to work up to a climax in the argument, and to bring home the conclusion clearly and at a timely moment. The 'Contents' list of any great didactic work, such as the

[1] The structure and form of the short story has been brilliantly analysed by Sean O'Faolain (*The Short Story*, Devin-Adair). The student is particularly recommended to his analysis of Robert Louis Stevenson's short story, *The Sire de Malétroit's Door*, which concludes:

'So much for the analysis, admittedly sketchy, of Stevenson's treatment of this subject. So analysed it looks straightforward and simple. "Anybody could do it." If he could think of it. But what did Stevenson think? That we cannot know. What was the subject in the crudest alloy before Stevenson refined it to this perfection? That is the essential question about the construction of stories; not how a writer handles what one reads but what matter it was that he handled. What angle did the writer adopt to that matter? What line, what simplification, compression or distillation was it that made the subject fit into the mould of the short-story and so become a short-story? Perhaps the only answer is that given by Stevenson himself in *Memories and Portraits*, an answer which is sybilline but suggestive. (I italicize the parts which seem to me the more suggestive):

' "The threads of a story *come from time to time together and make a picture* in the web; the characters fall from time to time into *some attitude to each other or to nature*, which stamps the story home *like an illustration*. Crusoe recoiling from the footprint, Achilles shouting over against the Trojans, Ulysses bending the great bow, Christian running with his fingers in his ears—these are each *culminating moments in the legend* and each has been printed on the mind's eye for ever. . . . This, then, is the plastic part of literature: *to embody character, thought or emotion in some act or attitude* that shall be remarkably striking to the mind's eye." '

'Sybilline, to us, because we would know what moment, which attitude, and which picture allured him in this tale, if, indeed, it "came off" as he foresaw, and was not (as so often happens) replaced by some other arrangement which "came together" or happily "fell" into position, unplanned. At least, however, we see the dramatic approach, and the compactness that resulted, as distinct from the discursive way of, say, Henry James. It would seem, in fact, that because of this approach Stevenson might be considered a better writer of episodes than of novels, as James was certainly a better writer of novels than of episodes.'

Summa Theologica of St. Thomas Aquinas, the *Ethics* of Spinoza, or the *Ecclesiastical Polity* of Hooker, will admirably illustrate this skeleton structure.

The perfection of a structure of this kind secures the logical arrangement of ideas and so preserves the unity of the thesis; without such a logical framework, irrelevant matter might be introduced under cover of some passing association of ideas; the wild goose and the red herring are common pests in logical writing, and nets must be constructed to exclude them. The *Biographia Literaria* of Coleridge is a standing example of confusion due to the lack of a logical ordering or preliminary disposition of material. In his first paragraph Coleridge gives us the motives of his work:

I have used the narrative chiefly for the purpose of giving a continuity to the work, in part for the sake of the miscellaneous reflections suggested to me by particular events, but still more as introductory to a statement of my principles in Politics, Religion and Philosophy, and an application of the rules, deduced from philosophical principles, to poetry and criticism. But of the objects which I proposed to myself, it was not the least important to effect, as far as possible, a settlement of the long continued controversy concerning the true nature of poetic diction; and at the same time to define with the utmost impartiality the real poetic character of the poet, by whose writings this controversy was first kindled, and has been since fuelled and fanned.

The *Biographia Literaria* is admittedly the most considerable work of literary criticism in English literature; but that does not exempt it from the charge of being confused in motive, ill-arranged in method and disproportionate in treatment. The confusion is inherent in this preliminary statement of aim. A narrative form was chosen in order to give continuity to certain miscellaneous reflections of a personal application— and this aim is kept in view for four chapters. These are followed by five chapters which are in no sense a narrative, and though they may be taken as 'introductory to a statement of my principles in Politics, Religion, and Philosophy', they are in reality a disproportionate and incongruous divagation on 'the law of Association'. The tenth chapter is called by the author 'a chapter of digressions and anecdotes', but actually it fits well enough into the narrative scheme of the first four chapters. The eleventh chapter is *sui generis*—a delightful 'exhortation to those who in early life feel themselves disposed to become authors'. The twelfth and thirteenth chapters return to the metaphysical strain, and then with the fourteenth chapter we begin that treatise on English poetics, with special reference to the poetry of Wordsworth, to which the book owes its great place in English criticism. The book then returns, in 'Satyrane's Letters', to the autobiographical mood, passes on to the quite irrelevant 'Critique on Bertram', and concludes in a metaphysical mood.

It is comparatively easy to rewrite other people's books, and the kind of criticism I am applying here may seem gratuitous. But obviously there are at least three distinct methods of writing embodied in *Biographia Literaria*, and these methods are incongruous and mutually detracting. The book might, conceivably, have been written entirely from the biographical or narrative angle; in that case much of the poetics and most of the metaphysics would have been sacrificed. Or it might conceivably have been written from the metaphysical angle, in which case the narrative scheme would have been abandoned, and the poetics introduced in a corollary and subordinate sense. But historically and critically the main value of the book resides in its poetics, and it is quite fair to say that ideally Coleridge should have selected this way of approach to his subject—that he should have disciplined all his thoughts and fancies to this end. The result would have been the most complete and most profound theory of poetry yet given to the world; instead of which we have only a shapeless haystack of a book, which tends to exasperate us with its futilities quite as often as it enlightens us with its wisdom.

This insistence on a unity of approach, on a coherence of plan, on an ordering of material—is a salutary exhortation, and not intended as an encouragement to the roundheads of literature. Once the plan is made and the material parcelled out, then the dry skeleton of this structure should be hidden beneath a surface which is all variety and interest. And that, of course, is the virtue of a good style. It intervenes between the bare structures of the intellect and those regions of the mind which are only open to sensuous perceptions.

The structure of a prose book which is not a single unity like an essay or short story, has been discussed with reference to a work of discursive reasoning. It may be asked whether the principles here suggested are applicable to an elaborate work of prose fiction such as the novel, and the question raises a very interesting problem. The craft of the novel has been so uncertain and indefinite in its development that perhaps we have not yet reached a stable type which can make the discussion of the problem profitable. There are two schools of thought. The first may be represented by Henry James, who both in his criticism and in his novels evolved a theory and practice of fiction which applies all the canons of coherence, structure, plan, that are possible for the work of discursive reasoning, to the novel. In effect the novel, in his conception, takes over the framework of the classical drama, and a new system of unities and a new theory of structure, more rigorous even than the rules of classical drama, are applied to the art of fiction. The aim, however, is not to imprison the fluidity and variety of life in some rigid framework. 'There is life and life', as Henry James said in his Preface to *The Tragic Muse*, 'and as waste is only life sacrificed and thereby prevented from "counting", I delight in a deep-breathing and an organic form.'

What James meant by 'an organic form' is vividly illustrated in his Preface to *The Wings of the Dove*[1]:

There was the 'fun', to begin with, of establishing one's successive centres—of fixing them so exactly that the portions of the subject commanded by them as by happy points of view, and accordingly treated from them, would constitute, so to speak, sufficiently solid *blocks* of wrought material, squared to the sharp edge, as to have weight and mass and carrying power; to make the construction, that is, to conduce to effect and to provide for beauty. Such a block, obviously, is the whole preliminary presentation of Kate Croy, which, from the first, I recall, absolutely declined to enact itself save in terms of amplitude. Terms of amplitude, terms of atmosphere, those terms, and those terms only, in which images

[1] Macmillan. By permission of John Farquharson on behalf of the Estate of the late Henry James.

assert their fulness and roundness, their power to revolve, so that
they have sides and backs, parts in the shade as true as parts in
the sun—these were plainly to be my conditions, right and left,
and I was so far from overrating the amount of expression the
whole thing, as I saw and felt it, would require, that to retrace
the way at present is, alas, more than anything else, but to mark
the gaps and the lapses, to miss, one by one, the intentions that,
with the best will in the world, were not to fructify. I have just
said that the process of the general attempt is described from the
moment the 'blocks' are numbered, and that would be a true
enough picture of my plan. Yet one's plan, alas, is one thing
and one's result another; so I am perhaps nearer the point in
saying that this last strikes me at present as most characterised by
the happy features that *were*, under my first and most blest illusion,
to have contributed to it. I meet them all, as I renew acquaintance,
I mourn for them all as I remount the stream, the absent values,
the palpable voids, the missing links, the mocking shadows, that
reflect, taken together, the early bloom of one's good faith. Such
cases are of course far from abnormal—so far from it that some
acute mind ought surely to have worked out by this time the 'law'
of the degree in which the artist's energy fairly depends on his
fallibility. How much and how often, and in what connections
and with what almost infinite variety, must he be a dupe, that of
his prime object, to be at all measurably a master, that of his
actual substitute for it—or in other words at all appreciably to
exist? He places, after an earnest survey, the piers of his bridge—
he has at least sounded deep enough, heaven knows, for their
brave position; yet the bridge spans the stream, after the fact, in
apparently complete independence of these properties, the principal
grace of the original design. *They* were an illusion, for their
necessary hour; but the span itself, whether of a single arch or of
many, seems by the oddest chance in the world to be a reality;
since, actually, the rueful builder, passing under it, sees figures
and hears sounds above: he makes out, with his heart in his throat,
that it bears and is positively being 'used'.

Fiction, another school would argue, is not a formal art at
all, but the transcript of life, a direct representation, not
ordered, but actually reflective. Not Flaubert nor Henry
James is the exemplar of this method, but Stendhal, Balzac,
Dostoevsky, or James Joyce. Style as such becomes irrelevant;
structure and arrangement actually destructive of reality; all
that matters is the vitality and humanity of the narrated
action. If this is really to be our standard, then English
literature is rich in triumphs. Fielding, Smollett, Richardson,

Thackeray, Trollope, George Eliot, Dickens, Meredith, Hardy—there is a vivid immediacy in the work of all these authors. There is a quickness of observation, a fund of comedy or humour, an invention of character or plot, and—in different degrees—a philosophy of life. These are the more obvious qualities of English fiction, and it will be observed that they are almost entirely rhetorical qualities; they are all various aspects of the art of persuasion. Their appeal is not to universal ideas, not to an abstract ideal of unity or harmony, but to human sensibilities.

Perhaps both theories are extreme. Some selection of the material of fiction, even though this material be 'raw life', seems essential: otherwise fiction would be co-extensive with existence, a claim no one makes for it. But where there is selection there must be arrangement, and where there is arrangement there must be a technique of expression. Fiction may therefore be regarded as an art which must translate life into words, put life into a definite shape, without in any way destroying its vital quality. Drama is different in that it abstracts the universal elements from life and constructs from these a rarefied and artificial life of the intellect, which is also in some undetermined way the life of the instincts.[1]

---

[1] 'I believe *the drama is not strictly literature at all*' is the venturesome opinion of one philosopher of art (Susanne Langer, 'The Primary Illusions and the Great Orders of Art', *Hudson Review* (New York), III, 2, 233 (1950)). 'It has a different origin, and uses words only as *utterances*. It is a kindred art, for it produces the same primary illusion as literature, namely the semblance of experienced events, but in a different mode: instead of creating a virtual Past it creates a virtual Present. It is related to literature as sculpture and architecture are related to the graphic arts.'

PART II
RHETORIC

Rhetoric

ARISTOTLE DEFINED RHETORIC as 'the power to see the possible ways of persuading people about any given subject'. At that time Rhetoric was confined almost exclusively to the study of persuasive *speech*. It was the application of dialectic to the material of politics, and it would have been difficult for a Greek to distinguish between the art of prose and the art of oratory. It is possible that if he had considered prose separately as an art, he would have done so under the heading of Poetics, and our first concern must therefore be to justify the use of the term Rhetoric in our present context.

The justification is simply that during the course of history the emphasis has gradually shifted from the spoken to the written word. It is true that there was an art of prose writing before the invention of printing; and indeed the almost complete declension of oratory is merely a recent development due to the spread of education and the growth of journalism. But this book is concerned with the art of prose not historically but in its state of actual development, as a present means, and from this point of view we must admit that the art includes all 'the possible ways of persuading people about any given subject'. Some of these ways, such as Exposition and Eloquence, it has in common with the ancient oratory; others, such as Fancy and Imagination, were already present in ancient prose (as we can see by considering together Herodotus and Sir Thomas Browne); but the special complexity and the special power of modern prose writing comes from the welding of these two arts of oratory and prose into a single art which we still call prose.

The powers of rhetoric are distinguished firstly by the mode of their operation, and afterwards by the fact that each mode forms a contrasting type according as it proceeds by discursive or non-discursive logic. There is a logic of thought (discursive) which gives us the power of exposition, producing intellectual assent; and a logic of sensibility (non-discursive or symbolic) which gives us the power of persuasion, producing emotional assent. These two types of rhetoric (which correspond to Books I-II and Book III of Aristotle's treatise) may be related to opposed directions of mental activity—the two directions of psychic energy which Jung has called 'extraversion' and 'introversion'. Though it is not easy, as Jung says, 'to characterize this contrasting relationship to the object in a way that is lucid and intelligible', and though 'there is a danger of reaching paradoxical formulations which would create more confusion than clarity', one can quite generally 'describe the introverted standpoint as one that under all circumstances sets the self and the subjective psychological processes above the object and the objective process, or at any rate holds the ground against the object—the extraverted standpoint, on the other hand, sets the subject below the object, whereby the object receives the predominant value'. He adds that 'every human being possesses both mechanisms as an expression of his natural life-rhythm. . . . A rhythmical alternation of both forms of psychic activity may correspond with the normal course of life. But the complicated external conditions under which we live, as well as the presumably even more complex conditions of our own individual psychic disposition, frequently favour the one mechanism and restrict and hinder the other; whereby a predominance of one mechanism naturally arises. If this condition becomes in any way chronic, a *type* is produced, namely an habitual attitude, in which the one attitude permanently predominates; not, of course, that the other can ever be completely suppressed, inasmuch as it also is an integral factor in psychic activity. . . .'[1]

Just as certainly as these psychic conditions produce a *type*, so as certainly they produce a *style*, and are the scientific justification for Buffon's famous aphorism. In the chapters that follow I shall follow a scheme determined by these considerations. If we take the four "psychic functions"

[1] *Psychological Types* (London, 1938), 12–13.

usually distinguished in psychology, and adopted by Jung,[1]
and relate them to the extraverted and introverted standpoints,
we can then denominate a type of rhetoric to correspond to each
of the eight possibilities—thus:

	EXTRAVERSION	INTROVERSION
THINKING -	exposition	— narrative
FEELING -	fancy	— imagination (invention)
SENSATION -	impressionism	— expressionism
INTUITION -	eloquence	— unity

It is not necessary for the student of prose style to accept

[1] 'I distinguish four basic functions in all, two rational and two irrational—viz.
thinking and *feeling, sensation* and *intuition.* I can give no a priori reason for
selecting just these four as basic functions; I can only point to the fact that this
conception has shaped itself out of many years' experience': Jung: *Psychological
Types,* p. 547. Jung gives a careful definition of each function, which the reader,
who wishes to pursue the psychological basis of literary styles, should consult.
In the present context I must limit myself to a few illuminating phrases.
   Intuition 'is that psychological function which transmits perceptions *in an
unconscious way.* Everything, whether outer or inner objects or their associations,
can be the object of this perception. Intuition has this peculiar quality: it is
neither sensation, nor feeling, nor intellectual conclusion, although it may appear
in any of these forms. Through intuition any one content is presented as a
complete whole, without our being able to explain or discover in what way this
content has been arrived at. Intuition is a kind of instinctive apprehension,
irrespective of the nature of its contents.'
   Sensation 'is that psychological function which transmits a physical stimulus
to perception. It is, therefore, identical with perception. . . . Sensation is
related not only to the outer stimuli, but also to the inner, i.e. to changes in the
internal organs.'
   Feeling 'is primarily a process that takes place between the ego and a given
content, a process, moreover, that imparts to the content a definite *value* in the
sense of acceptance or rejection ("like" or "dislike"); but it can also appear, as it
were, isolated in the form of "mood", quite apart from the momentary contents
of consciousness or momentary sensations. . . . Feeling is an entirely *subjective*
process, which may be in every respect independent of external stimuli, though
chiming in with every sensation . . . feeling is also a kind of *judging,* differing,
however, from intellectual judgment, in that it does not aim at establishing an
intellectual connection but is solely concerned with the setting up of a subjective
criterion of acceptance or rejection.'
   Thinking 'is that psychological function which, in accordance with its own
laws, brings given presentations into conceptual connection . . . must be differentiated into *active* and *passive* thought-activity. Active thinking is an act of the
will, passive thinking an occurrence. . . . Active thinking would correspond
. . . with my idea of directed thinking. Passive thinking. . . . I would term . . .
intuitive thinking. . . . The faculty of directed thinking I term *intellect*: the faculty
of passive, or undirected, thinking, I term *intellectual* intuition.'

this particular psychological basis for the varieties of rhetoric. I adopt it myself because I have found it illuminating in my study of all the arts, and it serves as a framework for critical observations that might otherwise appear to be arbitrary. The other general distinction which underlies these observations—that between discursive and non-discursive logic—is based on a different field of study: that of symbolic logic. Discursive thought, the normal process of logical reasoning, 'intellect' in Jung's phraseology, needs no explanation. But we have already seen, in our discussion of the paragraph and larger units of arrangement, how a persuasive effect may be obtained, not by rational conviction, but by the emotional impact of a significant form. Such forms are in effect *symbols*, and the existence of a symbolic mode of thought is now generally recognized by logicians. The subject in its entirety, and in its application to the field of aesthetics, must be studied in a work such as Susanne Langer's *Philosophy in a New Key*,[1] where it is made very clear that the forms of art are in effect unanalysable symbols corresponding to feelings—they are "patterns of sentience". The significance of any work of art lies in its formal organization: the form has the ability to present the feeling, and by virtue of such form we apprehend the nature of the feeling.

Such symbols 'are just as capable of *articulation*, i.e. of complex combination, as words. But the laws that govern this sort of articulation are altogether different from the laws of syntax that govern language'—that is to say, language as a discursive thought process. But they are not altogether different from the laws of rhetoric and composition by means of which words themselves become symbols, and a re organized to become works of art. Works of verbal art may therefore be described as systems of symbolism, subject to their own logic. As such they constitute a non-discursive mode of thought, and when their aim is persuasive rather than expressive, they may be differentiated in the manner described in the following chapters.

[1] Harvard Univ. Press, 1942.

CHAPTER VII

*

Exposition

THE ART OF EXPRESSING oneself in a logical manner we call *exposition*, but 'logical' is not used here in any precise scientific sense. Indeed, we might say that exposition is the art of expressing oneself *clearly*, logic being implied in the structure of the sentences employed.

Knowledge is either empirical or innate (*a priori*), and logic is the analysis of the perceptions or beliefs which constitute knowledge. The subject-matter of formal logic is now regarded as identical with the subject-matter of pure mathematics, and its method is deduction. But modern logic also includes methodology ('scientific method') and induction, and has become a very complex science.[1] But with logic in this sense we are not concerned, though we must not ignore the existence of an immense field of enquiry concerning the nature of the relation of our knowledge to the symbols in which that knowledge is expressed.[2]

The use of symbols in an exact and consistent way is the foundation of unequivocal expression, and therefore of good prose. Good prose is not confined to unequivocal expression: it also has emotive uses, as we shall see.[3] But good expository prose is the organization of symbols into a structure which we call *reasoning*.

[1] For a general introduction to the subject, see *A Preface to Logic* by Morris R. Cohen (Holt).

[2] The nature of this problem is defined in *The Meaning of Meaning*, by C. K. Ogden and I. A. Richards (Harcourt, Brace). Cf. also *Symbolism*, by A. N. Whitehead (Cambridge University Press, 1928).

[3] Cf. I. A. Richards, *Principles of Literary Criticism* (Harcourt, Brace): 'A statement may be used for the sake of the *reference*, true or false, which it causes. This is the *scientific* use of language. But it may also be used for the sake of the effects in emotion and attitude produced by the reference it occasions. This is the *emotive* use of language. This distinction once clearly grasped is simple. We may either use words for the sake of the references they promote, or we may use them for the sake of the attitudes and emotions which ensue.'

Reasoning is again a mental process that has never been adequately defined. It has a certain structure, which is to some extent a stylistic structure and has therefore been dealt with in Part I; and it is to some extent a logical structure, as I have already indicated. But apart from its structure, reasoning has an inherent quality, and our first concern is to attempt to analyse this quality. We may find that it is merely a bye-product of a logical structure.

Let us examine the following passage:

The tragedy of Massinger is interesting chiefly according to the definition given before; the highest degree of verbal excellence compatible with the most rudimentary development of the senses. Massinger succeeds better in something which is not tragedy; in the romantic comedy. *A Very Woman* deserves all the praise that Swinburne, with his almost unerring gift for selection, has bestowed upon it. The probable collaboration of Fletcher had the happiest result; for certainly that admirable comic personage, the tipsy Borachia, is handled with more humour than we expect of Massinger. It is a play which would be enjoyable on the stage. The form, however, of romantic comedy is itself inferior and decadent. There is an inflexibility about the poetic drama which is by no means a matter of classical, or neoclassical, or pseudoclassical law. The poetic drama might develop forms highly different from those of Greece or England, India or Japan. Conceded the utmost freedom, the romantic drama would yet remain inferior. The poetic drama must have an emotional unity, let the emotion be whatever you like. It must have a dominant tone; and if this be strong enough, the most heterogeneous emotions may be made to reinforce it. The romantic comedy is a skilful concoction of inconsistent emotion, a *revue* of emotion. *A Very Woman* is surpassingly well plotted. The debility of romantic drama does not depend upon extravagant setting, or preposterous events, or inconceivable coincidences; all these might be found in a serious tragedy or comedy. It consists in an internal incoherence of feelings, a concatenation of emotions which signifies nothing. From this type of play, so eloquent of emotional disorder, there was no swing back of the pendulum. Changes never come by a simple reinfusion into the form which the life has just left. The romantic drama was not a new form. Massinger dealt not with emotions so much as with the social abstractions of emotions, more generalised and therefore more quickly and easily interchangeable within the confines of a single action. He was not guided by direct communications through the nerves. Romantic drama tended, accordingly, toward what is sometimes called the 'typical', but which is not the truly typical; for the *typical* figure in a drama is always particularised—an individual. The tendency of the romantic drama was toward a form which continued it in removing its more conspicuous vices, was toward a more severe external order. This form was the Heroic Drama. We look into Dryden's *Essay on Heroic Plays*, and we find that 'love and valour ought to be the subject of a heroic poem'. Massinger, in his destruction of the old drama, had prepared the way for Dryden. The intellect had perhaps exhausted the old conventions. It was not able to supply the impoverishment of feeling.

T. S. ELIOT, *The Sacred Wood*, pp. 123-4.[1]

If we dissect this argument we shall see that it consists in the main of direct statements, followed by an explanatory analysis or an amplification of these statements; or the statement may be a summary or synthesis of previous observations. But every sentence is a statement of fact, or an unequivocal statement of opinion supported by fact. This clarity of statement can only be maintained if there exists in the writer's mind a sufficient fund or reservoir of knowledge from which he can draw in order to effect a liaison between otherwise seemingly independent facts. This process involves more than a power of generalization, more than the scientific methods of induction and deduction; it involves also the capacity to discern a pattern in events (which power we might perhaps call 'intuition', if intuition is to have any meaning not covered by the word 'perception'), and it also involves the capacity to see the significant among a series of events (which power we might call 'insight'). Reasoning is, in short, the reference of detached observations to a general background of knowledge, with the result that these observations can be brought into a mutual relationship and therefore into a unity of argument by the all-embracing resources of this background. And this fact it is which gives to reasoning that coherence and movement which is directly reflected in the quality of the style.

It has sometimes been asserted that the style is a test of the reasoning; that what is well thought is well written, and therefore what is well written must have been well thought. But this argument is not valid; good writing has often been

[1] Methuen.

expended on false premisses, and though it is somewhat difficult to see how this comes about, it can nevertheless be explained by the psychological hypothesis known as 'rationalization'. There may exist in the writer an emotional bias which compels him towards a certain attitude in life. Such a bias may not be in the present awareness of the writer; he may have dismissed it from his conscious life. We need not commit ourselves too deeply to any particular psychological theory to see that such an emotional bias can 'colour' existence without always being an active agent in our thoughts; and it may start us on a line of thought which thenceforward proceeds by a process of impeccable reasoning. Nevertheless the first premiss has been the emotional attitude (such as a fear of death) and this premiss throws forward a control of the development of the subsequent reasoning. Milton's *Doctrine and Discipline of Divorce* is a sufficient example of this type of rhetoric.

The only thing that is indispensable for the possession of a good style is personal sincerity. A sincere mind can and does reject facts which do not fit into its hypotheses. The lines of effective reasoning are as unlimited as the possible constructions that a well-informed and facile mind can place on events. Those who would persuade us of the truth of a statement must rely, not on an air of conviction or a show of reason, but on the compelling force of an emotional attitude. The only way of judging these emotional attitudes is by the historical method; bad emotional attitudes are shown up by their practical effects. Because such attitudes are usually vague, prejudiced and personal, some philosophers have thought that it would be well to rely on open dogmas, however arbitrary these dogmas might seem to critical minds.

Reasoning that depended entirely on true knowledge would form a closed circle. It would be impossible to break the chain of reasoning at any point and say, here is an unresolved factor. Everything should be, in the words of Sir Henry Maine, 'lucidity, simplicity and system'. Works which fulfil this ideal are necessarily very rare; they demand both aesthetic sensibility and a scientific temper. I shall, therefore, conclude this chapter by analysing in some detail Sir Henry Maine's *Ancient Law*, a book in which the quality of an expository style is seen in its perfection.

The book begins with a clear statement of purpose:

The chief object of the following pages is to indicate some of the earliest ideas of mankind, as they are reflected in Ancient Law, and to point out the relation of those ideas to modern thought.

This is the first sentence of the preface. The rest of the preface explains why, in such an enquiry, Roman law must be taken as a typical system and therefore seem to be treated disproportionately. It is the foundation on which the system of the book is built, and the method of building is the Historical Method. The Historical Method is nothing but the mode of reasoning we have defined, applied to past events; that is to say, it takes account of all the relevant facts, searches until it is satisfied that all possible facts have been brought to light, and then, and then only, constructs hypotheses to explain these facts. But the facts of history are so diverse, the departments of life are so interrelated, that the spheres of knowledge foreign to history are few, and works of history conspicuous for their all-embracing rationality and imaginative insight extremely rare.

The materials to be dealt with in a work like *Ancient Law* are first classified according to their common aspects or mutual relevance, that is to say, general categories emerge and the facts are included within them. Within the categories the facts will be disposed chronologically, and an evolutionary thesis will gradually be formed to explain this chronological disposition. The categories themselves will then be arranged so as best to fulfil the general purpose of the book. The simplest, and therefore perhaps the earliest, categories will come first, and, as the argument of the book develops, it will include the latter and more complex categories into which the subject has been divided. Thus in *Ancient Law* the first chapter deals with those Ancient Codes which are the first stable evidence of law and civilization, and which developed from the primitive rule of superstition and custom. The second chapter on 'Legal Fictions' shows by what means these sacrosanct codes became modified. The third chapter on 'The Law of Nature and Equity' shows how the older law was gradually superseded by a set of legal principles which were supposed to have an inherent or natural force. The fourth chapter traces the historical consequences of the theory of a law of nature down to modern times. These four chapters give us the general characteristics of ancient law, and the fifth chapter carries forward the object of the book by showing us the connection of this law with the early history of society. We have now all the elements necessary to trace the further development of ancient law—the interplay of the elements of social organization and the underlying principles of ancient law. The remaining chapters are therefore more detailed, tracing out the early history of such categories of law as Testementary Succession, Property, Contract, Delict and Crime, but taking into account all the time the really fructifying purpose of the book, which is to relate these early ideas of mankind to modern thought, and leave patent the philosophical implication of such a comparison.

The prose style in which this method is embodied is marked by that sustained perspicuity and even tenor which we noticed in connection with the passage from *The Sacred Wood*, as well as by that rare intellectual delectation which comes from the sense of surprise and satisfaction which we experience at finding so many discrete facts subsumed under one theory. That is, in such a style we find, not only 'lucidity' and 'simplicity', but also 'system', or that 'fine sense of analogy and harmony' which Sir Henry Maine admired in the French jurists. Clear explanations, acute distinctions, the invention of descriptive phrases, perfect definitions—these are but the minor characteristics of such a style; they are present at every turn, but above all is a unity of approach, a harmony of mood, and that even tenor which can only be illustrated by successive quotations, taken almost at random from different parts of the book.

The eighteenth century was half over when the most critical period in the history of Natural Law was reached. Had the discussion of the theory and of its consequences continued to be exclusively the employment of the legal profession, there would possibly have been an abatement of the respect which it commanded; for by this time the *Esprit des Lois* had appeared. Bearing in some exaggerations the marks of the excessive violence with which its author's mind had recoiled from assumptions usually suffered to pass without scrutiny, yet showing in some ambiguities the traces of a desire to compromise with existing prejudice, the book of Montesquieu, with all its defects, still proceeded on that Historical Method before which the Law of Nature has never maintained its footing for an instant. Its influence on thought ought to have been as great as its general popularity; but, in fact, it was never allowed time to put it forth, for the counter-hypothesis which it seemed destined to destroy passed suddenly from the forum to the street, and became the key-note of controversies far more exciting than are ever agitated in the courts or the schools. The person who launched it on its new career was that remarkable man who, without learning, with few virtues, and with no strength of character, has nevertheless stamped himself ineffaceably on history by the force of a vivid imagination, and by the help of a geniune and burning love for his fellowmen, for which much will always have to be forgiven him. We have never seen in our own generation—indeed the world has not seen more than once or twice in all the course of history—a literature which has exercised such prodigious influence over the minds of men, over every cast and shade of intellect, as that which emanated from Rousseau between 1749 and 1762. It was the first attempt to re-erect the edifice of human belief after the purely iconoclastic efforts commenced by Bayle, and in part by our own Locke, and consummated by Voltaire; and besides the superiority which every constructive effort will always enjoy over one that is merely destructive, it possessed the immense advantage of appearing amid an all but universal scepticism as to the soundness of all foregone knowledge in matters speculative.

When we go forward to the state of society in which these early legal conceptions show themselves as formed, we find that they still partake of the mystery and spontaneity which must have seemed to characterise a despotic father's commands, but that at the same time, inasmuch as they proceed from a sovereign, they presuppose a union of family groups in some wider organisation. The next question is, what is the nature of this union and the degree of intimacy which it involves. It is just here that archaic law renders us one of the greatest of its services and fills up a gap which otherwise could only have been bridged by conjecture. It is full, in all its provinces, of the clearest indications that society in primitive times was not what it is assumed to be at present, a collection of *individuals*. In fact, and in the view of the men who composed it, it was *an aggregation of families*. The contrast may be most forcibly expressed by saying that the *unit* of an ancient society was the Family, of a modern society the Individual. We must be prepared to find in ancient law all the consequences of this difference. It is so framed as to be adjusted to a system of small independent corporations. It is therefore scanty, because it is supplemented by the despotic commands of the heads of households. It is ceremonious, because the transactions to which it pays regard resemble international concerns much more than the quick play of intercourse between individuals. Above all it has a peculiarity of which the full importance cannot be shown at present. It takes a view of *life* wholly unlike any which appears in developed jurisprudence. Corporations *never die*, and accordingly primitive law considers the entities with which it deals, i.e. the patriarchal or family groups, as perpetual and inextinguishable. This view is closely allied to the peculiar aspect under which, in very ancient times, moral attributes present themselves. The moral elevation and moral debasement of the individual appear to be confounded with, or postponed to, the merits and offences of the group to which the individual belongs. If the community sins, its guilt is much more than the sum of the offences committed by its members; the crime is a corporate act, and extends in its consequences to many more persons than have shared in its actual perpetration. If, on the other hand, the individual is conspicuously guilty, it is his children, his kinsfolk, his tribesmen, or his fellow-citizens, who suffer with him, and sometimes for him. It thus happens that the ideas of moral responsibility and retribution often seem to be more clearly realised at very ancient than at more advanced periods, for, as the family group is immortal, and its liability to punishment indefinite, the primitive mind is not perplexed by the questions which become troublesome as soon as the individual is conceived as altogether separate from the group.

The science of Moral Theology, as it was first called, and as it is still designated by the Roman Catholic divines, was undoubtedly constructed, to the full knowledge of its authors, by taking principles of conduct from the system of the Church, and by using the language and methods of jurisprudence for their expression and expansion. While this process went on, it was inevitable that jurisprudence, though merely intended to be the vehicle of thought, should communicate its colour to the thought itself. The tinge received through contact with legal conceptions is perfectly perceptible in the earliest ethical literature of the modern world, and it is evident, I think, that the Law of Contract, based as it is on the complete reciprocity and indissoluble connection of rights and duties, has acted as a wholesome corrective to the predispositions of writers

who, if left to themselves, might have exclusively viewed a moral
obligation as the public duty of a citizen in the Civitas Dei.

———

It is a singular result of that ignorance of Roman law which
Englishmen readily confess, and of which they are sometimes not
ashamed to boast, that many English writers of note and credit
have been led by it to put forward the most untenable of paradoxes
concerning the condition of human intellect during the Roman
Empire. It has been constantly asserted, as unhesitatingly as if
there were no temerity in advancing the proposition, that from the
close of the Augustan era to the general awakening of interest on
the points of the Christian faith, the mental energies of the civilized
world were smitten with a paralysis. Now there are two subjects
of thought—the only two perhaps with the exception of physical
science—which are able to give employment to all the powers and
capacities which the mind possesses. One of them is Metaphysical
inquiry, which knows no limits as long as the mind is satisfied to
work on itself; the other is Law, which is as extensive as the concerns
of mankind. It happens that, during the very period indicated,
the Greek-speaking provinces were devoted to one, the Latin-
speaking provinces to the other, of these studies. I say nothing of
the fruits of speculation in Alexandria and the East, but I confidently
affirm that Rome and the West had an occupation in hand fully
capable of compensating them for the absence of every other
mental exercise, and I add that the results achieved, so far as we
know them, were not unworthy of the continuous and exclusive
labour bestowed on producing them. Nobody except a professional
lawyer is perhaps in a position completely to understand how
much of the intellectual strength of individuals Law is capable of
absorbing, but a layman has no difficulty in comprehending why
it was that an unusual share of the collective intellect of Rome
was engrossed by jurisprudence. The proficiency of a given
community in jurisprudence depends in the long run on the same
conditions as its progress in any other line of inquiry; and the
chief of these are the proportion of the national intellect devoted
to it, and the length of time during which it is so devoted. Now,
a combination of all the causes, direct and indirect, which contribute to the advancing and perfecting of a science continued to
operate on the jurisprudence of Rome through the entire space
between the Twelve Tables and the severance of the two Empires,—
and that not irregularly or at intervals, but in steadily increasing
force and constantly augmenting number. We should reflect that
the earliest intellectual exercise to which a young nation devotes
itself is the study of its laws. As soon as the mind makes its first
conscious efforts towards generalization, the concerns of every-day
life are the first to press for inclusion within general rules and

comprehensive formulas. The popularity of the pursuit on which all the energies of the young commonwealth are bent is at the outset unbounded; but it ceases in time. The monopoly of mind by law is broken down. The crowd at the morning audience of the great Roman jurisconsult lessens. The students are counted by hundreds instead of thousands in the English Inns of Court. Art, Literature, Science, and Politics, claim their share of the national intellect; and the practice of jurisprudence is confined within the circle of a profession, never indeed limited or insignificant, but attracted as much by the rewards as by the intrinsic recommendations of their science. This succession of changes exhibited itself even more strikingly at Rome than in England. To the close of the Republic the law was the sole field for all ability except the special talent of a capacity for generalship. But a new stage of intellectual progress began with the Augustan age, as it did with our own Elizabethan era. We all know what were its achievements in poetry and prose; but there are some indications, it should be remarked, that, besides its efflorescence in ornamental literature, it was on the eve of throwing out new aptitudes for conquest in physical science. Here, however, is the point at which the history of mind in the Roman State ceases to be parallel to the routes which mental progress had since then pursued. The brief span of Roman literature, strictly so called, was suddenly closed under a variety of influences, which though they may partially be traced it would be improper in this place to analyse. Ancient intellect was forcibly thrust back into its old courses, and law again became no less exclusively the proper sphere for talent than it had been in the days when the Romans despised philosophy and poetry as the toys of a childish race. Of what nature were the external inducements which, during the Imperial period, tended to draw a man of inherent capacity to the pursuits of the jurisconsult may best be understood by considering the option which was practically before him in his choice of a profession. He might become a teacher of rhetoric, a commander of frontier-posts, or a professional writer of panegyrics. The only other walk of active life which was open to him was the practice of the law. Through that lay the approach to wealth, to fame, to office, to the council-chambers of the monarch—it may be to the very throne itself.

Sir Henry Maine, *Ancient Law.*

CHAPTER VIII

*

Narrative

NARRATIVE IS OF TWO kinds, being descriptive either of *events* (what *is taking place*) or of *objects* (what *has taken place*); that is to say, it is either *active* or *passive* in character.

The object of narrative is to transmit to the reader an exact visual account of the object or action represented. What is seen must be translated into symbols by the writer, and these symbols must in turn convey to the reader the impression of the things seen. We are fond of using the word 'impression' in such a connection, and as in most common predilections of the kind, there is virtue in the chosen word. Impression implies a material impressed; it supplies a causal connection between the events or things observed and the plastic mind of the observer. It implies a translation of this plastic impress into words, images, rhythms and all other modes of expression.

In this process of translation, the writer should convey to the reader the *speed* of events, and the *actuality* of objects. Both these effects are best secured by economy of expression: that is to say, the words used to convey the impression should be just sufficient. If there are too many words, the action is clogged, the actuality blurred. If too few, the impression is not conveyed in its completeness; the outlines are vague. In either case there is a lack of visual clarity.

These rules seem obvious, but they have seldom been observed, and good narrative writing is comparatively rare in English literature. There is a human failing which urges us to elaborate and decorate our descriptions; it is perhaps merely the desire to infuse an objective activity with something of the personality of the narrator. There is, too, the irresistible attraction of words in themselves, urging us to use them for their own sakes rather than as exact symbols of the things they stand for. With these various dangers waylaying him, the writer can rarely exercise sufficient restraint to enable him to keep his eye on the object, and give to the reader the concreteness of the things he perceives. But if the eye should *distort* what it sees, and give a fictitious vitality to things that are really lifeless, the reader will begin to feel uneasy. The following paragraph from the beginning of Rudyard Kipling's *Love-o'-Women* is worth consideration from this point of view:

> 'The horror, the confusion, and the separation of the murderer from his comrades were all over before I came. There remained only on the barrack-square the blood of man calling from the ground. The hot sun had dried it to a dusky goldbeater-skin film, cracked lozenge-wise by the heat; and as the wind rose, each lozenge, rising a little, curled up at the edges as if it were a dumb tongue. Then a heavier gust blew all away down wind in grains of dark-coloured dust. It was too hot to stand in the sunshine before breakfast. The men were in barracks talking the matter over. A knot of soldiers' wives stood by one of the entrances to the married quarters, while inside a woman shrieked and raved with wicked filthy words.'

> RUDYARD KIPLING, *Many Inventions*, p. 261.[1]

We can readily admit that an accent of violence was needed and is very effective at the outset of this story, and that the heat of the tropical sun must be conveyed to the reader. But a melodramatic phrase like 'the blood of man' gives a warning that all is *not* well. 'A dusky goldbeater-skin film' is excellent; we see that film and can see it cracking lozenge-wise in the heat. But then the vision gets distorted. The 'dumb tongues' are not eloquent; merely stage properties. And did the author really see those grains of dark-coloured dust which a heavier gust blew all away? There is, admittedly, an effective device in prose style which we might call 'the microscopic eye'—see the extract from *An English Farmhouse* by Geoffrey Grigson given in the Appendix (page 209). Here, however, there is no distortion, but a minute and precise observation.

We find the best narrative prose in ages when the epic spirit has prevailed, that is to say, in writers who have been more conscious of their theme than of their own feelings and

[1] Macmillan.

opinions. The narrative is essentially addressed to an audience: it is not a self-revelation or a self-expression. It is accurate reporting. It is therefore devoid of comment and the only point of view it represents is the point of view of an interested observer. These qualities of objectivity, concreteness and impersonality are a natural possession of our earliest writers, and will be clearly observed in the following typical passages:

And some men say that in the Isle of Lango is yet the daughter of Ypocras, in form and likeness of a great dragon, that is a hundred fathom of length, as men say: for I have not seen her. And they of the Isles call her Lady of the Land. And she lieth in an old castle, in a cave, and sheweth twice or thrice in the year. And she doth no harm to no man, but if men do her harm. And she was thus changed and transformed, from a fair damsel, into likeness of a dragon, by a goddess, that was cleped Diana. And men say, that she shall so endure in that form of a dragon, unto the time that a knight come, that is so hardy, that dare come to her and kiss her on the mouth: and then shall she turn again to her own kind, and be a woman again, but after that she shall not live long.

And it is not long since, that a knight of Rhodes, that was hardy and doughty in arms, said that he would kiss her. And when he was upon his courser, and went to the castle, and entered into the cave, the dragon lift up her head against him. And when the knight saw her in that form so hideous and so horrible, he fled away. And the dragon bare the knight upon a rock, maugre his head; and from that rock she cast him into the sea: and so was lost both horse and man.

And also a young man, that wist not of the dragon, went out of a ship, and went through the Isle, till that he came to the castle, and came in to the cave, and went so long till that he found a chamber, and there he saw a damsel that combed her head, and looked in a mirror; and she had much treasure about her. And he trowed, that she had been a common woman, that dwelled there to receive men to folly. And he abode, till the damsel saw the shadow of him in the mirror. And she turned her toward him, and asked him, what he would. And he said, he would be her leman or paramour. And she asked him if that he were a knight. And he said, nay. And then she said, that he might not be her leman: but she bade him go again unto his fellows, and make him knight, and come again upon the morrow, and she should come out of the cave before him, and then come and kiss her on the mouth, and have no dread; 'for I shall do thee no manner of harm, albeit that thou see me in likeness of a dragon. For though thou see me hideous and horrible to look on, I do thee to witness, that it is made by enchantment. For without doubt, I am none other than thou seest now, a woman; and therefore dread thee nought. And if thou kiss me, thou shalt have all this treasure, and be my lord, and lord also of all the isle'.

And he departed from her and went to his fellows to ship, and let make him knight, and came again upon the morrow, for to kiss this damsel. And when he saw her come out of the cave in form of a dragon, so hideous and so horrible, he had so great dread, that he fled again to the ship, and she followed him. And when she saw that he turned not again, she began to cry, as a thing that had much sorrow; and then she turned again into her cave; and anon the knight died. And sithen hitherward might no knight see her, but that he died anon. But when a knight cometh, that is so hardy to kiss her, he shall not die; but he shall turn the damsel into her right form and kindly shape, and he shall be lord of all the countries and isles abovesaid.

Sir John Mandeville, *The Travels*, Ch. IV.

A certain man had two sons and the younger said to the Father, Father, give me the portion of substance that befalleth to me. And the father departed to him the substance. And after not many days this younger son gathered all that fell to him, and went in pilgrimage into a far country; and there he wasted his substance in living lecherously. And after that he had ended all things, a strong hunger was made in that land, and he began to have need. And he went out and cleaved to one of the citizens of that country, and this citizen sent him into his town, that he should feed hogs. And he coveted to fill his womb of these cods which the hogs eat, and no man gave to him. And he turned again in to himself, said, How many hired men in my father's house have plenty of loaves, and I perish here through hunger. I shall rise, and I shall go to my father, and say to him, Father, I have sinned against Heaven and before thee; now I am not worthy to be cleped thy son, make me as one of thy hired men. And he rising came to his father. And when he was yet far, his father saw him, and was stirred by mercy, and running against his son, fell on his neck and kissed him. And the son said to him, Father, I have sinned against Heaven and before thee; now I am not worthy to be cleped thy son. And the father said to his servants anon, Bring ye forth the first stole, and clothe ye him, and give ye a ring in his hand, and shoon unto his feet. And bring ye a calf made fat, and slay him, and eat we, and make we feast; for this my son was dead, and is quickened again, and he perished, and is found. And all began to eat plenteously. And his elder son was in the field; and when he came and was nigh the house, he heard a symphony and a croud. And he cleped one of the servants, and asked what were these things. And he said to him, Thy brother is come, and thy father hath slain a fat calf, for he hath received him safe. But he was wroth and would not come in; therefore his father went out, and began to pray him. And he answering to his father said, Lo, so many years I serve to thee, I broke never thy commandment; and thou never gave to me a kid, that I should eat largely with my friends. But after that this thy son, which devoured his substance with hooris, is come, thou hast slain to him a fat calf. And the father said to him, Son, thou art ever with me, and all my things be thine. But it behoved to make feast and have joy, for this thy brother was dead, and liveth again; he perished, and is found.

> JOHN WYCLIFFE, *St. Luke*, Ch. xv.
> (after Forshall and Madden's
> edition, Oxford, 1850).

It is interesting to compare this passage from Wycliffe with the parallel passage from the Authorized Version of the Bible. The differences are small, but though the Authorized Version gains in rhythm (and gains, too, because it is so familiar to us), it has lost a little in concreteness; we have 'riotous living' for 'living lecherously', 'the best robe for 'the first stole',' 'musick and dancing' for 'a symphony and a croud'.

And he said, A certain man had two sons: and the younger of them said to his Father, Father, give me the portion of goods that falleth to me. And he divided unto them his living. And not many days after the younger son gathered all together, and took his journey into a far country, and there wasted his substance with riotous living. And when he had spent all, there arose a mighty famine in that land; and he began to be in want. And he went and joined himself to a citizen of that country; and he sent him into his fields to feed swine. And he would fain have filled his belly with the husks that the swine did eat: and no man gave unto him. And when he came to himself, he said, how many hired servants of my father's have bread enough and to spare, and I perish with hunger! I will arise and go to my father, and will say unto him, Father, I have sinned against heaven, and before thee, and am no more worthy to be called thy son: make me as one of thy hired servants. And he arose, and came to his father. But when he was yet a great way off, his father saw him, and had compassion, and ran, and fell on his neck, and kissed him. And the son said unto him, Father, I have sinned against heaven, and in thy sight, and am no more worthy to be called thy son. But the father said to his servants, Bring forth the best robe, and put it on him; and put a ring on his hand, and shoes on his feet: and bring hither the fatted calf, and kill it; and let us eat, and be merry: for this my son was dead, and is alive again; he was lost, and is found. And they began to be merry. Now his elder son was in the field: and as he came near and drew nigh to the house, he heard musick and dancing. And he called one of the servants, and asked what these things meant. And he said unto him, Thy brother is come; and thy father hath killed the fatted calf, because he hath received him safe and sound. And he was angry, and would not go in: therefore came his father out, and intreated him. And he answering said to his father, Lo, these many years do I serve thee, neither transgressed I at any time thy commandment: and yet thou never gavest me a kid, that I might make merry with my friends: but as soon as this thy son was come, which hath devoured thy living with harlots, thou hast killed for him the fatted calf. And he said unto him, Son, thou art ever with me, and all that I have is thine. It was meet that we should make merry and be glad: for this thy brother was dead, and is alive again; and was lost, and is found.

St. Luke's Gospel, xv. 11–32.

But Sir Thomas Malory's *Morte d'Arthur* is the best and most sustained example of this early narrative prose:

Then afore him he saw come riding out of a castle a knight, and his horse trapped all red, and himself in the same colour. When this knight in the red beheld Balin, him thought it should be his brother Balin because of his two swords, but because he knew not his shield, he deemed it was not he. And so they aventryd their spears, and came marvellously fast together, and they smote each other in the shields, but their spears and their course were so big that it bare down horse and man, that they both lay in a swoon. But Balin was bruised sore with the fall of his horse, for he was weary of travel. And Balan was the first that rose on foot and drew his sword, and went toward Balin, and he arose and went against him, but Balan smote Balin first, and he put up his shield, and smote him through the shield and tamed his helm. Then Balin smote him again with that unhappy sword, and well nigh had felled his brother Balan, and so they fought there together till their breaths failed. Then Balin looked up to the castle, and saw the towers stand full of ladies. So they went to battle again, and wounded each other dolefully, and then they breathed oft-times, and so went unto battle, that all the place there as they fought was blood red. And at that time there was none of them both but they had either smitten other seven great wounds, so that the least of them might have been the death of the mightiest giant in this world. Then they went to battle again so marvellously that doubt it was to hear of that battle for the great bloodshedding, and their hauberks unnailed, that naked they were on every side. At the last Balan, the younger brother, withdrew him a little and laid him down. Then said Balin le Savage, What knight art thou?

for or now I found never no knight that matched me. My name is, said he, Balan, brother to the good knight Balin. Alas! said Balin, that ever I should see this day. And therewith he fell backward in a swoon. Then Balan yede on all four feet and hands, and put off the helm of his brother, and might not know him by the visage it was so full hewn and bled; but when he awoke he said, O Balan, my brother, thou hast slain me and I thee, wherefore all the wide world shall speak of us both. Alas! said Balan, that ever I saw this day, that through mishap I might not know you, for I espied well your two swords, but because ye had another shield I deemed you had been another knight. Alas! said Balin, all that made an unhappy knight in the castle, for he caused me to leave mine own shield to our both's destruction, and if I might live I would destroy that castle for ill customs. That were well done, said Balan, for I had never grace to depart from them since that I came hither, for here it happened me to slay a knight that kept this island, and since might I never depart, and no more should ye brother, and ye might have slain me as ye have, and escaped yourself with the life.

Right so came the lady of the tower with four knights and six ladies and six yeomen unto them, and there she heard how they made their moan either to other, and said, We came both out of one womb, and so shall we lye both in one pit. So Balan prayed the lady of her gentleness, for his true serveice that she would bury them both in that same place there the battle was done. And she granted them with weeping it should be done richly in the best manner. Now will ye send for a priest that we may receive our sacrament and receive the blessed body of our Lord Jesus Christ? Yea, said the lady, it shall be done. And so she sent for a priest and gave them their rites. Now, said Balin, when we are buried in one tomb, and the mention made over us how two brethren slew each other, there will never good knight nor good man see our tomb but they will pray for our souls. And so all the ladies and gentlewomen wept for pity. Then anon Balan died, but Balin died not till the midnight after, and so were they buried both, and the lady let make a mention of Balan how he was there slain by his brother's hands, but she knew not Balin's name.

It is the quality of passages such as this which makes the *Morte d'Arthur* seem like the source of all that is vigorous and subtle in our narrative prose.

The various editions of the English Bible, from Coverdale's in 1539 to the Authorized Version of 1611, consolidated and established the English idiom which had gradually been formed during the fourteenth and fifteenth centuries; they exemplify all the characteristics of a true narrative style—

concreteness, economy and speed. But although the English Bible has been the greatest single influence on the development of English prose style, two other influences which spread rapidly during the sixteenth century, the Renaissance and the Revival of Learning, tended in another direction. It is, of course, not possible to regard these two influences as separate forces—they are different aspects of the same movement of ideas; but by the Renaissance we denote more obviously the externals of an egoistic or individualistic spirit which sought to express itself in ornateness and fantasy; and by the Revival of Learning we denote those direct influences upon the structure of prose which came as a consequence of devotion to Latin models. Both these forces operated against the direct simplicity of the original English idiom; both acted to the detriment of a good narrative style. And whether because of these influences, or because the actual desire for expression in a narrative form declined, we find a great poverty of good narrative prose in the succeeding century. Bunyan and Defoe are exceptions (and we may be sure that Dryden would have been another, had he thought of writing in this manner), and both these authors were free from the influences of classical models. Bunyan at any rate derived his style directly from the English Bible and such early sources as Foxe's *Acts and Monuments*. Defoe was subject to more miscellaneous influences, but he was singularly free from the vanities and pretensions which beset even the best of his contemporaries.[1]

As I walk'd through the wilderness of this world, I lighted on a certain place, where was a Den; and I laid me down in that place to sleep: and as I slept I dreamed a Dream. I dreamed, and behold *I saw a man clothed with Rags, standing in a certain place, with his face from his own House, a Book in his hand, and a great burden upon his back. I looked, and saw him open the Book,* and read therein; and as he read, he wept and trembled: and not being able longer to contain, he brake out with a lamentable cry; saying, *what shall I do?*
In this plight therefore he went home, and refrained himself as

---

[1] Pepys is another exception; and an interesting one, for here we see how a man, writing with no sense of literary tradition, no thoughts of literary fame, guided only by a sincere and intense interest in himself, falls naturally into habits of precision, economy and concreteness. Pepys is no 'author', but some of his narratives, such as that of the Great Fire (2nd September 1666) and of his visit to Epsom Downs (14th July, 1667) cannot easily be matched for vitality and ease.

long as he could, that his Wife and Children should not perceive his distress; but he could not be silent long, because that his trouble increased: wherefore at length he brake his mind to his Wife and Children; and thus he began to talk to them, *O my dear Wife,* said he, *and you the Children of my bowels, I your dear friend, am in myself undone, by reason of a burden that lieth hard upon me: moreover, I am for certain informed that this our City will be burned with fire from Heaven, in which fearful overthrow, both myself, with thee, my Wife, and you my sweet babes, shall miserably come to ruin; except (the which yet I see not) some way of escape can be found, whereby we may be delivered.* At this his Relations were sore amazed; not for that they believed that what he had said to them was true, but because they thought that some frenzy distemper had got into his head: therefore, it drawing towards night, and they hoping that sleep might settle brains, with all haste they got him to bed; but the night was as troublesome to him as the day: wherefore instead of sleeping, he spent it in sighs and tears. So when the morning was come, they would know how he did; he told them, worse and worse. He also set to talking to them again, but they began to be hardened; they also thought to drive away his distemper by harsh and surly carriage to him: sometimes they would deride, sometimes they would chide, and sometimes they would quite neglect him: wherefore he began to retire himself to his Chamber to pray for, and pity them; and also to condole his own misery, he would also walk solitarily in the Fields, sometimes reading, and sometimes praying: and thus for some days he spent his time.

JOHN BUNYAN, *The Pilgrim's Progress.*

I had dressed myself up in a very mean habit, for as I had several shapes to appear in, I was now in an ordinary stuff-gown, a blue apron, and a straw hat; and I placed myself at the door of the Three Cups Inn, in St. John Street. There were several carriers used the inn, and the stage-coaches for Barnet, for Totteridge, and other towns that way stood always in the street in the evening, when they prepared to set out, so that I was ready for anything that offered, for either one or other. The meaning was this: people come frequently with bundles and small parcels to those inns, and call for such carriers or coaches as they want, to carry them into the country; and there generally attend women, porters' wives or daughters, ready to take in such things for their respective people that employ them.

It happened very oddly that I was standing at the inn gate, and a woman that had stood there before, and which was the porter's wife belonging to the Barnet stage-coach, having observed me, asked if I waited for any of the coaches. I told her Yes, I waited for my mistress, that was coming to go to Barnet. She asked me who was my mistress, and I told her any madam's name that came next me; but as it seemed, I happened upon a name, a family of which name lived at Hadley, just beyond Barnet.

I said no more to her, or she to me, a good while; but by and by, somebody calling her at a door a little way off, she desired me that if anybody called for the Barnet coach, I would step and call her at the house, which it seems was an alehouse. I said Yes, very readily, and away she went.

She was no sooner gone but comes a wench and a child, puffing and sweating, and asks for the Barnet coach. I answered presently, 'Here'. 'Do you belong to the Barnet coach?' says she. 'Yes, sweetheart', said I; what do ye want?' I want room for two passengers', says she. 'Where are they, sweetheart?' said I. 'Here's this girl, pray let her go into the coach', says she, 'and I'll go and fetch my mistress.' 'Make haste, then, sweetheart', says I, 'for we may be full else.' The maid had a great bundle under her arm; so she put the child into the coach, and I said, 'You had best put your bundle into the coach too.' 'No', says she, 'I am afraid somebody should slip it away from the child.' 'Give it me, then', said I, 'and I'll take care of it.' 'Do, then', says she, 'and be sure you take care of it'. 'I'll answer for it', said I, 'if it were for £20 value.' 'There, take it, then', says she, and away she goes.

As soon as I had got the bundle, and the maid was out of sight, I goes on towards the alehouse, where the porter's wife was, so that if I had met her, I had then only been going to give her the bundle, and to call her to her business, as if I was going away, and could stay no longer; but as I did not meet her, I walked away, and turning into Charterhouse Lane, made off through Charter-house Yard, into Long Lane, then crossed into Bartholomew Close, so into Little Britain, and through the Bluecoat Hospital, into Newgate Street.

To prevent my being known, I pulled off my blue apron, and wrapped the bundle in it, which before was made up in a piece of painted calico, and very remarkable; I also wrapped up my straw hat in it, and so put the bundle upon my head; and it was very well that I did this, for coming through the Bluecoat Hospital, who should I meet but the wench that had given me the bundle to hold. It seems she was going with her mistress, whom she had been gone to fetch, to the Barnet coaches.

I saw she was in haste, and I had no business to stop her; so away she went, and I brought my bundle safe home to my governess. There was no money, nor plate, or jewels in the bundle, but a very good suit of Indian damask, a gown and petticoat, a laced head and ruffles of very good Flanders lace, and some linen and other things, such as I knew very well the value of.

DANIEL DEFOE, *Moll Flanders.*

When we come to the next phase of English literature—that which may be said to begin with Swift and to end with

Smollett—there is a revival of narrative prose, due mainly to
the growth of the novel. But the novel brought with it its
own pitfalls. In the older forms of narrative, such as the
Fable, the Allegory, and the Parable, the action is coherent
and unimpeded. This holds good not only of the Biblical
narratives and of the early Romances, but also of a comparatively late writer like Defoe. It is true that in Defoe we get
moral reflections, but these are now allowed to impede the
action of the narrative: they are so much 'eye-wash' and can
be ignored without any detriment to the book as a whole.
They may, however, offend our sense of economy, and even,
by their insincerity, our sense of decency. A great writer,
like Swift, will not trifle in this way. He has his moral
reflections to make, and with a vengeance, but they will be
implicit in his story. Swift, therefore, can keep his narrative
as direct and unobstructed as a Fable, and has even no need
to point the moral. But Swift did more than preserve the
English idiom; he purified it. It came to him, chiefly in the
form of the English Bible, as an instinctive mode of expression—
direct because it was simple and unconscious, powerful
because it was *felt*. Swift accepted it for these simple virtues,
but he made it the instrument of his mighty intelligence; and
Swift's greatness consists in this fact, more than in anything
else, that however widely his vision might extend, however
deep his insight, his mode of expression remained simple, and
single, and clearly comprehensible.

I have already given an example of his narrative style
(see Chapter III, pp. 24-5.) to which the reader can refer;
but the fact that he is not quoted again at this point should
not blind us to the cardinal importance of Swift's narrative
style. It is the norm to which we must return again and
again if we are to preserve an English idiom, for never again
has that idiom been expressed in such purity and strength.[1]

The narrative style of Fielding, who is the best representative

---

[1] Cf. George Saintsbury, *History of English Prose Rhythm*, p. 242: 'His prose is
never, to a sound taste well cultivated, inharmonious, or monotonous, or mean;
but there never, in English, has been a prose in which harmony was secured
with so few means taken to secure it, and monotony avoided with so little apparent
effort to safeguard the avoidance.'

of the eighteenth century novelists, can be as direct and simple as the narrative style of Defoe or Swift.

He had not gone above two miles, charmed with the hope of shortly seeing his beloved Fanny, when he was met by two fellows in a narrow lane, and ordered to stand and deliver. He readily gave them all the money he had, which was somewhat less than two pounds; and told them he hoped they would be so generous as to return him a few shillings, to defray his charges on his way home.

One of the ruffians answered with an oath, 'Yes, we'll give you something presently: but first strip and be d—n'd to you'.—'Strip', cried the other, 'or I'll blow your brains to the devil.' Joseph remembering that he had borrowed his coat and breeches of a friend, and that he should be ashamed of making any excuse for not returning them, replied, he hoped they would not insist on his clothes, which were not worth much, but consider the coldness of the night. 'You are cold, are you, you rascal?' said one of the robbers: 'I'll warm you with a vengeance'; and, damning his eyes, snapped a pistol at his head; which he had no sooner done than the other levelled a blow at him with his stick, which Joseph, who was expert at cudgel-playing, caught with his, and returned the favour so successfully on his adverary, that he laid him sprawling, at his feet, and at the same instant received a blow from behind with the butt end of a pistol, from the other villain, which felled him to the ground, and totally deprived him of his senses.

The thief who had been knocked down had now recovered himself; and both together fell to belabouring poor Joseph with their sticks, till they were convinced they had put an end to his miserable being: they then stripped him entirely naked, threw him into a ditch, and departed with their booty.

HENRY FIELDING, *Adventures of Joseph Andrews*.

But the eighteenth century narrative does not always go at this speed; it is interspersed with the author's commentary, his side glances and quizzings, his 'philosophical reflections, the like not to be found in any light French romance', and eventually, as in the case of Sterne, with any idea that comes into the author's head.[1] This all makes for a certain density of interest, a charm, and even, we must admit, for a higher

[1] Cf. Graham Greene: 'However much we hate the man, or hate rather his coy whimsical defences, he is more "readable" than Fielding by virtue of that most musical style, the day-dream conversation of a man with a stutter in a world of his imagination where tongue and teeth have no problems to overcome, where no syllables are harsh, where mind speaks softly to mind with infinite subtlety of tone.' *The Lost Childhood* (London, Eyre and Spottiswoode, 1951), p. 62.

type of literary art. But the type is only higher in virtue of being different; it is no longer in the same category. It has lost unity of action, economy and concreteness,—all the essentials that have been laid down for good narrative prose, which is the prose of action, not of meditation.

Fiction did not really recover its directness for about a century, though there is an admirable concreteness about the prose of Jane Austen. There is a certain kind of economy too, but nothing so violent as speed. The characteristics, indeed, of her style are rather those of the essayist. The action is reduced to a minimum, and mind turns instead to analysis, to decoration (scene-painting), to mildly ironic comment:

It was hot; and after walking some time over the garden in a scattered, dispersed way, scarcely any three together, they insensibly followed one another to the delicious shade of a broad short avenue of limes, which, stretching beyond the garden at an equal distance from the river, seemed the finish of the pleasure grounds. It led to nothing; nothing but a view at the end over a low stone wall with high pillars, which seemed intended, in their erection, to give the appearance of an approach to the house, which had never been there. Disputable, however, as might be the taste of such a termination, it was in itself a charming walk, and the view which closed it extremely pretty. The considerable slope, at nearly the foot of which the Abbey stood, gradually acquired a steeper form beyond its grounds; and at half a mile distant was a bank of considerable abruptness and grandeur, well clothed with wood;— and at the bottom of this bank, favourably placed and sheltered, rose the Abbey-Mill Farm, with meadows in front, and the river making a close and handsome curve around it.

It was a sweet view—sweet to the eye and the mind. English verdure, English culture, English comfort, seen under a sun bright, without being oppressive.

JANE AUSTEN, *Emma*.

Descriptive prose of this kind is not written in any mood of compulsion. A skilful writer may be able to disguise this lack of internal necessity by means of various 'tricks of the trade,' and the result is merely a 'dead' perfection of phrase and rhythm. Jane Austen was not a skilled writer in this sense, and her lack of expertness betrays itself either in mere clumsiness, such as the repetition of the words 'seemed' and 'considerable' in the passage quoted here, or in a simplicity

or naivety of phrasing which is perhaps the secret of the
attraction which her style undoubtedly has for a large number
of people.

There are many 'quiet' situations for which this style is
adequate enough; but under the strain of dramatic action it
becomes almost ludicrous:

> There was too much wind to make the high part of the new Cobb
> pleasant for the ladies, and they agreed to get down the steps to
> the lower; and all were contented to pass quietly and carefully
> down the steep flight, excepting Louisa: she must be jumped
> down them by Captain Wentworth. In all their walks he had had
> to jump her from the stiles; the sensation was delightful to her.
> The hardness of the pavement for her feet made him less willing
> upon the present occasion; he did it however. She was safely
> down, and instantly, to show her enjoyment, ran up the steps to
> be jumped down again. He advised her against it, thought the
> jar too great; but no, he reasoned and talked in vain; she smiled
> and said, 'I am determined I will'. He put out his hands; she was
> precipitate by half a second; she fell on the pavement on the lower
> Cobb, and was taken up lifeless!
> There was no wound, no blood, no visible bruise; but her eyes
> were closed, she breathed not, her face was like death. The horror
> of that moment to all who stood around!
> Captain Wentworth, who had caught her up, knelt with her in
> his arms, looking on her with a face as pallid as her own, in an
> agony of silence. 'She is dead! she is dead!' screamed Mary,
> catching hold of her husband, and contributing with his own
> horror to make him immovable; and in another moment Henrietta,
> sinking under the conviction, lost her senses too, and would have
> fallen on the steps but for Captain Benwick and Anne, who caught
> and supported her between them.
> 'Is there no one to help me?' were the first words which burst
> from Captain Wentworth in a tone of despair, and as if all his own
> strength were gone.
> 'Go to him, go to him', cried Anne—'for Heaven's sake, go to
> him. I can support her myself. Leave me and go to him. Rub
> her hands, rub her temples; here are salts—take them, take them'.
> Captain Benwick obeyed, and Charles at the same moment
> disengaging himself from his wife, they were both with him; and
> Louisa was raised up and supported more firmly between them,
> and everything was done that Anne had prompted, but in vain;
> while Captain Wentworth, staggering against the wall for his
> support, exclaimed in the bitterest agony,—
> 'O God! her father and mother!'
> 'A surgeon!' said Anne.

He caught the word—it seemed to rouse him at once; and
saying only, 'True, true; a surgeon this instant!' was darting away,
when Anne eagerly suggested,—
'Captain Benwick—would not it be better for Captain Benwick?
He knows where a surgeon is to be found.'
Every one capable of thinking felt the advantage of the idea,
and in a moment (it was all done in rapid moments) Captain
Benwick had resigned the poor corpse-like figure entirely to the
brother's care, and was off for the town with the utmost rapidity.

JANE AUSTEN, Persuasion.

This atmosphere of a marionnette's opera[1] is entirely a
question of style.   In conception and development the scene
is right enough; it is rendered ludicrous by polite phrases like
'sinking under the conviction', 'disengaging himself from his
wife', 'every one capable of thinking felt the advantage of the
idea', 'the utmost rapidity', etc., which are not congruous
with the tragedy of the situation.   How bathetic, too, are
those apostrophes, 'The horror of that moment to all who
stood around', 'O God! her father and mother!' how absurdly
cooing Captain Wentworth's 'True, true'.

We have only to compare this style with a style which,
though equally simple, is nevertheless wrought in a mood of
emotional intensity, to see how such intensity compels the
expression to economy, directness and speed:

The following evening was very wet, indeed it poured down till
day-dawn; and, as I took my morning walk round the house,
I observed the master's window swinging open, and the rain
driving straight in.   He cannot be in bed, I thought: those showers
would drench him through.   He must either be up or out.   But
I'll make no more ado, I'll go boldly and look.
Having succeeded in obtaining entrance with another key, I ran
to enclose the panels, for the chamber was vacant; quickly pushing
them aside, I peeped in.   Mr. Heathcliff was there—laid on his
back.   His eyes met mine so keen and fierce, I started; and then
he seemed to smile.   I could not think him dead: but his face and
throat were washed with rain; the bedclothes dripped, and he was
perfectly still.   The lattice, flapping to and fro, had grazed one
hand that rested on the sill; no blood trickled from the broken

---

[1] An atmosphere that explains the charm which Jane Austen undeniably
exercises on people whose particular need is to be amused in a recondite way.
Such people have a sophisticated love of mere 'quaintness', and seek this quality
in all the arts.

skin, and when I put my fingers to it, I could doubt no more: he was dead and stark!

I hasped the window; I combed his long black hair from his forehead; I tried to close his eyes: to extinguish, if possible, that frightful, life-like gaze of exultation before anyone else beheld it. They would not shut: they seemed to sneer at my attempts, and his parted lips and sharp white teeth sneered too!

EMILY BRONTË, *Wuthering Heights*.

With the Brontës (the remark is true, at any rate of Charlotte as well as of Emily), a new vitality and stricter realism came into English fiction; it was a return to Swift and Defoe, or rather, to the fount of even these writers, for we know that the Bible was the most considerable literary influence in Emily Brontë's life. In prose fiction there has been since the middle of the last century no general lapse from this original English idiom among writers of distinction. This idiom, moreover, has been made the basis of American narrative style, not only in authors like Hawthorne, who may be said to belong to the English tradition, but in modern writers like Ernest Hemingway and William Faulkner, who owe little or nothing directly to this tradition.

We floated past the stump. Silas Foster plied his rake manfully, poking it as far as he could into the water, and immersing the whole length of his arm besides. Hollingsworth at first sat motionless, with the hooked pole elevated in the air. But, by and by, with a nervous and jerky movement, he began to plunge it into the blackness that upbore us, setting his teeth, and making precisely such thrusts, methought, as if he were stabbing at a deadly enemy. I bent over the side of the boat. So obscure, however, so awfully mysterious, was that dark stream, that—and the thought made me shiver like a leaf—I might as well have tried to look into the enigma of the eternal world, to discover what had become of Zenobia's soul, as into the river's depths, to find her body. And there, perhaps, she lay, with her face upward, while the shadow of the boat, and my own pale face peering downward, passed slowly betwixt her and the sky!

Once, twice, thrice, I paddled the boat up stream, and again suffered it to glide, with the river's slow funereal motion, downward. Silas Foster had raked up a large mass of stuff, which, as it came towards the surface, looked somewhat like a flowing garment, but proved to be a monstrous tuft of water-weeds. Hollingsworth, with a gigantic effort, upheaved a sunken log. When once free of the bottom, it rose partly out of water,—all weedy and slimy, a devilish-looking object, which the moon had not shone upon for half a hundred years,—then plunged again, and sullenly returned to its old resting-place, for the remnant of the century.

NATHANIEL HAWTHORNE, *The Blithedale Romance.*

The characteristics of good narrative prose, which we have considered mainly in relation to fiction, apply in some degree to other forms of narrative writing, such as history, biography, books of travel and books descriptive of natural phenomena. History, in so far as it is a description of events, has nothing to lose by giving a semblance of actuality to these events, and the same is true of biography. This may be stated as a general principle, but it is extremely difficult to find an example of historical writing which adequately illustrates these virtues; most historians have considered it necessary to eke out the scantiness of their facts with personal affectations; the narrative is subordinated to theoretical disquisitions and hypothetical motivations. The historian makes no attempt to see the events in their concreteness, but reacts to what he considers the historical significance of these events. We are given, not a narrative of facts, but a contemporaneous philosophy of history—an amalgam of politics, psychology, metaphysics and prejudice. As politics, or psychology or metaphysics, these writings may have great value and interest, but considered solely from our present point of view, considering, that is to say, history as a narrative of past events, they are prolix and indefinite. This is true of our greatest historians, of Gibbon and Grote, of Carlyle, Freeman and Green. These defects are not so obvious in a military historian like Sir William Napier. I shall, however, take this opportunity of giving a specimen from the writings of Robert Southey, whose style is a model of consistent 'workmanlike' qualities—the style of a man who writes swiftly and voluminously, and who has discovered the true economy of a clear mind and a clean pen:

The General now proceeded to the 42nd. 'Highlanders', said he, 'remember Egypt!' They rushed on, and drove the French before them, till they were stopped by a wall: Sir John accompanied them in this charge. He now sent Captain Hardinge to order up a battalion of Guards to the left flank of the 42nd. The officer commanding the light infantry conceived, at this, that they were to be relieved by the Guards, because their ammunition was nearly expended, and he began to fall back. The General, discovering the mistake, said to them, 'My brave 42nd, join your comrades: ammunition is coming, and you have your bayonets!' Upon this, they instantly moved forward. Captain Hardinge returned, and pointed out to the General where the Guards were advancing. The enemy kept up a hot fire, and their artillery played incessantly on the spot where they were standing. A cannon-shot struck Sir John, and carried away his left shoulder and part of his collar-bone, leaving the arm hanging by the flesh. He fell from his horse on his back, his countenance did not change, neither did he betray the least sensation of pain. Captain Hardinge, who dismounted, and took him by the hand, observed him anxiously watching the 42nd, which was warmly engaged, and told him they were advancing; and upon that intelligence his countenance brightened. Colonel Graham, who now came up to assist him, seeing the composure of his features, began to hope that he was not wounded, till he saw the dreadful laceration. From the size of the wound, it was vain to make any attempt at stopping the blood; and Sir John consented to be removed in a blanket to the rear. In raising him up, his sword, hanging on the wounded side, touched his arm, and became entangled between his legs. Captain Hardinge, observing his composure, began to hope that the wound might be not mortal, and said to him he trusted he might be spared to the army, and recover. Moore turned his head, and looking steadfastly at the wound for a few seconds, replied, 'No, Hardinge, I feel that to be impossible.'

As the soldiers were carrying him slowly along, he made them frequently turn round, that he might see the field of battle, and listen to the firing; and he was well pleased when the sound grew fainter. A spring waggon came up, bearing Colonel Wynch, who was wounded: the Colonel asked who was in the blanket, and being told it was Sir John Moore, wished him to be placed on the waggon. Sir John asked one of the Highlanders whether he thought the waggon or the blanket was best? and the man said the blanket would not shake him so much, as he and the other soldiers would keep the step, and carry him easy. So they proceeded with him to his quarters at Corunna, weeping as they went.

ROBERT SOUTHEY, *The History of the Peninsular War*.

Southey's excellencies are no less patent in his biographical works, and *The Life of Nelson* is often quoted as the best short biography in the language. There are no special observations to make on the particular characteristics of biography: a good biography is a direct narrative and demands the very qualities of visual clarity, concreteness and speed that we have assigned

to narrative in general, and it has often inspired them.   Here
are two most admirable examples:

Mr. Hastings, by his quality, being the son, brother, and uncle
to the Earls of Huntingdon, and his way of living, had the first
place amongst us.   He was peradventure an original in our age,
or rather the copy of our nobility in ancient days in hunting and
not warlike times; he was low, very strong and very active, of a
reddish flaxen hair, his clothes always green cloth, and never all
worth when new five pounds.   His house was perfectly of the old
fashion, in the midst of a large park well stocked with deer, and
near the house rabbits to serve his kitchen, many fish-ponds, and
great store of wood and timber; a bowling-green in it, long but
narrow, full of high ridges, it being never levelled since it was
ploughed; they used round sand bowls, and it had a banqueting-
house like a stand, a large one built in a tree.   He kept all manner
of sport-hounds that ran buck, fox, hare, otter, and badger, and
hawks long and short winged; he had all sorts of nets for fishing:
he had a walk in the New Forest and the manor of Christ Church.
This last supplied him with red deer, sea and river fish; and indeed,
all his neighbours' grounds and royalties were free to him, who
bestowed all his time in such sports, but what he borrowed to
caress his neighbours' wives and daughters, there being not a
woman in all his walks of the degree of a yeoman's wife or under,
and under the age of forty, but it was extremely her fault if he were
not intimately acquainted with her.   This made him very popular,
always speaking kindly to the husband, brother, or father, who was
to boot very welcome to his house whenever he came.   There he
found beef pudding and small beer in great plenty, a house not so
neatly kept as to shame him or his dirty shoes, the great hall
strewed with marrow bones, full of hawks' perches, hounds,
spaniels, and terriers, the upper sides of the hall hung with the
fox-skins of this and the last year's skinning, here and there a
polecat intermixed, guns and keepers' and huntsmen's poles in
abundance.   The parlour was a large long room, as properly
furnished; on a great hearth paved with brick lay some terriers
and the choicest hounds and spaniels; seldom but two of the great
chairs had litters of young cats in them, which were not to be
disturbed, he having always three or four attending him at dinner,
and a little white round stick of fourteen inches long lying by his
trencher, that he might defend such meat as he had no mind to
part with to them.   The windows, which were very large, served
for places to lay his arrows, crossbows, stonebows, and other such
like accoutrements; the corners of the room full of the best chose
hunting and hawking poles; an oyster-table at the lower end,
which was of constant use twice a day all the year round, for he
never failed to eat oysters before dinner and supper through all

seasons: the neighbouring town of Poole supplied him with them. The upper part of this room had two small tables and a desk, on the one side of which was a church Bible, on the other the Book of Martyrs; on the tables were hawks' hoods, bells, and such like, two or three old green hats with their crowns thrust in so as to hold ten or a dozen eggs, which were of a pheasant kind of poultry he took much care of and fed himself; tables, dice, cards, and boxes were not wanting. In the hole of the desk were store of tobacco-pipes that had been used. On one side of this end of the room was the door of a closet, wherein stood the strong beer and the wine, which never came thence but in single glasses, that being the rule of the house exactly observed, for he never exceeded in drink or permitted it. On the other side was a door into an old chapel not used for devotion; the pulpit, as the safest place, was never wanting of a cold chine of beef, pasty of venison, gammon of bacon, or great apple-pie, with thick crust extremely baked. His table cost him not much, though it was very good to eat at, his sports supplying all but beef and mutton, except Friday, when he had the best sea-fish as well as other fish he could get, and was the day that his neighbours of best quality most visited him. He never wanted a London pudding, and always sung it in with 'my part lies therein-a. He drank a glass of wine or two at meals, very often syrrup of gilliflower in his sack, and had always a tun glass without feet stood by him holding a pint of small beer, which he often stirred with a great sprig of rosemary. He was well natured, but soon angry, calling his servants bastard and cuckoldy knaves, in one of which he often spoke truth to his own knowledge, and sometimes in both, though of the same man. He lived to a hundred, never lost his eyesight, but always writ and read without spectacles, and got to horse without help. Until past fourscore he rode to the death of a stag as well as any.

1ST EARL OF SHAFTESBURY, *Fragment on the Character of Mr. Henry Hastings.*

Three white wands had been stuck in the sand to mark the Poet's grave, but as they were at some distance from each other, we had to cut a trench thirty yards in length, in the line of the sticks, to ascertain the exact spot, and it was nearly an hour before we came upon the grave.

In the meantime Byron and Leigh Hunt arrived in the carriage, attended by soldiers, and the Health Officer, as before. The lonely and grand scenery that surrounded us so exactly harmonised with Shelley's genius, that I could imagine his spirit soaring over us. The sea, with the islands of Gorgona, Capraji, and Elba, was before us; old battlemented watch-towers stretched along the coast, backed by the marble-crested Appenines glistening in the sun, picturesque from their diversified outlines, and not a human dwelling was in sight. As I thought of the delight Shelley felt in such scenes of loneliness and grandeur whilst living, I felt we were no better than a herd of wolves or a pack of wild dogs, in tearing out his battered and naked body from the pure yellow sand that lay so lightly over it, to drag him back to the light of day; but the dead have no voice, nor had I power to check the sacrilege—the work went on silently in the deep and unresisting sand, not a word was spoken, for the Italians have a touch of sentiment, and their feelings are easily excited into sympathy. Even Byron was silent and thoughtful. We were startled and drawn together by a dull hollow sound that followed the blow of a mattock; the iron had struck a skull, and the body was soon uncovered. Lime had been strewn on it; this, or decomposition, had the effect of staining it a dark and ghastly indigo colour. Byron asked me to preserve the skull for him; but remembering that he had formerly used one as a drinking-cup, I was determined Shelley's should not be so profaned. The limbs did not separate from the trunk, as in the case of Williams's body, so that the corpse was removed entire into the furnace. I had taken the precaution of having more and larger pieces of timber, in consequence of my experience of the day before of the difficulty of consuming a corpse in the open air with our apparatus. After the fire was well kindled we repeated the ceremony of the previous day; and more wine was poured over Shelley's dead body than he had consumed during his life. This with the oil and salt made the yellow flames glisten and quiver. The heat from the sun and fire was so intense that the atmosphere was tremulous and wavy. The corpse fell open and the heart was laid bare. The frontal bone of the skull, where it had been struck with the mattock, fell off; and, as the back of the head rested on the red-hot bottom bars of the furnace, the brains literally seethed, bubbled, and boiled as in a cauldron, for a very long time.

Byron could not face this scene, he withdrew to the beach and swam off to the *Bolivar*. Leigh Hunt remained in the carriage. The fire was so fierce as to produce a white heat on the iron, and to reduce its contents to grey ashes. The only portions that were not consumed were some fragments of bones, the jaw, and the skull, but what surprised us all, was that the heart remained entire. In snatching this relic from the fiery furnace, my hand was severely burnt; and had anyone seen me do the act I should have been put into quarantine.

E. J. TRELAWNY, *Last Days of Shelley and Byron*.

Finally, as an example of narrative prose used in the description of travels, and as a more extensive illustration of the virtues of a good narrative style, I cannot do better than quote a chapter from *The Bible in Spain*:

I arrived at Padron late in the evening, on my return from
Pontevedra and Vigo. It was my intention at this place to send
my servant and horses forward to Santiago, and to hire a guide to
Cape Finisterre. It would be difficult to assign any plausible
reason for the ardent desire which I entertained to visit this place;
but I remembered that last year I had escaped almost by a miracle
from shipwreck and death on the rocky sides of this extreme point
of the Old World, and I thought that to convey the Gospel to a
place so wild and remote might perhaps be considered an acceptable
pilgrimage in the eyes of the Maker. True it is that but one copy
remained of those which I had brought with me on this last journey;
but this reflection, far from discouraging me in my projected
enterprise, produced the contrary effect, as I called to mind that,
ever since the Lord revealed Himself to man, it had seemed good
to Him to accomplish the greatest ends by apparently the most
insufficient means; and I reflected that this one copy might serve
as an instrument for more good than the four thousand nine hundred
and ninety-nine copies of the edition of Madrid.

I was aware that my own horses were quite incompetent to
reach Finisterre, as the roads or paths lie through stony ravines,
and over rough and shaggy hills, and therefore determined to
leave them behind with Antonio, whom I was unwilling to expose
to the fatigues of such a journey. I lost no time in sending for an
alquilador, or person who lets out horses, and informing him of my
intention. He said he had an excellent mountain pony at my
disposal, and that he himself would accompany me; but at the
same time observed, that it was a terrible journey for man and
horse, and that he expected to be paid accordingly. I consented
to give him what he demanded, but on the express condition that
he would perform his promise of attending me himself, as I was
unwilling to trust myself four or five days amongst the hills with
any low fellow of the town whom he might select, and who it was
very possible might play me some evil turn. He replied by the
term invariably used by the Spaniards when they see doubt or
distrust exhibited: '*No tengra usted cuidado*, I will go myself'. Having
thus arranged the matter perfectly satisfactorily, as I thought, I
partook of a slight supper, and shortly afterwards retired to
repose.

I had requested the *alquilador* to call me the next morning at
three o'clock; he, however, did not make his appearance till five,
having, I suppose, overslept himself, which was indeed my own
case. I arose in a hurry, dressed, put a few things in a bag, not
forgetting the Testament, which I had resolved to present to the
inhabitants of Finisterre. I then sallied forth and saw my friend
the *alquilador*, who was holding by the bridle the pony or *jaca*
which was destined to carry me in my expedition. It was a beautiful little animal, apparently strong and full of life, without one

single white hair in its whole body, which was black as the plumage
of a crow.

Behind it stood a strange-looking figure of the biped species, to
whom, however, at the moment, I paid little attention, but of
whom I shall have plenty to say in the sequel.

Having asked the horse-lender whether he was ready to proceed,
and being answered in the affirmative, I bade adieu to Antonio,
and putting the pony in motion, we hastened out of the town,
taking at first the road which leads towards Santiago. Observing
that the figure which I had previously alluded to was following
close at our heels, I asked the *alquilador* who it was, and the reason
of its following us; to which he replied that it was a servant of his,
who would proceed a little way with us and then return. So we
went on at a rapid rate, till we were within a quarter of a mile
of the Convent of the Esclavitud, a little beyond which he had
informed me that we should have to turn off from the high-road;
but here he suddenly stopped short, and in a moment we were all
at a standstill. I questioned the guide as to the reason of this, but
received no answer. The fellow's eyes were directed to the ground,
and he seemed to be counting with the most intense solicitude the
prints of the hoofs of the oxen, mules, and horses in the dust of the
road. I repeated my demand in a louder voice; when, after a
considerable pause, he somewhat elevated his eyes, without,
however, looking me in the face, and said that he believed that I
entertained the idea that he himself was to guide me to Finisterre,
which if I did, he was very sorry for, the thing being quite impossible, as he was perfectly ignorant of the way, and, moreover,
incapable of performing such a journey over rough and difficult
ground, as he was no longer the man he had been; and, over and
above all that, he was engaged that day to accompany a gentleman
to Pontevedra, who was at that moment expecting him. 'But',
continued he, 'as I am always desirous of behaving like a *caballero*
to everybody, I have taken measures to prevent your being
disappointed. This person', pointing to the figure, 'I have engaged
to accompany you. He is a most trustworthy person, and is well
acquainted with the route to Finisterre, having been thither several
times with this very *jaca* on which you are mounted. He will,
besides, be an agreeable companion to you on the way, as he speaks
French and English very well, and has been all over the world.'
The fellow ceased speaking at last; and I was so struck with his
craft, impudence, and villany, that some time elapsed before I
could find an answer. I then reproached him in the bitterest
terms for his breach of promise, and said that I was much tempted
to return to the town instantly, complain of him to the *alcade*, and
have him punished at any expense. To which he replied, 'Sir
Cavalier, by so doing you will be nothing nearer Finisterre, to
which you seem so eager to get. Take my advice, spur on the

jaca, for you see it is getting late, and it is twelve long leagues
from hence to Corcuvion, where you must pass the night; and from
thence to Finisterre is no trifle. As for the man, *no tenga usted
cuidado*, he is the best guide in Galicia, speaks English and French,
and will bear you pleasant company.'

By this time I had reflected that by returning to Padron I should
indeed be only wasting time, and that by endeavouring to have
the fellow punished no benefit would accrue to me; moreover, as
he seemed to be a scoundrel in every sense of the word, I might as
well proceed in the company of any person as in his. I therefore
signified my intention of proceeding, and told him to go back, in
the Lord's name, and repent of his sins. But having gained one
point, he thought he had best attempt another; so placing himself
about a yard before the *jaca*, he said that the price which I had
agreed to pay him for the loan of his horse (which, by-the-by, was
the full sum he had demanded) was by no means sufficient, and
that before I proceeded I must promise him two dollars more,
adding that he was either drunk or mad when he had made such
a bargain. I was now thoroughly incensed, and without a moment's
reflection, spurred the *jaca*, which flung him down in the dust,
and passed over him. Looking back at the distance of a hundred
yards, I saw him standing in the same place, his hat on the ground,
gazing after us, and crossing himself most devoutly. His servant,
or whatever he was, far from offering any assistance to his principal,
no sooner saw the *jaca* in motion than he ran by its side, without
word or comment, further than striking himself lustily on the
thigh with his right palm. We soon passed the Esclavitud, and
presently afterwards turned to the left into a stony broken path
leading to fields of maize. We passed by several farm-houses, and
at last arrived at a dingle, the sides of which were plentifully
overgrown with dwarf oaks, and which slanted down to a small
dark river shaded with trees, which we crossed by a rude bridge.
By this time I had had sufficient time to scan my odd companion
from head to foot. His utmost height, had he made the most of
himself, might perhaps have amounted to five feet one inch; but
he seemed somewhat inclined to stoop. Nature had gifted him
with an immense head, and placed it clean upon his shoulders,
for amongst the items of his composition it did not appear that a
neck had been included. Arms long and brawny swung at his
sides, and the whole of his frame was as strong built and powerful
as a wrestler's; his body was supported by a pair of short but very
nimble legs. His face was very long, and would have borne
some slight resemblance to a human countenance had the nose been
more visible, for its place seemed to have been entirely occupied
by a wry mouth and large staring eyes. His dress consisted of three
articles: an old and tattered hat of the Portuguese kind, broad at
the crown and narrow at the eaves, something which appeared to

be a shirt, and dirty canvas trousers. Willing to enter into conversation with him, and remembering that the *alquilador* had informed me that he spoke languages, I asked him, in English, if he had always acted in the capacity of guide. Whereupon he turned his eyes with a singular expression upon his face, gave a loud laugh, a long leap, and clapped his hands thrice above his head. Perceiving that he did not understand me, I repeated my demand in French, and was again answered by the laugh, leap, and clapping. At last he said, in broken Spanish, 'Master mine, speak Spanish in God's name, and I can understand you, and still better if you speak Gallegan, but I can promise no more. I heard what the *alquilador* told you, but he is the greatest *embustero* in the whole land, and deceived you then as he did when he promised to accompany you. I serve him for my sins; but it was an evil hour when I left the deep sea and turned guide'. He then informed me that he was a native of Padron, and a mariner by profession, having spent the greater part of his life in the Spanish navy, in which service he had visited Cuba and many parts of the Spanish Americas, adding, 'when my master told you that I should bear you pleasant company by the way, it was the only word of truth that has come from his mouth for a month; and long before you reach Finisterre you will have rejoiced that the servant, and not the master, went with you: he is dull and heavy, but I am what you see.' He then gave two or three first-rate somersaults, again laughed loudly, and clapped his hands. 'You would scarcely think', he continued, 'that I drove that little pony yesterday, heavily laden, all the way from Corunna. We arrived at Padron at two o'clock this morning; but we are nevertheless both willing and able to undertake a fresh journey. *No tenga usted cuidado*, as my master said, no one ever complains of that pony or of me.' In this kind of discourse we proceeded a considerable way through a very picturesque country, until we reached a beautiful village at the skirt of a mountain. 'This village', said my guide, 'is called Los Angeles, because its church was built long since by the angels; they placed a beam of gold beneath it, which they brought down from heaven, and which was once a rafter of God's own house. It runs all the way under the ground from hence to the cathedral of Compostella.'

Passing through the village, which he likewise informed me possessed baths, and was much visited by the people of Santiago, we shaped our course to the north-west, and by so doing doubled a mountain which rose majestically over our heads, its top crowned with bare and broken rocks, whilst on our right, on the other side of a spacious valley, was a high range connected with the mountains to the northward of Saint James. On the summit of this range rose high embattled towers, which my guide informed me were those of Altamira, an ancient and ruined castle, formerly the principal

residence in this province of the counts of that name. Turning
now due west, we were soon at the bottom of a steep and rugged
pass, which led to more elevated regions. The ascent cost us nearly
half an hour, and the difficulties of the ground were such that I
more than once congratulated myself on having left my own horses
behind, and being mounted on the gallant little pony, which,
accustomed to such paths, scrambled bravely forward, and eventually brought us in safety to the top of the ascent.

Here we entered a Gallegan cabin, or *choza*, for the purpose of
refreshing the animal and ourselves. The quadruped ate some
maize, whilst we two bipeds regaled ourselves on some *broa* and
aguardiente, which a woman whom we found in the hut placed
before us. I walked out for a few minutes to observe the aspect
of the country, and on my return found my guide fast asleep on
the bench where I had left him. He sat bolt upright, his back
supported against the wall, and his legs pendulous, within three
inches of the ground, being too short to reach it. I remained
gazing upon him for at least five minutes, whilst he enjoyed
slumbers seemingly as quiet and profound as those of death itself.
His face brought powerfully to my mind some of those uncouth
visages of saints and abbots which are occasionally seen in the
niches of the walls of ruined convents. There was not the slightest
gleam of vitality in his countenance, which for colour and rigidity
might have been of stone, and which was as rude and battered as
one of the stone heads at Icolmkill, which have braved the winds
of twelve hundred years. I continued gazing on his face till I
became almost alarmed, concluding that life might have departed
from its harassed and fatigued tenement. On my shaking him
rather roughly by the shoulder he slowly awoke, opening his eyes
with a stare, and then closing them again. For a few moments
he was evidently unconscious of where he was. On my shouting
to him, however, and inquiring whether he intended to sleep all
day, instead of conducting me to Finisterre, he dropped upon his
legs, snatched up his hat, which lay on the table, and instantly ran
out of the door, exclaiming, 'Yes, yes, I remember; follow me,
captain, and I will lead you to Finisterre in no time'. I looked
after him, and perceived that he was hurrying at a considerable
pace in the direction in which we had hitherto been proceeding.
'Stop', said I, 'stop! Will you leave me here with the pony?
Stop; we have not paid the reckoning. Stop!' He, however,
never turned his head for a moment, and in less than a minute
was out of sight. The pony, which was tied to a crib at one end
of the cabin, began now to neigh terrifically, to plunge, and to
erect its tail and mane in a most singular manner. It tore and
strained at the halter till I was apprehensive that strangulation
would ensue. 'Woman', I exclaimed, 'where are you, and what
is the meaning of all this?' But the hostess had likewise dis-

appeared, and though I ran about the *choza*, shouting myself
hoarse, no answer was returned. The pony still continued to
scream and to strain at the halter more violently than ever. 'Am
I beset with lunatics?' I cried, and flinging down a *peseta* on the
table, unloosed the halter, and attempted to in roduce the bit
into the mouth of the animal. This, however, I found impossible
to effect. Released from the halter, the pony made at once for
the door, in spite of all the efforts which I could make to detain it.
'If you abandon me', said I, 'I am in a pretty situation; but there
is a remedy for everything!' with which words I sprang into the
saddle, and in a moment more the creature was bearing me at a
rapid gallop in the direction, as I supposed, of Finisterre. My
position, however diverting to the reader, was rather critical to
myself. I was on the back of a spirited animal, over which I had
no control, dashing along a dangerous and unknown path. I could
not discover the slightest vestige of my guide, nor did I pass anyone
from whom I could derive any information. Indeed, the speed
of the animal was so great, that even in the event of my meeting
or overtaking a passenger, I could scarcely have hoped to exchange
a word with him. 'Is the pony trained to this work?' said I,
mentally. 'Is he carrying me to some den of banditti, where my
throat will be cut, or does he follow his master by instinct?' Both
of these suspicions I, however, soon abandoned. The pony's
speed relaxed; he appeared to have lost the road. He looked
about uneasily: at last, coming to a sandy spot, he put his nostrils
to the ground, and then suddenly flung himself down, and wallowed
in true pony fashion. I was not hurt, and instantly made use of
this opportunity to slip the bit into his mouth, which previously
had been dangling beneath his neck; I then remounted in quest of
the road.

This I soon found, and continued my way for a considerable
time. The path lay over a moor, patched with heath and furze,
and here and there strewn with large stones, or rather rocks.
The sun had risen high in the firmament, and burned fiercely.
I passed several people, men and women, who gazed at me with
surprise, wondering, probably, what a person of my appearance
could be about, without a guide, in so strange a place. I inquired
of two females whom I met whether they had seen my guide; but
they either did not or would not understand me, and, exchanging
a few words with each other in one of the hundred dialects of the
Gallegan, passed on. Having crossed the moor, I came rather
abruptly upon a convent, overhanging a deep ravine, at the bottom
of which brawled a rapid stream.

It was a beautiful and picturesque spot: the sides of the ravine
were thickly clothed with wood, and on the other side a tall hill
uplifted itself. The edifice was large, and apparently deserted.
Passing by it, I presently reached a small village, as deserted, to

all appearance, as the convent, for I saw not a single individual, nor so much as a dog to welcome me with his bark. I proceeded, however, until I reached a fountain, the waters of which gushed from a stone pillar into a trough. Seated upon this last, his arms folded, and his eyes fixed upon the neighbouring mountain, I beheld a figure which still frequently recurs to my thoughts, especially when asleep and oppressed by the nightmare. This figure was my runaway guide.

GEORGE BORROW, *The Bible in Spain.*

CHAPTER IX

*

Fantasy (Fancy)

IN THE TABLE ON p. 85, extraverted feeling was shown as giving rise to "fancy", introverted feeling as giving rise to "imagination". These two words, with their near synonyms 'fantasy' and 'invention', are extremely confusing, and I must begin by trying to give them a clear meaning within the present context.

The *New English Dictionary* points out, with reference to the word *fantasy*, and the almost identical word *phantasy*, that 'in modern use *fantasy* and *phantasy*, in spite of their identity in sound and in ultimate etymology, tend to be apprehended as separate words, the predominant sense of the former being "caprice, whim, fanciful invention", while that of the latter is "imagination, visionary notion"'. This distinction is implied in the use of the word *fantasy* in the present context, and indeed it will be necessary in this chapter to define the special connotation of the word with some precision, in order to distinguish a mode of rhetoric which has not yet been given separate recognition.

Fantasy should not be confused with those separate, disparate and unorganized expressions which give form to a '*passing*' whim or caprice and which are more properly called 'conceits'. A fantasy is more than a conceit, implying a sustained invention in the realm of fancy. Before we can demonstrate its characteristics as a type of rhetoric we must further distinguish it from imagination.

Fantasy is extraverted feeling:[1] imagination is introverted

1 I should confess at this point that Jung would scarcely sanction this statement, for he has remarked (*Psychological Types*, p. 547) that 'phantasy-activity, or reverie . . . is a peculiar form of activity which can manifest itself in all the four functions'. But by his use of the word 'reverie' as a synonym for 'phantasy' Jung shows that he has in mind something quite different from the English meaning of *fancy*. In German the words *Phantasie*, *phantasieren* are associated primarily with the phenomenon of 'day-dreaming', which is far from the sense of Coleridge's 'fixities and definites'.

feeling. If in pursuit of the extraversion of feeling, the mind turns to speculation, the result is fantasy. When, however, feeling is introverted, the product of speculation is imaginative. The distinction follows the lines of discursive and non-discursive logic. Fantasy may be visionary, but it is deliberate and rational; imagination is sensuous and symbolic. Each mode has its characteristic style, but the style of fantasy is analogous to that of exposition, while the style of imagination is analogous to that of narrative. Fantasy may be identified with fancy, though it is customary to apply the word fancy to the mental activity as such, the word fantasy to the product of that activity. Of fancy as a mental process I have no desire to improve on the definition given by Coleridge:

> Fancy . . . has no other counters to play with, but fixities and definites. The fancy is, indeed, no other than a mode of memory emancipated from the order of time and space; while it is blended with, and modified by that empirical phenomenon of the will, which we express by the word Choice. But equally with the ordinary memory the Fancy must receive all its materials ready made from the law of association.
>
> *Biographia Literaria*, chapter xiii.

It is necessary, however, to comment on this definition with special reference to prose composition. We must try to distinguish pure fantasy, and to describe its rhetorical properties.

We notice in the first place that fancy is concerned with fixities and definites. In other words, it is an objective faculty. It does not deal with vague entities; it deals with things which are concrete, clearly perceptible, visibly defined.

Secondly, it is 'a mode of memory emancipated from the order of time and space'. This clearly distinguishes fancy from exposition and narrative, for it deliberately avoids the logic and consistency of these types of rhetoric and creates a new and arbitrary order of events. It is, as the next clause in Coleridge's definition points out, an exercise of choice, an expression of the will. Psychologically the will may follow a direction given to it by the conditions of our mental and physical environment; it may be merely a pattern of behaviour. Coleridge perceived something of this, and added as a qualification that 'Fancy must receive all its materials ready made from the law of association'—meaning thereby that nothing comes to the mind except in some connection with the world of which it is but one unit. But this consideration does not affect the present argument; we are dealing with a mode of expression, with the definite and observable facts constituted by a series of words; and such words do sometimes present that arbitrary appearance which we ascribe to the will and to the exercise of conscious choice.

Fantasy, then, the product of Fancy, is distinguished by two qualities which we may briefly summarize as objectivity and apparent arbitrariness. In what form of literature do we find these two qualities notably expressed? I think only in one, essentially, and that is the fairy tale. But there is more than one kind of fairy tale.

The fairy tale is originally a folk creation. Its analogue in verse is the ballad. It is a common characteristic of these forms of expression, which are handed down from generation to generation by word of mouth, that the slow changes they undergo are all in the direction of the elements with which Coleridge has distinguished Fancy: they become emancipated from the order of time and space because the memory does not carry literally from generation to generation, but only essentially. The idea of theme is constant, but there is a gradual accretion of subsidiary details. And the memory that reaches from one generation to another tends to select only those elements of the story which are vivid and actual, and these will naturally be objective elements, rather than the descriptions of emotional or individual reactions. There is a natural tendency, therefore, for the ballad and folk tale to develop a clear objective narrative, but a narrative encumbered with odd inconsequential but startlingly vivid and concrete details.

At St. Mary's of the Wolf-pits in Suffolk, a boy and his sister were found by the inhabitants of that place near the mouth of a pit which is there, who had the form of all their limbs like to those of other men, but they differed in the colour of their skin from all the people of our habitable world; for the whole surface of their skin was tinged of a green colour. No one could understand their speech. When they were brought as curiosities to the house of a certain knight, Sir Richard de Caine, at Wikes, they wept bitterly. Bread and other victuals were set before them, but they would touch none of them, though they were tormented by great hunger, as the girl afterwards acknowledged. At length, when some beans just cut, with their stalks, were brought into the house, they made signs, with great avidity, that they should be given to them. When they were brought, they opened the stalks instead of the pods, thinking the beans were in the hollow of them; but not finding them there, they began to weep anew. When those who were present saw this, they opened the pods, and showed them the naked beans. They fed on these with great delight, and for a long time tasted no other food. The boy however was always languid and depressed, and he died within a short time. The girl enjoyed continual good health, and becoming accustomed to various kinds of food, lost completely the green colour, and gradually recovered the sanguine habit of her entire body. She was afterwards regenerated by the laver of holy baptism, and lived for many years in the service of that knight (as I have frequently heard from him and his family), and was rather loose and wanton in her conduct. Being frequently asked about the people of her country, she asserted that the inhabitants, and all they had in that country, were of a green colour; and that they saw no sun, but enjoyed a degree of light like what is after sunset. Being asked how she came into this country with the aforesaid boy, she replied, that as they were following their flocks they came to a certain cavern, on entering which they heard a delightful sound of bells; ravished by whose sweetness, they went for a long time wandering on through the cavern until they came to its mouth. When they came out of it, they were struck senseless by the excessive light of the sun, and the unusual temperature of the air; and they thus lay for a long time. Being terrified by the noise of those who came on them, they wished to fly, but they could not find the entrance of the cavern before they were caught.

The Green Children.[1]

A story such as this is the norm to which all types of Fantasy should conform. The only difference is, that in the conscious literary inventions with which we are nowadays concerned, the will or intention of the writer has to take the part of the age long and impersonal forces of folk tradition. That this can be achieved is beyond doubt, and Southey's immortal story may be given as a proof of it:

[1] From T. Keightley, *The Fairy Mythology*, p. 281.

Once upon a time there were Three Bears, who lived together in a house of their own, in a wood. One of them was a Little, Small, Wee Bear; and one was a Middle-sized Bear, and the other was a Great, Huge Bear. They had each a pot for their porridge, a little pot for the Little, Small Wee Bear; and a middle-sized pot for the Middle Bear; and a great pot for the Great, Huge Bear. And they had each a chair to sit in; a little chair for the Little, Small, Wee Bear; and a middle-sized chair for the Middle Bear; and a great chair for the Great, Huge Bear. And they had each a bed to sleep in; a little bed for the Little, Small, Wee Bear; and a middle-sized bed for the Middle Bear; and a great bed for the Great, Huge Bear.

One day, after they had made the porridge for their breakfast, and poured it into their porridge-pots, they walked out into the wood while their porridge was cooling, that they might not burn their mouths, by beginning too soon to eat it. And while they were walking a little old Woman came to the house. She could not have been a good, honest old Woman; for first she looked in at that window, and then she peeped in at the keyhole; and seeing nobody in the house, she lifted the latch. The door was not fastened, because the Bears were good Bears, who did nobody any harm, and never suspected that any body would harm them. So the little old Woman opened the door, and went in; and well pleased she was when she saw the porridge on the table. If she had been a good little old Woman, she would have waited till the Bears came home, and then, perhaps, they would have asked her to breakfast; for they were good Bears,—a little rough or so, as the manner of Bears is, but for all that very good natured and hospitable. But she was an impudent, bad old Woman, and set about helping herself.

So first she tasted the porridge of the Great, Huge Bear, and that was too hot for her; and she said a bad word about that. And then she tasted the porridge of the Middle Bear, and that was too cold for her; and she said a bad word about that, too. And then she went to the porridge of the Little, Small, Wee Bear, and tasted that; and that was neither too hot, nor too cold, but just right; and she liked it so well, that she ate it all up: but the naughty old Woman said a bad word about the little porridge-pot, because it did not hold enough for her.

Then the little old Woman sate down in the chair of the Great, Huge Bear, and that was too hard for her. And then she sate down in the chair of the Middle Bear, and that was too soft for her. And then she sate down in the chair of the Little, Small, Wee Bear, and that was neither too hard, nor too soft, but just right. So she seated herself in it, and there she sate till the bottom of the chair came out, and down came hers, plump upon the ground. And the naughty old Woman said a wicked word about that too.

Then the little old Woman went up stairs into the bed-chamber in which the three Bears slept. And first she lay down upon the bed of the Great, Huge Bear; but that was too high at the head for her. And she next lay down upon the bed of the Middle Bear; and that was too high at the foot for her. And then she lay down upon the bed of the Little, Small, Wee Bear; and that was neither too high at the head, nor at the foot, but just right. So she covered herself up comfortably, and lay there till she fell fast asleep.

By this time the Three Bears thought their porridge would be cool enough; so they came home to breakfast. Now the little old Woman had left the spoon of the Great, Huge Bear standing in his porridge.

'SOMEBODY HAS BEEN AT MY PORRIDGE!'

said the Great, Huge Bear, in his great, rough, gruff voice. And when the Middle Bear looked at his, he saw that the spoon was standing in it too.. They were wooden spoons; if they had been silver ones, the naughty old Woman would have put them in her pocket.

'Somebody has been at my porridge!'

said the Middle Bear, in his middle voice.

Then the Little, Small, Wee Bear looked at his, and there was the spoon in the porridge-pot, but the porridge was all gone.

'*Somebody has been at my porridge, and has eaten it all up!*'

said the Little, Small, Wee Bear, in his little, small, wee voice.

Upon this the Three Bears, seeing that someone had entered their house, and eaten up the Little, Small, Wee Bear's breakfast, began to look about them. Now the little old Woman had not put the hard cushion straight when she rose from the chair of the Great, Huge Bear.

'SOMEBODY HAS BEEN SITTING IN MY CHAIR!'

said the Great, Huge Bear, in his great, rough, gruff voice.

And the little old Woman had squatted down the soft cushion of the Middle Bear.

'Somebody has been sitting in my chair!'

said the Middle Bear, in his middle voice.

And you know what the little old Woman had done to the third chair.

'*Somebody has been sitting in my chair, and has sate the bottom of it out!*'

said the Little, Small, Wee Bear, in his little, small, wee voice.

Then the Three Bears thought it necessary that they should make farther search; so they went up stairs into their bed-chamber. Now the little old Woman had pulled the pillow of the Great, Huge Bear out of its place.

'SOMEBODY HAS BEEN LYING IN MY BED!'

said the Great, Huge Bear, in his great, rough, gruff voice.

And the little old Woman had pulled the bolster of the Middle
Bear out of its place.

'Somebody has been lying in my bed!'

said the Middle Bear, in his middle voice.

And when the Little, Small, Wee Bear came to look at his bed,
there was the bolster in its place; and the pillow in its place upon
the bolster; and upon the pillow was the little old Woman's ugly,
dirty head,—which was not in its place, for she had no business
there.

'Somebody has been lying in my bed,—and here she is!'

said the Little, Small, Wee Bear, in his little, small, wee voice.

The little old Woman had heard in her sleep the great, rough,
gruff voice of the Great, Huge Bear; but she was so fast asleep
that it was no more to her than the roaring of wind, or the rumbling
of thunder.   And she had heard the middle voice of the Middle
Bear, but it was only as if she had heard someone speaking in a
dream.   But when she heard the little, small, wee voice of the Little,
Small, Wee Bear, it was so sharp, and so shrill, that it awakened
her at once.   Up she started; and when she saw the Three Bears
on one side of the bed, she tumbled herself out at the other, and
ran to the window.   Now the window was open, because the
Bears, like good, tidy Bears, as they were, always opened their
bed-chamber window when they got up in the morning.   Out the
little old Woman jumped; and whether she broke her neck in the
fall; or ran into the wood and was lost there; or found her way
out of the wood, and was taken up by the constable and sent to
the House of Correction for a vagrant as she was, I cannot tell.
But the Three Bears never saw anything more of her.

ROBERT SOUTHEY, *The Doctor.*

This story so perfectly conforms to the requirements of a
folk tale that it has actually been adopted as such, and is
everywhere and in almost every language reprinted and
retold with little consciousness of the fact that it is a deliberate
creation of an English writer of the early nineteenth century.

The perfection of 'The Three Bears' is a rare one.   Almost
all other fairy tales which are not traditional fail in some way,
and their failure can, I think, always be traced to an ignorance
of the canons of fantasy.   Kingsley's *Water Babies*, for example,
has one of the true elements of fantasy—arbitrariness, but it
lacks objectivity: it has a subjective, or moralizing, intent,
and this not only destroys its rhetorical purity but in so doing

destroys its rhetorical effect, as any child will tell you. *Alice in Wonderland* comes much nearer to perfection—it is magnificently arbitrary, and is in a large measure objective. A good deal of satirical thought underlies the fantasy, and though the fantasy is pervasive enough to allow children (and perhaps adults) to ignore the satire (as also in a more recent example of fantasy—George Orwell's *Animal Farm*), the adult is generally aware of the sophistication. *Alice* has a suppressed background of culture which a true fairy tale never has. *Alice* will always delight our particular civilization: it will hardly become a part of our traditional folk-lore, like 'The Three Bears'.

A primitive, or at least an innocent, outlook seems essential to a good fairy tale, and it is among the civilizations which to-day retain something of their primitive spirit that we naturally find the best Fairy Tales. I refer in particular to Alexey Michailovich Remizov, whose tales 'Her Star-Bear' and 'Hare Ivanitch' are perfect examples of their kind. The following short passage from the former tale will illustrate their fantastical nature:

Alyónushka's little star was a long time flying through the air, and, at last, it fell down into the heart of a wood, where the trees were thickest, where the firs intertwined their shaggy branches and made an eerie humming noise.

A thick blue-grey mist woke up and crawled across the sky, and the winter night was over.

And the sun, dressed in a scarlet cloak and a laced hat, came down from his crystal watch-tower.

Alyónushka's little star was lying, all transparent, with melancholy blue eyes, on the soft pine needles, not far from a hare's form, and Jack Frost began to breathe on things.

And the old sun marched on and on, over the wood, and went home to his crystal watch-tower.

Snow clouds appeared and lay across the sky, and it began to grow dark.

In a trembling voice the grumbling wind struck up his old winter song.

The dumb snow-storm sprang up, and, dumb though she was, she shrieked.

The snow began to dance.

The poor little star was dozing by the hare's form, and the thaw of a little tear rolled down her star cheek and then froze again.

And it seemed to her that once more she was flying round in the dancing chorus with her little golden friends, and they were so merry and laughed out loud, like Alyónushka. And the cloudy night—an old Nannie, like Vlasyevna—was taking care of them.

.   .   .   .   .

The blinds were being pulled up.

All day Alyónushka stood by the open window. Strange people were walking past, furniture removers were jogging along, and look! a waggon is crawling past, piled up with mattresses and tables and beds.

'That means that somebody is off to the country!' decided Alyónushka. The sky was blue and clear, and the sky smiled at Alyónushka.

'Mummie! I say, Mummie! When are *we* going to the country?' she kept asking.

'We'll get ready, darling, and pack up everything and go off far away, farther than last summer!' said Mummie: Mummie was making Alyónushka a dressing-gown, and she was busy.

'Oh! if only we could go quickly,' teased Alyónushka.

She couldn't as much as look at her toys—they were so wooden and dull. The toys, too, had had enough of winter.[1]

To pass to more sophisticated types of fantasy, written as deliberate artifices, it is easy to quote many quasi-fantastical compositions, but very few have the purity of traditional fairy tales. A 'Utopia', or description of a fantastical country and its civilization, might well exhibit all the characteristics of pure fantasy, but rarely does so because the writer has some ulterior satirical or moral aim, which aim directs his composition, fixes it in space and time, gives it a basis of subjective intolerance. Such objections apply to *Utopia* itself, to *News from Nowhere* and *The Dream of John Ball*, to *Erewhon*, *A Crystal Age* and Orwell's *1984*.[2] They do not apply to some of the fantasies of H. G. Wells, who comes as near as any modern writer to a sense of pure fantasy. He errs, as in *The Time Machine*, by imparting to his fantasies a pseudo-scientific logicality; it is as though having conceived one

[1] From *The Book of the Bear*, being Twenty-one Tales newly translated from the Russian by Jane Harrison and Hope Mirrlees. (Nonesuch Press, 1926.)

[2] W. H. Hudson, in his Preface to the second edition of *A Crystal Age*, remarks: 'In going through this book after so many years I am amused at the way it is coloured by the little cults and crazes, and modes of thought of the 'eighties of the last century. They were so important then, and now, if remembered at all, they appear so trivial.'

arbitrary fantasy he were compelled by the habits of his scientific training to work out the consequences of this fantasy. Real fantasy is bolder than this; it dispenses with all logic and habit, and relies on the force of wonder alone.

The Thousand and One Nights, with its magnificent apparatus of genii and afrits, is the greatest work of fantasy that has ever been evolved by tradition, and given literary form. But it, alas, is not English, and has no English equivalent. The Western world does not seem to have conceived the necessity of fairy-tales for grown-ups—though it has been suggested that the modern detective story is an equivalent—and that is perhaps why it condemns them to a life of unremitted toil. In *Vathek* William Beckford produced a counterfeit of an Arabian Nights' Entertainment which almost deserves to be incorporated in the Eastern collection. But a counterfeit is a counterfeit, and though *Vathek* is one of the best fantasies in the language,[1] I prefer not to give it as a model because I would rather envisage the possibility of a fantasy that is racial in its origins and part, not only of the English language, but of English traditions. Meanwhile I can only suggest that the possibility of such a fantasy is foreshadowed in the dramatic nightmare which makes the climax of James Joyce's *Ulysses*. The first 'stage direction' illustrates the strain of fantasy which is sustained throughout the episode:

The Mabbot street entrance of nighttown, before which stretches an uncobbled tramsiding set with skeleton tracks, red and green will-o'-the-wisps and danger signals. Rows of flimsy houses with gaping doors. Rare lamps with faint rainbow-fans. Round Rabaiotti's halted ice gondola stunted men and women squabble. They grab wafers between which are wedged lumps of coal and copper snow. Sucking, they scatter slowly. Children. The swancomb of the gondola, highreared, forges on through the murk, white and blue under a lighthouse. Whistles call and answer.[2]

The only fault of this fantasy is its incoherence, which is not the incoherence of arbitrariness (which is always

---

[1] *Vathek* was written in French by its author, so the Rev. Samuel Henley, who translated it, should have a share in these encomiums.

[2] P. 408.

simple[1]) but of sophistication. This fantasy from *Ulysses* needs for its appreciation an intellectual standpoint of a most exclusive kind; it needs a temper of metaphysical disillusion. As a fantasy it is not therefore completely emancipated from the order of time and space; nor is it completely concrete in its expression. *Finnegan's Wake*, with its reliance on arbitrary word associations, is a better example, but one that is far too complex and sophisticated for the common reader.

Fancy has suffered a certain denigration from its association of contrast to imagination, which latter faculty has been enhanced ever since writers of the Romantic Movement took it as their special endowment. But this aspersion of fancy is entirely sentimental in origin; as I have shown, fancy and imagination are rather to be regarded as equal and opposite faculties, directly related to the general opposition of discursive and non-discursive thought. When a less romantic age has realized this distinction, perhaps it will turn to fantasy as to a virgin soil, and give to English literature an entertainment comparable to the *Thousand and One Nights*.

[1] Compare, for example, Samuel Foote's delightful oddity:

THE
GREAT
PANJANDRUM
HIMSELF

So she went into the garden
to cut a cabbage-leaf
to make an apple-pie;
and at the same time
a great she-bear, coming down the street,
pops its head into the shop.
What! no soap?
So he died,
and she very imprudently married the Barber:
and there were present
the Picninnies,
and the Joblillies,
and the Garyulies,
and the great Panjandrum himself,
with the little round button at top;
and they all fell to playing the game
of catch-as-catch-can,
till the gunpowder ran out at the heels of their boots.

CHAPTER X

*

Imagination or Invention

WE SHALL FIND IT necessary to consider the subjects of the following two chapters in close association, since it is not always easy to discriminate between the speculative use of sensibility and the intelligent control of emotion (by such devices as rhythm and structural form). The ordered use of perceptual images is one rhetorical function; it is the subject of the present chapter. The control of emotion by thought is another rhetorical function, really quite distinct from the first function, but not often distinguished. It will be the subject of Chapter XI, but in this first chapter we must cover a certain amount of ground common to both subjects and vaguely described by the most dangerous word in our critical vocabulary—imagination.

Hazlitt made a distinction between the "inventive and refined" and the "impressive and vigorous" styles, which will perhaps serve to underline this distinction. The first style, which we call inventive, is used to introduce new ideas; the second, which we call impressive, is used to infuse life and energy into existing ideas:

There are two very different ends which a man of genius may propose to himself either in writing or speaking, and which will accordingly give birth to very different styles. He can have but one of these two objects; either to enrich, or strengthen the mind; either to furnish us with new ideas, to lead the mind into new trains of thought, to which it was before unused, and which it was incapable of striking out for itself; or else to collect and embody what we already knew, to rivet our old impressions more deeply; to make what was before plain still plainer, and to give to that which was familiar all the effect of novelty. In the one case we receive an accession to the stock of our ideas; in the other, an additional degree of life and energy is infused into them: our thoughts continue to flow in the same channels, but their pulse is quickened and invigorated. I do not know how to distinguish these different styles better than by calling them severally the inventive and refined, or the impressive and vigorous styles.

WILLIAM.HAZLITT, Essay on *Edmund Burke*.

The definition of imagination which Coleridge opposes to that of fancy, quoted in the last chapter, is not so useful for our present purpose. It is much vaguer, and couched in the terms of a transcendentalism which, to say the least of it (and the best), is no longer in fashion. Imagination is considered as either primary or secondary.

The primary Imagination I hold to be the living power and prime agent of all human perception, and as a repetition in the finite mind of the eternal act of creation in the infinite I AM. The secondary Imagination I consider as an echo of the former, co-existing with the conscious will, yet still as identical with the primary in the *kind* of its agency, and differing only in *degree*, and in the *mode* of its operation. It dissolves, diffuses, dissipates, in order to recreate: or where this process is rendered impossible, yet still at all events it struggles to idealize and to unify. It is essentially *vital*, even as all objects (*as* objects) are essentially fixed and dead.

It is very difficult to apply this definition. The primary imagination is apparently identified with the general principle of creative thought, and the secondary imagination is that same creative principle in the degree that it becomes conscious activity. Later on in the *Biographia Literaria* (towards the end of Chapter XIV) it appears that imagination as defined here is largely identified with the poetic principle. With this identification I should agree in so far as imagination is a 'creative' activity.[1] In the moment of its origination the word is poetry. Let this be the primary sense of imagination. But then I think that in its secondary sense the word must be held to cover more factors than are implied in Coleridge's definition. Or rather, I think that some of the factors which Coleridge would describe as secondary are really primary, in that they are moments of origination or creativity; the

---

[1] I put creative within these marks which so conveniently suggest ambiguity because it is only by analogy that the word can be used in such a context. A thought is born—a thought that never existed before—but it always comes into the world with a pedigree, and generally finds itself among near relations.

secondary process is really the conscious arrangement of these moments into an expressive pattern, as Coleridge recognizes in his emphasis on 'the conscious will' and on unification.

There is a famous phrase in the second passage dealing with imagination (the one to which I have just referred) which describes exactly what I wish more particularly to connote by the word Imagination in the present context. Coleridge says that this power of imagination reveals itself, among other ways, in the balance and reconciliation of 'a judgment ever awake and steady self-possession with enthusiasm more than usual state of emotion with more than usual order, and feeling profound or vehement'.

The *predominance* which is given on the one hand to order or judgment and on the other hand to emotion or feeling determines those opposed types of expression which are given the historical terms 'classical' or 'romantic'. The *priority* of either of these qualities determines the distinction between prose and poetry. If the thought is of a discursive or speculative origin, with creation or feeling subsumed or induced within its framework, then the form of expression is prosaic; if the thought is of an immediate or intuitive origin, if it is 'essentially vital', but nevertheless assumes order and harmony, then the form of expression is poetic.

For as the rain cometh down, and the snow from heaven, and returneth not thither, but watereth the earth, and maketh it bring forth and bud, that it may give seed to the sower, and bread to the eater: so shall my word be that goeth forth out of my mouth: it shall not return unto me void, but it shall accomplish that which I please, and it shall prosper in the thing whereto I sent it. For ye shall go out with joy, and be led forth with peace: the mountains and the hills shall break forth before you into singing, and all the trees of the field shall clap their hands. Instead of the thorn shall come up the fir tree, and instead of the brier shall come up the myrtle tree: and it shall be to the Lord for a name, for an everlasting sign that shall not be cut off.

Isaiah, lv. 10–13.

This example, though printed as prose, is essentially poetry, and I think it will be found that all such lyrical expressions, though they resemble prose in their typographical arrangement and lack of metrical regularity, are nevertheless purely poetical expressions, following the distinction between Poetry and Prose which I have made in the Introduction.

To be more precise: Imagination is 'the creative faculty of the mind' (*Concise Oxford Dictionary*). It is creative, if we keep to the etymological significance of the word, in that it bodies forth 'images'. In this sense I maintain that it is a poetical faculty. The 'maker' of imagery is the poet. That is the plain significance of the words and their historical origin. But what of that other faculty, operative alike in poetry and prose, which consists in the invention of all those 'imaginary' beings, things, events and conversations which make up a good part of our prose literature? It is true that we use the word 'imaginary' to describe conceptions such as these, but that is because the word has become so debased, and confused with the quite different word 'imaginative', that we cannot possibly associate it with any strict description of the processes involved either in 'creative' thought or in invention. Invention, indeed, is the word which can most appropriately be used to describe the faculty now in question.

But the texture must be persuasive, else there is no art, no literature. In what way, then, shall we qualify the inventive faculty in prose style in order to distinguish it from inventions which are merely mechanical and ineffective? Coleridge's word 'vital' gives us a clue, though it must be made clear that Coleridge had no prevision of the uses that this good word was to be put to by an evolutionary philosophy. 'Vital' is perhaps not a word that can be used with any comfort nowadays, and it is not really essential. All that it is necessary to make clear is that, just as in Fancy the speculative will of the writer *arbitrarily* disposes the fixities and definitudes of thought, so in Invention the speculative will fixes and makes definite the impressions or perceptions received from the senses. Prose, which as I have said before, has mainly if not entirely a *descriptive* function, thus becomes at this stage the description of sensible impressions. But so multiform and multitudinous are these impressions that to communicate them in any effective or persuasive way it is necessary to select, segregate and arrange. I do not refer to those logical arrangements which we have already dealt with in Chapters VII and VIII, but to the rhetorical arrangement of sense impressions in the art of writing.

It is time to resort to a practical demonstration:

They decided to bury him in our churchyard at Greymede under the beeches; the widow would have it so, and nothing might be denied her in her state.

It was a magnificent morning in early spring when I watched among the trees to see the procession come down the hillside. The upper air was woven with the music of the larks, and my whole world thrilled with the conception of summer. The young pale wind-flowers had arisen by the woodgale, and under the hazels, when perchance the hot sun pushed his way, new little suns dawned, and blazed with real light. There was a certain thrill and quickening everywhere, as a woman must feel when she has conceived. A sallow stree in a favoured spot looked like a pale gold cloud of summer dawn; nearer it had poised a golden, fairy busby on every twig, and was voiced with a hum of bees, like any sacred golden bush, uttering its gladness in the sacred murmur of bees, and in warm scent. Birds called and flashed on every hand; they made off exultant with streaming strands of grass, or wisps of fleece, plunging into the dark spaces of the wood, and out again into the blue.

A lad moved across the field from the farm below with a dog trotting behind him,—a dog, no, a fussy, black-legged lamb trotting along on its toes, with its tail swinging behind. They were going to the mothers on the common, who moved like little grey clouds among the dark gorse.

I cannot help forgetting, and sharing the spink's triumph, when he flashes past with a fleece from a bramble bush. It will cover the bedded moss, it will weave among the soft red cowhair beautifully. It is a prize, it is an ecstasy to have captured it at the right moment, and the nest is nearly ready.

Ah, but the thrush is scornful, ringing out his voice from the hedge! He sets his breast against the mud, and models it warm for the turquoise eggs—blue, blue, bluest of eggs, which cluster so close and round against the breast, which round up beneath the breast, nestling content. You should see the bright ecstasy in the eyes of a nesting thrush, because of the rounded caress of the eggs against her breast!

What a hurry the jenny wren makes—hoping I shall not see her dart into the low bush. I have a delight in watching them against their shy little wills. But they have all risen with a rush of wings, and are gone, the birds. The air is brushed with agitation.

There is no lark in the sky, not one; the heaven is clear of wings or twinkling dot——.

Till the heralds come—till the heralds wave like shadows in the bright air, crying, lamenting, fretting forever. Rising and falling and circling round and round, the slow-waving peewits cry and complain, and lift their broad wings in sorrow. They stoop suddenly to the ground, the lapwings, then in another throb of anguish and protest, they swing up again, offering a glistening white breast to the sunlight, to deny it in black shadow, then a glisten of green, and all the time crying and crying in despair.

The pheasants are frightened into cover, they run and dart through the hedge. The cold cock must fly in his haste, spread himself on his streaming plumes, and sail into the wood's security.

There is a cry in answer to the peewits, echoing louder and stronger the lamentation of the lapwings, a wail which hushes the birds. The men come over the brow of the hill, slowly, with the old squire walking tall and straight in front; six bowed men bearing the coffin on their shoulders, treading heavily and cautiously, under the great weight of the glistening white coffin; six men following behind, ill at ease, waiting their turn for the burden. You can see the red handkerchiefs knotted round their throats, and their shirt-fronts blue and white between the open waistcoats. The coffin is of new unpolished wood, gleaming and glistening in the sunlight; the men who carry it remember all their lives after the smell of new, warm elm-wood.

Again a loud cry from the hill-top. The woman has followed thus far, the big, shapeless woman, and she cries with loud cries after the white coffin as it descends the hill, and the children that cling to her skirts weep aloud, and are not to be hushed by the other woman, who bends over them, but does not form one of the group. How the crying frightens the birds, and the rabbits; and the lambs away there run to their mothers. But the peewits are not frightened, they add their notes to the sorrow; they circle after the white, retreating coffin, they circle round the woman; it is they who forever 'keen' the sorrows of this world. They are like priests in their robes, more black than white, more grief than hope, driving endlessly round and round, turning, lifting, falling and crying always in mournful desolation, repeating their last syllables like the broken accents of despair.

The bearers have at last sunk between the high banks, and turned out of sight. The big woman cannot see them, and yet she stands to look. She must go home, there is nothing left.

They have rested the coffin on the gate posts, and the bearers are wiping the sweat from their faces. They put their hands to their shoulders on the place where the weight has pressed.

The other six are placing the pads on their shoulders, when a girl comes up with a jug, and a blue pot. The squire drinks first, and fills for the rest. Meanwhile the girl stands back under the hedge, away from the coffin which smells of new elm-wood. In imagination she pictures the man shut up there in close darkness, while the sunlight flows all outside, and she catches her breast with terror. She must turn and rustle among the leaves of the violets for the flowers she does not see. Then, trembling, she comes to herself, and plucks a few flowers and breathes them hungrily into her soul, for comfort. The men put down the pots beside her, with thanks, and the squire gives the word. The bearers lift up the burden again, and the elm-boughs rattle along the hollow white wood, and the pitiful red clusters of elm-flowers sweep along it as if they whispered in sympathy—'We are so sorry, so sorry——'; always the compassionate buds in their fulness of life bend down to comfort the dark man shut up in there. 'Perhaps', the girl thinks, 'he hears them, and goes softly to sleep.' She shakes the tears out of her eyes on to the ground, and, taking up her pots, goes slowly down, over the brooks.

In a while, I too got up and went down to the mill, which lay red and peaceful, with the blue smoke rising as winsomely and carelessly as ever. On the other side of the valley I could see a pair of horses nod slowly across the fallow. A man's voice called to them now and again with a resonance that filled me with longing to follow my horses over the fallow, in the still, lonely valley, full of sunshine and eternal forgetfulness. The day had already forgotten. The water was blue and white and dark-burnished with shadows; two swans sailed across the reflected trees with perfect blithe grace. The gloom that had passed across was gone. I watched the swan with his ruffled wings swell onwards; I watched his slim consort go peeping into corners and under bushes; I saw him steer clear of the bushes, to keep full in view, turning his head to me imperiously, till I longed to pelt him with the empty husks of last year's flowers, knapweed and scabious. I was too indolent, and I turned instead to the orchard.

There the daffodils were lifting their heads and throwing back their yellow curls. At the foot of each sloping, grey old tree stood a family of flowers, some bursten with golden fulness, some lifting their heads slightly, to show a modest, sweet countenance, others still hiding their faces, leaning forward pensively from the jaunty grey-green spears; I wished I had their language, to talk to them distinctly.

Overhead, the trees, with lifted fingers shook out their hair to the sun, decking themselves with buds as white and cool as a water-nymph's breasts.

I began to be very glad. The colts-foot discs glowed and laughed in a merry company down the path; I stroked the velvet faces, and laughed also, and I smelled the scent of black-currant leaves, which is full of childish memories.

The house was quiet and complacent; it was peopled with ghosts again; but the ghosts had only come to enjoy the warm place once more, carrying sunshine in their arms and scattering it through the dusk of gloomy rooms.

D. H. LAWRENCE, *The White Peacock*, pp. 237–42.[1]

I do not put this passage forward as a perfect example of prose writing (its tendency is to be too lyrical, a fault very patent in the fifth paragraph), but there is no doubting its effectiveness. There is present a strong emotional state, an intense feeling for a definite situation, and this emotion or feeling is 'dealt out' in a steady but always terse evocation of beauty. The object of this description is to convey the duration of an event or the perspective of a scene with sufficient density or solidity. The action itself, viewed without emotion, would appear insignificant enough if translated into barely sufficient words—into a 'bald statement'. Only when the action itself is swift and economical, leaving no time for emotional reactions, can the expression be swift and economical. Here the pace is funereal, the emotion brooding and passionate. The chapter in which the passage occurs is called 'A Shadow in Spring', and the experience to be conveyed is that of the passage of death through the earth at springtide. To do this most effectively the whole scene is conveyed through the medium of an adolescent sensibility—a sensibility sympathetically aware of the organic 'thrill and quickening everywhere'. Such a sensibility can conceive all those diverse and even disconcerting incidents with which the scene can be as it were *decorated*. For by means of decoration the essential density is achieved. The triumph of the spink (chaffinch) is not an irrelevance; it makes actual the indifference of renascent life to the dark shadow passing by. And this litany of bird life prepares us aptly for the sudden and shrill lamentation of the mourning woman. It would not have reached us so intensely but for this decorative preparation. The sensibility then shifts—from Spring to the Shadow. Yet still the density must be achieved, the passage of the shadow delayed. There is the smell of new, warm elm-wood; the peewits that are not frightened; the

[1] Duckworth.

girl with a jug, and a blue pot; the horses nodding slowly across the fallow. And then the shadow passes, delayed by a new series of impressions; the Spring returns, with glowing coltsfoot discs and the scent of black-currant leaves. The mood of sorrow is dissipated and sunshine is scattered through the dusk of gloomy rooms.

It is dangerous, and perhaps impertinent, to attempt to analyse the rhetoric of a passage so sensitive as this; we cannot pull the flower to pieces without destroying its charm. But it will perhaps be seen that there is more in such imaginative writing than a merely spontaneous jet of inspiration. There is an organization of, a speculation with feeling,—not feeling alone, nor yet feeling organized, but an inventive process through or by means of which the feeling is evoked. The speculative mind works and the sense-impressions are the material it works upon—memories of colours and scents and sounds, the subjective world within us.

*

CHAPTER XI

Impressionism

IN IMAGINATIVE WRITING the speculative organizing mind of the writer works with the data of perception. The process, if we can regard it for a moment so mechanically, still remains on the plane of sensation. But the sensations may cause certain powerful reactions which we describe generically as *emotions*. Sensations or emotions are the most complex factors in our psychical make-up; they are complex in that they involve not only the immediate perception, but also all that cluster of memories and associations which constitute the personality. When this cluster, like a hive of bees is roused by some stimulus coming from the physical world, its subsequent stirrings and evolutions are apt to be violent and uncontrollable. The direction of the sensation or emotion, being determined by so many factors of the mind, factors which are not usually present to our awareness at one and the same time, is apt to be unforeseen. These factors produce that blindness and vagueness which characterize all sensations in their 'raw' state, before they have become related to the normal level of consciousness.

'Impressions' are received and recorded by the nervous organism. They may be held in their sensational vividness (and the capacity so to hold them is a peculiarity of the artist) and then projected back into forms which match the impressions. But alternatively they may be allowed to 'sink in' and arouse whatever reactions and associations may linger in the memory. They then become transformed into expressive symbols of the experience of the receiving personality. In each case we have a structure of words—one extravert and objective, the other introvert and subjective.

The type of rhetoric which is the extravert expression of sensation or emotion obviously needs to be carefully distinguished from poetry, especially from poetry which is not regularly metrical. But the distinction can be made, though it is a subtle matter, and almost entirely a question of rhythm. I say 'almost entirely' because it is possible that an elaborate classification of 'specimens' might reveal the fact that subject-matter had something to do with it: in other words, that the type of the object determined the type of the emotion, and the type of the emotion the type of the rhetoric. Obviously there are sufficient possibilities in such a chain of relations. But we are concerned with the final expression in words, and if we analyse this the difference is revealed as rhythmical.

Natural rhythm ('sprung' rhythm, as Hopkins called it) is dictated by emotional tension; it is a kind of sensational 'pulse' given to the speaking voice. All forms of prose rhythm may be considered as modifications of this natural rhythm. If we take an 'illiterate' expression of strong emotional intensity, the rhythm is direct, dramatic, 'expressive':

> If it had not been for these thing, I might have live out my life, talking at street corners to scorning men. I might have die, unmarked, unknown, a failure. Now we are not a failure. This is our career and our triumph. Never in our full life can we hope to do such work for tolerance, for joostice, for man's onderstanding of man, as now we do by an accident. Our words,—our lives—our pains—nothing! The taking of our lives—lives of a good shoe-maker and a poor fish peddler—all! That last moment belong to us—that agony is our triumph!
>
> *Vanzetti to Judge Thayer.*

Though this speech is devoid of all 'artistry', of all deliberate structure, it has the elements of great prose. The rhythmical analysis of the passage alone is sufficient to convince one of this. The rhythm mounts in a tempo as triumphant as the mood it expresses; the simplicity and pathos of the words used do the rest.

There is an intimate biological connection between sensation and rhythm. Pain and sorrow are often expressed in rhythmical swaying movements; joy is expressed in rhythmical dances; religious emotions in ritual—there is no need to expatiate on such a commonplace of social psychology. The voice has its visceral controls, and though it would be rash to assume that the rhythmical reactions of the viscera and larynx to a strong emotion *are* the rhythms of the accompanying speech, yet these physical connections should be remembered since they are the basis of those refinements of expression which art introduces. What else is art, or conscience and intelligence for that matter, but a subtle extenuation and spiritualization of the gross physical responses of the body to its environment?

The beauty of rhetoric such as that uttered by Vanzetti is common enough in life, but it is not often recorded.   It dies on the air.   But such daily expressions are the rudiments of all literary art, whether they are written in direct dramatic 'outpouring', or as emotional meditation on past experience, or as simulated moods. The direct expression, except for such unconscious examples as those I have already referred to, must wait for inspiration, for a mood in which the writer actually experiences some form of trance *with the same effect* as a directly stimulated sensation.

The normal process of expression is recollective and associative. That the 'emotions recollected in tranquillity' do nevertheless involve a return to some degree of actual (visceral) feeling, need not be denied; but the essence of Wordsworth's definition (which should not be confined to poetry) is in the word tranquillity.   The 'emotions' come back to us as concrete experiences, ill-defined perhaps, but static, and powerless to overthrow our equanimity.   The intelligence has made ready for them, sees them objectively, and proceeds to 'set them in order'.   The intelligence gives us structure; the recollection of emotion *should* give us rhythm; and with rhythm and structure we have the elements of literary art.

But sometimes the rhythm also is given by the intelligence; what have we then?

Let us first consider the following passages:

I thought it was a Sunday morning in May; that it was Easter Sunday, and as yet very early in the morning.   I was standing, as it seemed to me, at the door of my own cottage.   Right before me lay the very scene which could really be commanded from that situation, but exalted, as was usual, and solemnised by the power of dreams.   There were the same mountains, and the same lovely valley at their feet; but the mountains were raised to more than Alpine height, and there was interspace far larger between them of savannahs and forest lawns; the hedges were rich with white roses; and no living creature was to be seen, excepting that in the green churchyard there were cattle tranquilly·reposing upon the verdant graves, and particularly round about the grave of a child whom I had once tenderly loved, just as I had really beheld them, a little before sunrise, in the same summer when that child died. I gazed upon the well-known scene, and I said to myself, 'It yet wants much of sunrise, and it is Easter Sunday; and that is the day on which they celebrate the first-fruits of Resurrection. I will walk abroad; old griefs shall be forgotten to-day: for the air is cool and still, and the hills are high, and stretch away to heaven; and the churchyard is as verdant as the forest lawns, and the forest lawns are as quiet as the churchyard; and with the dew I can wash the fever from my forehead; and then I shall be unhappy no longer'. I turned, as if to open my garden gate, and immediately saw upon the left a scene far different; but which yet the power of dreams had reconciled into harmony. The scene was an oriental one; and there also it was Easter Sunday, and very early in the morning. And at a vast distance were visible, as a stain upon the horizon, the domes and cupolas of a great city—an image or faint abstraction, caught perhaps in childhood from some picture of Jerusalem. And now a bow-shot from me, upon a stone, shaded by Judean palms, there sat a woman; and I looked, and it was— Ann! She fixed her eyes upon me earnestly; and I said to her at length, 'So, then, I have found you at last.' I waited; but she answered me not a word. Her face was the same as when I saw it last; the same, and yet, again, how different! Seventeen years ago, when the lamp-light of mighty London fell upon her face, as for the last time I kissed her lips (lips, Ann, that to me were not polluted), her eyes were streaming with tears. The tears were now no longer seen. Sometimes she seemed altered; yet again sometimes *not* altered; and hardly older. Her looks were tranquil, but with unusual solemnity of expression, and I now gazed upon her with some awe. Suddenly her countenance grew dim; and, turning to the mountains, I perceived vapours rolling between us: in a moment all had vanished; thick darkness came on; and in the twinkling of an eye I was far away from mountains, and by lamp-light in London, walking again with Ann—just as we had walked, when both children, eighteen years before, along the endless terraces of Oxford Street.

THOMAS DE QUINCEY, *Confessions of an
English Opium-Eater.*

Let me wither and weare out mine age in a discomfortable, in an unwholesome, in a penurious prison, and so pay my debts with my bones, and recompence the wastefulnesse of my youth, with the beggery of mine age; Let me wither in a spittle under sharpe, and

foule, and infamous diseases, and so recompence the wantonnesse
of my youth, with that loathsomenesse in mine age; yet, if God
with-draw not his spirituall blessings, his Grace, his Patience, If I
can call my suffering his Doing, my passion his Action, All this
that is temporall, is but a catterpiller got into one corner of my
garden, but a mill-dew fallen upon one acre of my Corne; the body
of all, the substance of all is safe, as long as the soule is safe. But
when I shall trust to that, which wee call a good spirit, and God
shall deject, and empoverish, and evacuate that spirit, when I shall
rely upon a morall constancy, and God shall shake, and enfeeble,
and enervate, destroy and demolish that constancy; when I shall
think to refresh my selfe in the serenity and sweet ayre of a good
conscience, and God shall call up the damps and vapours of hell
itselfe, and spread a cloud of diffidence, and an impenetrable crust
of desperation upon my conscience; when health shall flie from me,
and I shall lay hold upon riches to succour me, and comfort me in
my sicknesse, and riches shall flie from me, and I shall snatch
after favour, and good opinion, to comfort me in my poverty;
when even this good opinion shall leave me, and calumnies and
misinformations shall prevaile against me; when I shall need peace,
because there is none but thou, O Lord, that should stand for me,
and then shall finde, that all the wounds that I have, come from
thy hand, all the arrowes that stick in me, from thy quiver; when
I shall see, that because I have given my selfe to my corrupt nature,
thou hast changed thine; and because I am all evill towards thee,
therefore thou hast given over being good towards me; When it
comes to this height, that the fever is not in the humors, but in
the spirits, that mine enemy is not an imaginary enemy, fortune,
nor a transitory enemy, malice in great persons, but a reall, and an
irresistible, and an inexorable, and an everlasting enemy the Lord
of Hosts himselfe, The Almighty God himselfe, the Almighty God
himselfe onely knows the waight of this affliction, and except hee
put in that *pondus gloriae*, that exceeding waight of an eternall
glory, with his owne hand, into the other scale, we are waighed
downe, we are swallowed up, irreparably, irrevocably, irrecover-
ably, irremediably.

JOHN DONNE, *Sermon LXVI*.

Another time in a lowering and sad evening, being alone in the
field, when all things were dead and quiet, a certain want and
horror fell upon me, beyond imagination. The unprofitableness
and silence of the place dissatisfied me; its wideness terrified me;
from the utmost ends of the earth fears surrounded me. How did
I know but dangers might suddenly arise from the East, and
invade me from the unknown regions beyond the seas? I was a
weak and little child, and had forgotten there was a man alive in
the earth. Yet something also of hope and expectation comforted

me from every border. This taught me that I was concerned in all the world: and that in the remotest borders the causes of peace delight me, and the beauties of the earth when seen were made to entertain me: that I was made to hold a communion with the secrets of Divine Providence in all the world: that a remembrance of all the joys I had from my birth ought always to be with me: that the presence of Cities, Temples, and Kingdoms ought to sustain me, and that to be alone in the world was to be desolate and miserable. The comfort of houses and friends, the clear assurance of treasures everywhere, God's care and love, his goodness, wisdom, and power, His presence and watchfulness in all the ends of the earth, were my strength and assurance for ever: and that these things being absent to my eye, were my joys and consolations, as present to my understanding as the wideness and emptiness of the Universe which I saw before me.

THOMAS TRAHERNE, *Centuries of Meditations.*

Delightful is it to bathe in the *moonsea* on the sands, and to listen to tales of genii in the tent: but then in Arabia the anxious heart is thrown into fierce and desperate commotion, by the accursed veil that separates beauty from us. There we never see the blade of that sweet herbage rise day after day into light and loveliness, never see the blossom expand; but receive it unselected, unsolicited, and unwon. Happy the land where the youthful are without veils, the aged without suspicion; where the antelope may look to what resting-place she listeth, and bend her slender foot to the fountain that most invites her.

Odoriferous gales! whether of Deban or of Dafar, if ye bring only fragrance with you, carry it to the thoughtless and light-hearted! carry it to the drinker of wine, to the feaster and the dancer at the feast. If ye never have played about the beloved of my youth, if ye bring me no intelligence of her, pass on! away with you!

W. S. LANDOR, *Imaginary Conversations.* (Mahomet and Sergius.)

I shall make only a few remarks on his English, and a few preliminary on the importance of style in general, which none understood better than he. The greater part of those who are most ambitious of it are unaware of its value. Thought does not separate man from the brutes; for the brutes think: but man alone thinks beyond the moment and beyond himself. Speech does not separate them; for speech is common to all perhaps, more or less articulate, and conveyed and received through different organs in the lower and more inert. Man's thought, which seems imperishable, loses its form, and runs along from proprietor to impropriator, like any other transitory thing, unless it is invested so becomingly and nobly that no successor can improve upon it, by any new

fashion or combination. For want of dignity and beauty, many
good things are passed and forgotten; and much ancient wisdom
is over-run and hidden by a rampant verdure, succulent but
unsubstantial. It would be invidious to bring forward proofs of
this out of authors in poetry and prose, now living or lately dead.
A distinction must, however, be made between what falls upon
many, like rain, and what is purloined from a cistern or a conduit
belonging to another man's house. There are things which were
another's before they were ours, and are not the less ours for that;
not less than my estate is mine because it was my grandfather's.
There are features, there are voices, there are thoughts, very
similar in many; and when ideas strike the same chord in any two
with the same intensity, the expression must be nearly the same.
Let those who look upon style as unworthy of much attention,
ask themselves how many, in proportion to men of genius, have
excelled in it. In all languages, ancient and modern, are there
ten prose-writers at once harmonious, correct, and energetic?
Harmony and correctness are not uncommon separately, and force
is occasionally with each; but where, excepting in Milton, where,
among all the moderns, is energy to be found always in the right
place? Even Cicero is defective here, and sometimes in the most
elaborate of his orations. In the time of Milton it was not customary for men of abilities to address to the people at large what
might inflame their passions. The appeal was made to the serious,
to the well-informed, to the learned, and was made in the language
of their studies. The phraseology of our Bible, on which no
subsequent age has improved, was thought to carry with it solemnity
and authority; and even when popular feelings were to be aroused
to popular interest, the language of the prophets was preferred to
the language of the vulgar. Hence, amid the complicated anta-
gonisms of war there was more austerity than ferocity. The
gentlemen who attended the court avoided the speech as they
avoided the manners of their adversaries. Waller, Cowley, and
South were resolved to refine what was already pure gold, and
inadvertently threw into the crucible many old family jewels,
deeply enchased within it. Eliot, Pym, Selden, and Milton
reverenced their father's house, and retained its rich language
unmodified. Lord Brougham would make us believe that scarcely
a sentence in Milton is easy, natural, and vernacular. Nevertheless,
in all his dissertations, there are many which might appear to have
been written in our days, if indeed any writer in our days were
endowed with the same might and majesty. Even in his *Treatise
on Divorce*, where the Bible was most open to him for quotations,
and where he might be the most expected to recur to the grave
and antiquated, he has often employed, in the midst of theological
questions and juridical formularies, the plainest terms of his
contemporaries. Even his arguments against prelacy, where he

rises into poetry like the old prophets, and where his ardent words assume in their periphery the rounded form of verse, there is nothing stiff or constrained.

W. S. LANDOR, *Opinions of Caesar, Cromwell, Milton, and Buonaparte.*

These five passages are sufficient to give us the span between emotion and intelligence. If we compare the first of them with the simple utterance of Vanzetti, we shall at once be conscious of two differences: in de Quincey's prose the rhythms are much longer, much smoother, much subtler; and the vocabulary is much more exotic. The emotion, it seems to me, is genuine enough. A deep fund of longing and regret expresses itself in a day-dream which recreates the visual concreteness of the longed-for objects. The mind seeks instinctively (or intuitively) symbols that will satisfy the dominant emotion. It would be vain to attempt to explain the process: a principle of selection, animated by the emotion, is at work within a storehouse whose merchandise we can never account for nor exhaust. What we must note here is the literal result. The emotion is conveyed with perfect appropriateness: the words (with one or two exceptions, like 'verdant' and 'savannahs') are simple, and the rhythm is slow and pensive. As an expression of emotion it is much less direct, much less dramatic, than Vanzetti's speech; and the measure of this difference is the measure of the intervening intelligence.

If we now pass to Donne's famous sermon, and compare the paragraph quoted with De Quincey's prose, we shall notice a still greater progression away from directness and concrete dramatic expression. ('Dramatic' in a sense, the passage certainly is; but in a sense more exactly conveyed by 'eloquent'.) The rhythm has become extremely elaborate, indeed intricate, full of returns and repetitions, of cadence and syllabic counterpoint. The metaphors are far fetched, the symbols strange. Yet the emotion is still evident and direct. The whole passage is consistent; appropriateness of word or rhythm is never in question.

These two examples suggest that we are right in looking

upon the relation of intelligence to emotion as one of tension—a vibrant tension which becomes evident in variations of rhythm. The subtlest variations will occur when intelligence and emotion are almost equal forces, as they are occasionally in works of sincere religious meditation. The passage from Traherne will illustrate this quality, and the work from which it is quoted is throughout written in a sweetly modulated rhythm which has no parallel in English prose. It seems that only in writers who forget self but retain sensation, and whose thought is an inspired contemplation (which is to say, only in true mystics) do we get this rare quality of soft rhythmical emphasis. A state of tension depends on the fixed direction of the opposing forces. Should one of the forces be uncertain, the tension will break, the rhythm falter. The result may be merely insignificant, or decidedly confused. But when the intelligence is steadfast, and only the emotion uncertain, then the results may be more complicated, and deceptive. Consider the passage quoted from Landor's *Mahomet and Sergius*. The rhythmical structure is elaborate and even beautiful, but everything is sacrificed to this end. The inversions and apostrophes are artificial, but more particularly the rhythm itself has taken on a sing-song rise and fall which is foreign to prose. This brings us to the highly contentious question already referred to in the Introduction (pp. x-xii). True rhythm is dictated by emotional tension. Such rhythm may be either poetic or prosaic, but that is a question of immediacy and of the writer's intention. Immediacy—that is, direct expression, non-discursive ('sensational') thought—is always poetical, even when it has the appearance of prose. There is more essential 'poetry' in Vanzetti's speech than in many a Coronation Ode. In direct expression, with its instinctive rhythm, there is no question of the 'choice of a *means* of expression'. There is no question of deliberation: the word is act. This, however, does not preclude the possibility of originality *within* a deliberate structure, and so we may get brief phrases and stray lines of poetry even within a Coronation Ode. And we can freely admit that the deliberate structure is often the necessary cause of and only means to originality.

Without a deliberate structure creative activity tends to be fragmentary and disjointed. But *rhythm* is the accent of expression and its accompaniment. It is created in the act of expression. To justify an elaborate rhythm, therefore, there must be an underlying mental activity of corresponding complexity. To invent the rhythm and fill it up with syllabic sounds is to reverse the natural process, confusing sense and sound, literature and music. Thus all prose whose rhythm is, as it were, *a priori*, is false and artificial, and though like all artificialities it may be justified as a pastime, it is not to be confused with art, which is nothing if not sincere.[1] Under this condemnation, therefore, I think much of Landor's prose would fall, especially the much quoted passages with which we are all familiar. But I do not suggest that Landor was altogether devoid of emotional sincerity; indeed, the highly ornate rhythms familiar to the readers of anthologies do not really represent his normal style, which in the *Imaginary Conversations*, is at its best more dramatic, and elsewhere merely commonplace. Landor's emotion was perhaps most involved in questions of his own craft, and then, as will be seen from the eulogy of Milton which has been quoted, it exemplifies all the virtues which it upholds.

So much for impressionism as conveyed in the sensational impact of rhythm. But many other devices may be used to produce an impressionistic effect (punctuation, paragraph structure, disjointed syntax), so that the prose form as a whole becomes impressionistic. Essentially, an impressionistic style is one in which the logical structure appears to have been

---

[1] If 'sincerity' seems too like a moral test, let us say that 'art is nothing if too obvious'. It is not the artifice as such that we complain of; but only its obtrusion. Aristotle is very definite on this question: 'wherefore those who practise this artifice must conceal it and avoid the appearance of speaking artificially instead of naturally; for that which is natural persuades, but the artificial does not. For men become suspicious of one whom they think to be laying a trap for them, as they are of mixed wines. Such was the case with the voice of Theodorus as contrasted with that of the rest of the actors; for his seemed to be the voice of the speaker, that of the others the voice of someone else. Art is cleverly concealed when the speaker chooses his words from ordinary language and puts them together like Euripides, who was the first to show the way'. (*Rhetoric*, III. ii. 5–6. Trans. J. H. Freese, Loeb Library.) But it is not only a question of words, but also of rhythms; these too must be natural and ordinary, or only strange and remote in a subtle recombination of elements natural and ordinary.

distorted in order to produce a direct correspondence with the writer's sensations. The projection of sensations or emotions into a given form is known in aesthetics as 'empathy'[1] (feeling into), and impressionism is the creation of means that facilitate this process. An 'impressionist' painting, for example, is one into which the spectator 'enters' with all the sensations and emotions that accompany the actual scene depicted (girls dancing, horses racing, etc.). An impressionist prose style is one that gives the illusion that the reader is participating in the events, scenes or actions described. Like impressionism in painting, impressionism in writing is a specifically modern style, though Sterne might be regarded as a precursor. It is said of Balzac that he so lived with his characters that he experienced genuine emotions from the vicissitudes which he created for them, but he did not convey this feeling of identification in his style, which is of the 'thinking' type. It is only when we reach Proust in French literature, and Virginia Woolf in English, that a purely impressionistic style is created. *The Waves* is perhaps the best example of Mrs. Woolf's impressionistic style, but a more extreme example is provided by William Faulkner:

We left the road. Among the moss little pale flowers grew, and the sense of water mute and unseen. *I hold to use like this I mean I use to hold She stood in the door looking at us her hands on her hips*
You pushed me it was your fault it hurt me too
We were dancing sitting down I bet Caddy cant dance sitting down
Stop that stop that
I was just brushing the trash off the back of your dress
You keep your nasty old hands off me it was your fault you pushed me down I'm mad at you
I don't care she looked at us stay mad she went away We began to hear the shouts, the splashings; I saw a brown body gleam an instant.
Stay mad. My shirt was getting wet and my hair. Across the roof

[1] The following is the best description of empathy known to me: 'to glide with one's own feeling into the dynamic structure of an object, a pillar or a crystal or the branch of a tree, or even an animal or a man, and as it were to trace from within, understanding the formation and motoriality (Bewegtheit) of the object with the perceptions of one's own muscles; it means to "transpose" oneself over there and in there. Thus it means the exclusion of one's own concreteness, the extinguishing of the actual situation of life, the absorption in pure aestheticism of the reality in which one participates.' Martin Buber: *Between Man and Man,* (London, Routledge and Kegan Paul, 1947), p. 97.

*hearing the roof loud now I could see Natalie going through the garden
among the rain. Get wet I hope you catch pneumonia go on home Cowface.
I jumped hard as I could into the hogwallow and mud yellowed up to my
waist stinking I kept on plunging until I fell down and rolled over in it*
'Hear them in swimming, sister? I wouldn't mind doing that
myself.' If I had time. When I have time. I could hear my
watch. *mud was warmer than the rain it smelled awful. She had her
back turned I went around in front of her. You know what I was doing?
She turned her back I went around in front of her the rain creeping into the
mud flatting her bodice through her dress it smelled horrible. I was hugging
her that's what I was doing. She turned her back I went around in front
of her. I was hugging her I tell you.*
  I dont give a damn what you were doing
  *You don't you dont I'll make you I'll make you give a damn. She hit
my hands away I smeared mud on her with the other hand I couldn't feel the
wet smacking of her hand I wiped mud from my legs smeared it on her wet
hard turning body hearing her fingers going into my face but I couldn't feel
it even when the rain began to taste sweet on my lips*
They saw us from the water first, heads and shoulders. They
yelled and one rose squatting and sprang among them. They
looked like beavers, the water lipping about their chins, yelling.

WILLIAM FAULKNER: *The Sound and the Fury.*[1]

The final stage of impressionism is reached in the so-called
interior monologue, which James Joyce used with such brilliance
in the last section of *Ulysses*. All trace of the author's personality has disappeared: he is completely identified with the
character he is describing, and has no idiosyncrasies of his
own left. The style is no longer the man (i.e. the author)
but the character. The limitations of this style have been
pointed out by a French critic, Auguste Bailly:[2]

... a form of art, if it is to be more than a mere technical experiment,
should be judged on its merits, its veracity. As to its merits, let
us waive discussion; *de gustibus.* . . . But veracity is another
matter, and my opinion is that, though the analytic method may
give a partly false or artificial presentation of the stream of
consciousness, the silent monologue is just as artificial and just as
false. The necessity of recording the flow of consciousness by

[1] Reprinted by permission of Random House Inc. Copyright 1931 by William
Faulkner. A more extensive specimen of Faulkner's impressionistic style is given
in the Appendix, p. 202. Faulkner indulges in a plentiful use of italics, apparently to distinguish the more subjective consciousness of his characters from the
objective events. Punctuation is omitted in various passages, but it is difficult to
discover a consistent principle—perhaps the intention is to indicate different levels
of consciousness.

[2] Quoted by Stuart Gilbert: *James Joyce's Ulysses* (London, Faber, 1930), p. 26.

means of words and phrases compels the writer to depict it as a continuous horizontal line, like a line of melody. But even a casual examination of our inner consciousness shows us that this presentation is essentially false. We do not think on one plane, but on many planes at once. It is wrong to suppose that we follow only one train of thought at a time; there are several trains of thought, one above another. We are generally more aware, more completely conscious, of thoughts which take form on the higher plane; but we are also aware, more or less obscurely, of a stream of thoughts on the lower levels. We attend or own to one series of reflexions or images; but we are all the time aware of other series which are unrolling themselves on obscurer planes of consciousness. Sometimes there are interferences, irruptions, unforeseen contacts between these series. A stream of thought from a lower level suddenly usurps the bed of the stream which flowed on the highest plane of consciousness. By an effort of will-power we may be able to divert it; it subsides but does not cease to exist. At every instant of conscious life we are aware of such simultaneity and multiplicity of thought-streams.

CHAPTER XII

*

Expressionism

EXPRESSIONISM IS A WORD that has had much more vogue on the Continent than in England. In Austria and Germany in particular it has indicated a whole literary and artistic movement. The deliberate aim of this movement was to 'express' subjective emotional experiences as opposed to the recording of impressions derived from the external world. In other words, the aim of the writer became the expression of the uniqueness of his *personality*, his *individuality* or *idiosyncrasy*. 'Individuality' implies the contrast of a single being with the crowd: this sense *is* perhaps implied in the attitude to be analysed, but it is not the main sense. 'Idiosyncrasy' has better claims, since it very exactly stands for the mentality peculiar to a particular person, and therefore might be extended to the expression of that mentality in writing. But the act of writing involves an assertion of positive qualities which deserves the somewhat more dignified word 'personality'.

In a way, all the arts of rhetoric are personal, in that they depend on the particular instincts and mental habits of the writer. But the elements which we have been discussing in the last five chapters, and those which we have still to deal with, such as Eloquence and Taste, all involve the adaptation of these instincts and habits to some outer necessity: the personal force is interfered with, whether by logic, by intelligence, by emotional or speculative ends, or by various fantasies and fictions which we unconsciously create to deceive ourselves. The essence of all these different modes of subordination is persuasion to a static view of things, to a condition of logical, moral, rational or emotional satisfaction. The writer submits to a scale of values which he finds ready-made in the world he lives in. But another type of writer does not wish to measure himself against an objective reality; all he desires is to be assured of his own reality, of the positive existence

of his own individuality and his own unique reactions to the
phenomenal world. His aim is to project *himself*, to persuade
us not to this view or that view of the world, but to the micro-
cosm that he himself is.

Walter Pater, in his essay on 'Style', gave one of the best
descriptions of this kind of writing:

> . . . according to the well-known saying, 'The style is the man',
> complex or simple, in his individuality, his plenary sense of what
> he really has to say, his sense of the world; all cautions regarding
> style arising out of so many natural scruples as to the medium
> through which alone he can expose that inward sense of things,
> the purity of this medium, its laws or tricks of refraction: nothing
> is to be left there which might give conveyance to any matter
> save that. Style in all its varieties, reserved or opulent, terse,
> abundant, musical, stimulant, academic, so long as each is really
> characteristic or expressive, finds thus its justification, the sumptu-
> ous good taste of Cicero being as truly the man himself, and not
> another, justified, yet insured inalienably to him, thereby, as would
> have been his portrait by Raffaelle, in full consular splendour, on
> his ivory chair.
> A relegation, you may say perhaps—a relegation of style to the
> subjectivity, the mere caprice, of the individual, which must soon
> transform it into mannerism. Not so! since there is, under the
> conditions supposed, for those elements of the man, for every
> lineament of the vision within, the one word, the one acceptable
> word, recognisable by the sensitive, by others 'who have intelli-
> gence' in the matter, as absolutely as ever anything can be in the
> evanescent and delicate region of human language. The style,
> the manner, would be the man, not in his unreasoned and really
> uncharacteristic caprices, involuntary or affected, but in absolutely
> sincere apprehension of what is most real to him.
>
> WALTER PATER, *An Essay on Style.*

Two things are essential to an expressionistic rhetoric:
sensibility enough to be aware of one's individual reactions,
and *emotion* enough to enlarge this sensibility, to magnify and
exploit it in the interests of self-projection, self-expression,
self-'creation'.

A state of sensibility is generally a state of passivity. We
receive the impressions which stream in through the senses,
and our *body* automatically responds. We even go so far as
to express a state of satisfaction, or some other feeling aroused
in us. We look at a landscape, we 'feel' obscurely, and then

perhaps we say 'How lovely!' But this is not at all the process of a writer bent on self-expression. The obscure sensation which he experiences must itself be defined, analysed and described. It must be distinguished from all other sensations, whether of the writer or of other people.

Obscure emotions can be described obscurely, and then the result is sentimentality: the writer becomes the dupe of his emotions. But the writer can also, if the emotion is strong enough, and if his emotional reactions are supported by his sensibility, find objective equivalents for his emotion. He may not be able to define it graphically in the sense that one can define a curve or a chord of music; but he may be able to find a verbal equivalent which evokes approximately the same reaction in others as the original sensation evoked in him. This explains why much of this personal writing, as in Rousseau, Lamb and Stevenson, is of a very concrete and objective form. The extreme of personal writing can be deceptively like the extreme of impersonal writing. Both achieve a distinct clarity. The difference between them depends on what is seen through the clarity.

A personal style may be clear and concrete, but it is not *ordered*. The images, though hard and distinct, are haphazard. They form a picturesque ruin, not a symmetrical structure. The details of this disorder we may call the *idiom* of the writer. An idiom is, literally, what a man makes his own, just as an idiom in language is what a particular language makes its own. And just as the idiom of one language cannot be translated into the idiom of another without giving an impression of falsity, so a writer's idiom is personal to himself, and cannot be copied or assimilated by other writers.

Peculiar as it is, a writer's idiom is nevertheless difficult to analyse. Take the following passage:

Stage, Gentlemen, have a little patience, they are e'en upon coming instantly. He that should begin the play, Master Littlewit, the proctor, has a stitch new fallen in his black silk stocking; 'twill be drawn up ere you can tell twenty: he plays one o' the Arches that dwells about the hospital, and he has a very pretty part. But for the whole play, will you have the truth on't?—I am looking, lest the poet hear me, or his man, Master Brome, behind the arras—it is like to be a very conceited scurvy one, in plain English. When 't comes to the Fair once, you were e'en as good go to Virginia, for anything there is of Smithfield. He has not hit the humours, he does not know them; he has not conversed with the Bartholomew birds, as they say; he has ne'er a sword and buckler-man in his Fair; nor a little Davy, to take toll o' the bawds there, as in my time; nor a Kindheart, if anybody's teeth, should chance to ache, in his play; nor a juggler with a well educated ape, to come over the chain for a King of England, and back again for the Prince, and sit still on his arse for the Pope and the King of Spain. None of these fine sights! Nor has he the canvas cut in the night, for a hobby-horse-man to creep into his she neighbour, and take his leap there. Nothing! No: an some writer that I know had had but the penning o' this matter, he would have made you such a jig-a-jog in the booths, you should have thought an earthquake had been in the Fair! But these master-poets, they will have their own absurd courses; they will be informed of nothing. He has (sir reverence) kicked me three or four times about the tiring-house, I thank him, for but offering to put in with my experience. I'll be judged by you, gentlemen, now, but for one conceit of mine: would not a fine pump upon the stage have done well for a property now? and a punk set under upon her head, with her stern upward, and have been soused by my witty young masters of the Inns of Court? What think you of this for a show, now? he will not hear of this! I am an ass! I! And yet I kept the stage in Master Tarleton's time, I thank my stars. Ho! an that man had lived to have played in *Bartholomew Fair*, you should have seen him have come in, and have been cozened in the cloth-quarter, so finely! and Adams, the rogue, have leaped and capered upon him, and have dealt his vermin about, as though they had cost him nothing! and then a substantial watch to have stolen in upon them, and taken them away, with mistaking words, as the fashion is the stage-practice.

BEN JONSON, Bartholomew Fair.

All the individuality of Ben Jonson is there, and a good deal of his personality. But it would be difficult to fix these qualities on to particular phrases and periods. 'The Bartholo-mew bird', 'a well-educated ape', 'she neighbour', 'cozened in the cloth-quarter', 'a substantial watch'—there is something in the conjoining of these words which we can recognize as Jonsonian, and what these few words do obviously, many other words do subtly. They suggest the person of the author—who had, by the way, a theory about this very matter. We find the word 'humours' here in this very passage to remind us. A humour, according to Jonson, was to be observed in a character when

> Some one peculiar quality
> Doth so possess a man, that it doth draw
> All his effects, his spirits, and his powers,
> In their confluctions, all to run one way.

A humour is thus conceived as an active force: it is the dominance of one particular passion, the 'drive' of one particular disposition in a person. It cannot therefore be identified with idiom, and the theory is only referred to here to suggest that it is in characters such as Jonson had in mind, and of whom he himself was a sufficient example—in characters where a particular passion predominates, that we get a peculiar mode of expression. Not that we should stress the word 'passion' in this context—the dominant force is often a denial of passion, a determined effort to avoid anything personal or direct.[1]

A personal style being above all things *personal*, no further generalizations are possible. The style is the man, in the proper meaning of that phrase. We must be content to quote the man:

[1] This is brought out well in a passage from a letter which D. H. Lawrence wrote to Edward Garnett (5 June, 1914): 'When Marinetti writes: "It is the solidity of a blade of steel that is interesting by itself, that is, the incomprehending and inhuman alliance of its molecules in resistance to, let us say, a bullet. The heat of a piece of wood or iron is in fact more passionate, for us, than the laughter or tears of a woman"—then I know what he means. He is stupid, as an artist, for contrasting the heat of the iron and the laugh of the woman. Because what is interesting in the laugh of the woman is the same as the binding of the molecules of steel or their action in heat: it is the inhuman will, call it physiology, or like Marinetti—physiology of matter, that fascinates me. I don't so much care about what the woman *feels*—in the ordinary usage of the word. That presumes an *ego* to feel with. I only care about what the woman *is*—what she is—inhumanly, physiologically, materially—according to the use of the word: but for me, what she *is* as a phenomenon (or as representing some greater, inhuman will), instead of what she feels according to the human conception. That is where the futurists are stupid. Instead of looking for the new human phenomenon, they will only look for the phenomena of the science of physics to be found in human beings. They are crassly stupid. But if anyone would give them eyes, they would pull the apples right off the tree, for their stomachs are true in appetite.' *The Letters of D. H. Lawrence* (London, Heinemann, 1932), p. 198.
'What the woman *is*'—that is to say, her unique sensational reality, and not the author's own feelings about her. Lawrence is here contrasting the impressionistic, empathetic method described in the last chapter (which was his own aim), with the expressionistic method that is our present concern. Nevertheless, it is doubtful whether Lawrence ever succeeded in his aim, his characters being generally projections of his own ego.

Now my uncle Toby had one evening laid down his pipe upon the table, and was counting over to himself upon his finger ends (beginning at his thumb) all Mrs. Wadman's perfections one by one; and happening two or three times together, either by omitting some, or counting others twice over, to puzzle himself sadly, before he could get beyond his middle finger—Prithee, Trim! said he, taking up his pipe again,—bring me a pen and ink: Trim brought paper also.

Take a full sheet—Trim! said my uncle Toby, making a sign with his pipe at the same time to take a chair and sit down close by him at the table. The corporal obeyed—placed the paper directly before him—took a pen, and dipp'd it in the ink.

—She has a thousand virtues, Trim! said my uncle Toby—

Am I to set them down, an' please your honour? quoth the corporal.

—But they must be taken in their ranks, replied my uncle Toby; for of them all, Trim, that which wins me most, and which is a security for all the rest, is the compassionate turn and singular humanity of her character—I protest, added my uncle Toby, looking up, as he protested it, towards the top of the ceiling— That was I her brother, Trim, a thousandfold, she could not make more constant or more tender enquiries after my sufferings—though now no more.

The corporal made no reply to my uncle Toby's protestation, but by a short cough—he dipp'd the pen a second time into the inkhorn; and my uncle Toby, pointing with the end of his pipe as close to the top of the sheet at the left hand corner of it, as he could get it—the corporal wrote down the word HUMANITY—thus.

Prithee, corporal, said my uncle Toby, as soon as Trim had done it—how often does Mrs. Bridget enquire after the wound on the cap of thy knee, which thou received'st at the battle of *Landen?*

She never, an' please your honour, enquires after it at all.

That, corporal, said my uncle Toby, with all the triumph the goodness of his nature would permit—That shews the difference in the character of the mistress and maid—had the fortune of war allotted the same mischance to me, Mrs. Wadman would have enquired into every circumstance relating to it a hundred times— She would have enquired, an' please your honour, ten times as often about you honour's groin—The pain, Trim, is equally excruciating,—and Compassion has as much to do with the one as the other—

—God bless your honour! cried the corporal—what has a woman's compassion to do with a wound upon the cap of a man's knee? had your honour's been shot into ten thousand splinters at the affair of Landen, Mrs. Wadman would have troubled her head about it as little as Bridget; because, added the corporal, lowering his voice, and speaking very distinctly, as he assigned his reason—

'The knee is such a distance from the main body—whereas the groin, your honour knows, is upon the very *curtain* of the *place.*'

My uncle Toby gave a long whistle—but in a note which could scarce be heard across the table.

The corporal had advanced too far to retire—in three words he told the rest—

My uncle Toby laid down his pipe as gently upon the fender, as if it had been spun from the unravellings of a spider's web—

—Let us go to my brother Shandy's, said he.

LAURENCE STERNE, *Life and Opinions of Tristram Shandy.*

THE CABIN

(Ahab moving to go on deck; Pip catches him by the hand to follow.)

'Lad, lad, I tell thee thou must not follow Ahab now. The hour is coming when Ahab would not scare thee from him, yet would not have thee by him. There is that in thee, poor lad, which I feel too curing to my malady. Like cures like; and for this hunt, my malady becomes my most desired health. Do thou abide below here, where they shall serve thee, as if thou wert the captain. Aye, lad, thou shalt sit here in my own screwed chair; another screw to it, thou must be.'

'No, no, no! ye have not a whole body, sir; do ye but use poor me for your one lost leg; only tread upon me, sir: I ask no more, so I remain part of ye.'

'Oh! spite of million villains, this makes me a bigot in the fadeless fidelity of man!—and a black! and crazy!—but methinks like-cures-like applies to him too; he grows so sane again.'

'They tell me, sir, that Stubb did once desert poor little Pip, whose drowned bones now show white, for all the blackness of his living skin. But I will never desert ye, sir, as Stubb did him. Sir, I must go with ye.'

'If thou speakest thus to me much more, Ahab's purpose keels up in him. I tell thee no; it cannot be.'

'Oh good master, master, master!'

'Weep so, and I will murder thee! have a care, for Ahab too is mad. Listen, and thou wilt often hear my ivory foot upon the deck, and still know that I am there. And now I quit thee. Thy hand!—Met! True art thou, lad, as the circumference to its centre. So: God for ever bless thee; and if it come to that,—God for ever save thee, let what will befall.'

(Ahab goes; Pip steps one step forward.)

'Here he this instant stood; I stand in his air,—but I'm alone. Now were even poor Pipe here I could endure it, but he's missing. Pip! Pip! Ding, dong, ding! Who's seen Pip? He must be up here; let's try the door. What? neither lock, nor bolt, nor bar; and yet there's no opening it. It must be the spell; he told me to stay here: Aye, and told me this screwed chair was mine, Here, then, I'll seat me, against the transom, in the ship's full middle, all her keel and her three masts before me. Here, our old sailors say, in their black seventy-fours great admirals sometimes sit at table, and lord it over rows of captains and lieutenants. Ha! what's this? epaulets! epaulets! the epaulets all come crowding. Pass round the decanters; glad to see ye; fill up, monsieurs! What an odd feeling, now, when a black boy's host to white men with gold lace upon their coats!—Monsieurs, have ye seen one Pip?—a little negro lad, five feet high, hang-dog look, and cowardly! Jumped from a whale-boat once;—seen him? No! Well then, fill up again, captains, and let's drink shame upon all cowards! I name no names. Shame upon them! Put one foot upon the table. Shame upon all cowards.—Hist! above there, I hear ivory—Oh, master! master! I am indeed down-hearted when you walk over me. But here I'll stay, though this stern strikes rocks; and they bulge through; and oysters come to join me.'

HERMAN MELVILLE: *Moby Dick*, ch. cxxix.

Rain was universal; a thick robe of it swept from hill to hill; thunder rumbled remote, and between the ruffled roars the downpour pressed on the land with a great noise of eager gobbling, much like that of the swine's trough fresh filled, as though a vast assembly of the hungered had seated themselves clamorously and fallen to on meats and drinks in a silence, save of the chaps. A rapid walker poetically and humorously minded gathers multitudes of images on his way. And rain, the heaviest you can meet, is a lively companion when the resolute pacer scorns discomfort of wet clothes and squealing boots. South-western rain-clouds, too, are never long sullen: they enfold and will have the earth in a good strong glut of the kissing overflow; then, as a hawk with feathers on his beak of the bird in his claw lifts head, they rise and take veiled feature in long climbing watery lines: at any moment they may break the veil and show soft upper cloud, show sun on it, show sky, green near the verge they spring from, of the green of grass in early dew; or, along a travelling sweep that rolls asunder overhead, heaven's laughter of purest blue among titanic white shoulders: it may mean fair smiling for awhile, or be the lightest interlude; but the watery lines, and the drifting, the chasing, the upsoaring, all in a shadowy fingering of form, and the animation of the leaves of the trees pointing them on, the bending of the tree-tops, the snapping of branches, and the hurrahings of the stubborn hedge at wrestle with the flaws, yielding but a leaf at most, and that on a fling, make a glory of contest and wildness without aid of colour to inflame the man who is at home in them from old association on road, heath and mountain. Let him be drenched, his heart will sing. And thou, trim cockney, that jeerest, consider thyself, to whom it may occur to be out in such a scene, and with what steps of a nervous dancing master it would be thine to play the hunted rat of the elements, for the preservation of the one imagined dry spot about thee, somewhere on thy luckless person! The taking of rain and sun alike befits men of our climate, and he who would have the secret of a strengthening intoxication must court the clouds of the South-west with a lover's blood.

GEORGE MEREDITH, *The Egoist.*

I suggested that no generalizations were possible on the question of personal style, but in these three examples we may perceive a distinction between the first and the third. The first flows with a rapid and smooth ease which is the greatest virtue of a personal style. The words *seem* to take a line of least resistance; actually they are governed by fidelity to the author's sense of his own selfhood. That can be the most exacting of disciplines, and we know, for example, how long Sterne laboured at the perfecting of his easy style. If anything involving thought, with its deliberate structures and universal concepts, is allowed to intervene between the selfhood and the expression, then the flow is impeded by obstructions. These obstructions appear as awkwardness of diction, hesitances of rhythm, uncertainties of invention—flaws apparent in the third passage quoted above. An unimpeded style—the style of Sterne and of Lamb and the developed style of Henry James—is a matter for fowling-nets and stratagems. The register is so delicate that any *fixation* is fatal; a magnet of any kind will throw the instrument completely out of gear. It follows that a personal style in the sense in which we have defined it is a very rare achievement; and when achieved our reactions to the style are likely enough to be our reactions to the person, and not to the thing. How rarely does the critic see beyond the man Sterne to the triumph of his style—the greatest triumph (for flexibility, for fluidity, for delicacy) in the whole range of our prose. But for one erratic genius of this kind there are a hundred who adopt a code. It is a more possible and a more politic faith: it educes, in minds of sufficient humility, the great virtues of tradition.

[1] Oxford.

CHAPTER XIII

*

Eloquence

THE ART OF EXPOSITION is the mere logic of thought, but when this art is heightened in any way, we must seek other terms. The first of these is *eloquence*, which is the art of exposition animated by an intuitive grasp of the greatness of its theme.

Eloquence is either of words or ideas, but the eloquence that is merely of words, lacking force, would be better designated *elegance* or *wit*, and is that 'little frothy water on some gaudy day' of Bolingbroke's admirable definition:

Eloquence, that leads mankind by the ears, gives a nobler superiority than power that every dunce may use, or fraud that every knave may employ to lead them by the nose. But eloquence must flow like a stream that is fed by an abundant spring, and not sprout forth a little frothy water on some gaudy day, and remain dry the rest of the year.

BOLINGBROKE, *Spirit of Patriotism.*

Sterne makes the same distinction, with rather more elaboration; but, significantly, both Sterne and Bolingbroke use the word 'gaudy':

There are two sorts of eloquence; the one indeed scarce deserves the name of it, which consists chiefly in laboured and polished periods, an over-curious and artificial arrangement of figures, tinselled over with a gaudy embellishment of words, which glitter, but convey little or no light to the understanding. This kind of writing is for the most part much affected and admired by the people of weak judgment and vicious taste, but is a piece of affectation and formality the sacred writers are utter strangers to. It is a vain and boyish eloquence; and as it has always been esteemed below the great genuises of all ages, so much more so, with respect to those writers who were actuated by the spirit of infinite wisdom, and therefore wrote with that force and majesty with which never man writ. The other sort of eloquence is quite the reverse to this, and which may be said to be the true characteristic of the holy Scriptures; where the eloquence does not arise from a laboured and far-fetched elocution, but from a surprising mixture of simplicity and majesty, which is a double character, so difficult to be united, that it is seldom to be met with in compositions merely human.

LAURENCE STERNE, *Forty-second Sermon.*

Elegance is a play *with* words; wit a play *on* words. Elegance, which is concerned with the *position* of words, disposes them in various 'figures'; and among these we may distinguish *antithesis, apostrophe,* and *hypallage.* Wit is concerned with the *meaning* of words, which it deflects or deforms, as in *irony, allusion, parody, paronomasia* (puns, etc.) and *hyperbole.*[1]

Elegance is something more than mere affectation; it is *deliberately* artificial. But it need not be merely artificial: the writer of the following artifice pours out his figures of speech with a very pleasant gusto:

Good clothes are the embroidered trappings of pride, and good cheer the very eryngo-root of gluttony; so that fine backs and fat bellies are coach-horses to two of the seven deadly sins; in the boots of which coach Lechery and Sloth sit like the waiting-maid. In a most desperate state therefore do tailors and cooks stand, by means of their offices; for both those trades are apple-squires to that couple of sins. The one invents more fantastic fashions than France hath worn since her first stone was laid; the other more lickerish epicurean dishes than were ever served up to Gallonius' table. Did man, think you, come wrangling into the world about no better matters, than all his lifetime to make privy searches in Birchin-lane for whalebone doublets, or for pies of nightingale tongues in Helio-gabalus his kitchen? No, no! the first suit of apparel that ever mortal man put on came neither from the mercer's shop nor the merchant's warehouse: Adam's bill would have been taken then, sooner than a knight's bond now; yet was he great in nobody's books for satin and velvets: the silkworms had something else to do in those days than to set up looms and be free of the weavers: his breeches were not so much worth as King Stephen's, that cost but a poor noble; for Adam's holiday hose and doublet were of no better stuff than plain fig-leaves, and Eve's best gown of the same piece; there went but a pair of shears between them. An antiquary in this town has yet some of the powder of those leaves dried to show. Tailors then were none of the twelve Companies:

---

[1] In treatises on Rhetoric many other forms both of Elegance and of Wit have been distinguished; such as *anaphora, anastrophe, climax* and *anti-climax, oxymoron, litotes* and *meiosis.* It is not necessary to define or illustrate these in detail: they are mostly analytical definitions of effective word-play, and are rarely used deliberately and categorically by the writer himself. Many permutations and combinations of words within the grammatical structure of the sentence can be distinguished and defined; but the broad distinction here made between Elegance and Wit seems to be the only essential one.

their hall, that now is larger than some dorpes among the Nether-
lands, was then no bigger than a Dutch butcher's shop: they durst
not strike down their customers with large bills: Adam cared not
an apple-paring for all their lousy hems. There was then neither
the Spanish slop, nor the skipper's galligaskin; the Switzer's
blistered codpiece, nor the Danish sleeve sagging down like a
Welsh wallet; the Italian's close strosser, nor the French standing
collar: your treble-quadruple daedalian ruffs, nor your stiff-necked
rabatoes, that have more arches for pride to row under, than can
stand under five London bridges, durst not then set themselves
out in print; for the patent for starch could by no means be signed.
Fashions then was counted a disease, and horses died of it: but now,
thanks to folly, it is held the only rare physic, and the purest
golden asses live upon it.

THOMAS DEKKER, *The Gull's Hornbook*.

Wit is not so deliberately artificial as mere elegance; the
attitude is always a detached one, the thrust always in some
manner oblique, and the effect one of artifice. But intellect
or emotion is usually involved. Ironic wit such as Swift's,
even when engaged on the most trivial of subjects, is often a
mask for deep feelings:

Perhaps the critics may accuse me of a defect in my following
system of polite conversation; that there is one great ornament of
discourse, whereof I have not produced a single example; which
indeed I purposely omitted, for some reasons that I shall immediately offer; and, if those reasons will not satisfy the male part of
my gentle readers, the defect may be applied in some manner by
an appendix to the second edition; which appendix shall be printed
by itself, and sold for sixpence, stitched, and with a marble cover,
that my readers may have no occasion to complain of being
defrauded.

The defect I mean is, my not having inserted into the body of
my book all the oaths now most in fashion for embellishing discourse, especially since it could give no offence to the clergy, who
are seldom or never admitted to these polite assemblies. And it
must be allowed, that oaths well chosen are not only very useful
expletives to matter, but great ornaments of style.

What I shall here offer in my own defence upon this important
article, will, I hope, be some extenuation of my fault.

First, I reasoned with myself, that a just collection of oaths,
repeated as often as the fashion requires, must have enlarged this
volume at least to double the bulk, whereby it would not only
double the charge, but likewise make the volume less commodious
for pocket carriage.

Secondly, I have been assured by some judicious friends, that themselves have known certain ladies to take offence (whether seriously or not) at too great a profusion of cursing and swearing, even when that kind of ornament was not improperly introduced, which, I confess, did startle me not a little, having never observed the like in the compass of my own several acquaintance, at least for twenty years past. However, I was forced to submit to wiser judgments than my own.

Thirdly, as this most useful treatise is calculated for all future times, I considered, in this maturity of my age, how great a variety of oaths I have heard since I began to study the world, and to know men and manners. And here I found it to be true, what I have read in an ancient poet:

> For, now-a-days, men change their oaths
> As often as they change their clothes.

In short, oaths are the children of fashion; they are in some sense almost annuals, like what I have observed before of cant words; and I myself can remember about forty different sets. The old stock oaths, I am confident, do not amount to above forty-five, or fifty at most; but the way of mingling and compounding them is almost as various as that of the alphabet.

SIR JOHN PERROT was the first man of quality whom I find upon the record to have sworn by *God's wounds*. He lived in the reign of Queen Elizabeth, and was supposed to be a natural son of Henry VIII, who might also probably have been his instructor. This oath indeed still continues, and is a stock oath to this day; so do several others that have kept their natural simplicity; but infinitely the greater number has been so frequently changed and dislocated, that if the inventors were now alive, they could hardly understand them.

JONATHAN SWIFT, Introduction to *A Complete Collection of Genteel and Ingenious Conversation.*

Irony, however, is not always so universal in its basis, nor so intelligent in its aim, as with Swift. It is more often the weapon of an exclusive egotism, of a mean and esoteric spirit that lacks common understanding and sympathy. This explains why it is used but sparingly by writers of true eloquence, Swift notwithstanding. But Swift is more often sardonic, and irony is not to be confused with the sardonic, which is a passionate state of mind far removed from the detachment of irony.

The more innocent forms of wit play on unexpected conjunctions and oppositions of words. There is again a need for the sparing use of this type of wit; it grows wearisome and facetious if kept up too long. No one has better exploited both its uses and abuses than Mr. Chesterton:

Poetry deals with primal and conventional things—the hunger for bread, the love of woman, the love of children, the desire for immortal life. If men really had new sentiments, poetry could not deal with them. If, let us say, a man did not feel a bitter craving to eat bread; but did, by way of substitute, feel a fresh, original craving to eat brass fenders or mahogany tables, poetry could not express him. If a man, instead of falling in love with a woman, fell in love with a fossil or a sea anemone, poetry could not express him. Poetry can only express what is original in one sense—the sense in which we speak of original sin. It is original, not in the paltry sense of being new, but in the deeper sense of being old; it is original in the sense that it deals with origins.

G. K. CHESTERTON, *Robert Browning*, p. 99.[1]

But to return to true eloquence: it is intuitive in its nature, and is 'fed by an abundant spring'. It flows when some dominant idea has mastery of the mind and orders the expression to the single purpose of that idea. Everything, every subordination and subtlety of style, is driven into one persuasive unity.

These three conditions are necessary to Eloquence—firstly, an adequate theme; then a sincere and impassioned mind; and lastly a power of sustainment or pertinacity.

It is idle to use eloquence upon a mean subject, for the result is always ludicrous. We speak ironically of people who 'wax eloquent', implying that their enthusiasm for a particular theme has betrayed them into a disproportionate mode of expression:

He is about to be struck down. A dark hand, gloved at first in folly, now intervenes. Exit Czar. Deliver him and all he loved to wounds and death. Belittle his efforts, asperse his conduct, insult his memory; but pause then to tell us who else was found capable. Who or what could guide the Russian State? Men gifted and daring; men ambitious and fierce; spirits audacious and commanding—of these there was no lack. But none could answer the few plain questions on which the life and fame of Russia turned. With victory in her grasp she fell upon the earth, devoured alive, like Herod of old, by worms. But not in vain her valiant deeds. The giant mortally stricken had just time, with dying strength, to

[1] Methuen.

pass the torch eastward across the ocean to a new Titan long sunk
in doubt who now arose and began ponderously to arm. The
Russian Empire fell on March 16; on April 6 the United States
entered the war.

THE RT. HON. WINSTON CHURCHILL, *The World Crisis, 1916-1918*.
    Part I.[1]

Such eloquence is false because it is artificial: it is one of
the many pits into which a writer may fall if his conception of
'fine writing' is not supported by an inner structure of fine
thinking.   Here the images are stale, the metaphors violent.
The whole passage exhales a false dramatic atmosphere,
descending to a childish use of the very rubrics of drama with
'Exit Czar'.   There is a volley of rhetorical imperatives,
followed by an inevitable ironic question.   Then a volley of
epithets, high-sounding and redundant.   Then the simile of
Herod's worms, too familiar to produce the calculated shudder.
Then a line of verse ('But not in vain', etc.) and then a spate
of still staler images—giant, torch and Titan.   And to complete the bathos, a plain and very literal statement of the
cause of all this false eloquence.

Mr. Churchill has, of course, done better than this, and
under the stress of many a great occasion, his eloquence has
been purified and simplified.   Nevertheless, at its greatest,
as in the following famous passage, it never has the felicity
and dignity of Burke's eloquence:

Even though large tracts of Europe and many old and famous
States have fallen or may fall into the grip of the Gestapo and all
the odious apparatus of Nazi rule, we shall not flag or fail.   We
shall go on to the end.   We shall fight in France, we shall fight in
the seas and oceans, we shall fight with growing confidence and
growing strength in the air; we shall defend our Island, whatever
the cost may be.   We shall fight on the beaches, we shall fight on
the landing-grounds, we shall fight in the fields and in the streets,
we shall fight in the hills; we shall never surrender; and even if,
which I do not for a moment believe, this Island or a large part of
it were subjugated and starving, then our Empire beyond the seas,
armed and guarded by the British Fleet, would carry on the
struggle, until, in God's good time, the New World, with all its
power and might, steps forth to the rescue and the liberation of the
Old.

The Second World War.   Vol. II., *Their Finest Hour*, p. 104.

[1] Scribner.

This passage should be compared with the quotation from Burke's *Reflections on the French Revolution* given on pages 35-7.

When false eloquence has for its aim not so much an aggrandization of the theme as an aggrandization of the self, then it may be described as *declamation*. An enthusiasm for a poor theme may be genuine to the extent of the writer's intelligence—he is then eloquent because he cannot rejoice in restraint. But in this second order of mock-eloquence the writer, suspecting the meanness of his theme, attempts to magnify it by grand phrases, thereby hoping to invest his own poor thoughts with the quality of this magnificence:

The eye, most illustrious sons of the Muses, most learned Oxonians, whose fame I have heard celebrated in all parts of the globe, the eye, that most amazing, that stupendous, that comprehending, that miraculous organ, the eye is the Proteus of the passions, the herald of the mind, the interpreter of the heart, and the window of the soul. The world was made for the eye and the eye for the world.

My subject is light, most illustrious sons of literature, intellectual light. Ah, my philosophical, metaphysical, my classical, mathematical, mechanical, my theological, my critical audience, my subject is the eye. You are the eye of England!

England has two eyes, Oxford and Cambridge. They are the two eyes of England, and two intellectual eyes. You are the right eye of England, the elder sister in Science.

The eye is indefatigable. The eye is an angelic faculty. The eye in this respect is female.

CHEVALIER TAYLOR's *Oration at Oxford.*

The difference between true and false eloquence is easily perceived, and it is only under special conditions, such as those created by an excited crowd, that the pretence of eloquence can have any effect. It then serves to stir gross and uncriticized emotions into a state of self-intoxication which has no relation to the real content of the expression. Indeed, such eloquence when analyzed will usually be found to consist of many high-sounding phrases of little inherent meaning. The use of false eloquence is particularly prevalent in politics and the press:

TO THE DEAD AND TO THE LIVING

On this the ninth anniversary of the Armistice which ended the greatest and the most fateful of all wars, the heart of this world-wide Empire turns in a special manner to the memory of those whose lives were the price of our deliverance. As there has been no struggle in our annals so terrible and so exacting, no danger so prolonged and imminent, no cause so great, no sacrifices so cruel, and no victory on which larger and more lasting issues hung, so there is no day in our calendar like to this. For over four years we stood on the edge of the abyss, of ruin as an Empire, as a nation, perhaps of ruin as a race. The men we commemorate to-day saved us from that ruin by their death. The appeal is universal. Scarce a home in the land, from the most splendid of ancestral palaces to the humblest cottage or the poorest lodging in our towns, was unvisited in that dread time by the angel of death. He smote the best; a whole generation entering upon life in the flower of early manhood, and others already husbands and fathers, the stay and the guardians of the widows and the orphans they have left. To the bereaved, first of all, this is a day of days, dedicated to the memory of their dead, a memory ever living with them, but by time and the everyday duties and occupations of life mercifully softened with the years. The annual testimony to the fallen, celebrated with such solemn and befitting rites as Church and State can give, bears recurrent witness to the full measure in which Empire and nation share the grief and the gratitude of the mourners. There is no day on which all sorts and conditions of our people are so widely and so deeply moved by thoughts and feelings common to them all. The prayerful congregations in the churches on Sunday, the crowds which will gather round the Cenotaph or attend the services and visit the tomb of the Unknown Warrior to-day, and those other crowds which will assemble in their own churches or about their own local monuments through the provinces and through all lands where the flag flies, are filled according to their gifts and their experiences by the same spirit, the same memories, and the same hopes.

The London Times, November 11, 1927.

The writer of *ad hoc* eloquence such as this probably deserves our sympathy rather than our scorn. We need not analyze the passage in detail; it is rather better than Mr. Churchill's false eloquence, because it is not so violent. But it is interesting to note in what small but significant ways a writer in this mood betrays himself. Why, at the end of the second sentence, does he write 'no day in our calendar like *to* this'? 'Like this' is the natural expression; the 'to' is inserted either to swell out the rhythm, or as a reminiscence of the Biblical 'unto'. Violence was the general characteristic of the first example, exaggeration of the second; this third example is unctuous.

Eloquence may inhere in a phrase, as 'a noble and puissant
Nation rousing herself like a strong man after sleep, *and shaking
her invincible locks*' (Milton), but the two first-named conditions
of eloquence—an adequate theme and a sincere and impassioned
mind—really imply a mood which is sustained within the
extent of the subject. An adequate theme, like victory,
courage, beauty, God, nature, or the infinity of space, cannot
be confined to a few paltry phrases, but creates a mood of
expansive fury.

But there is another reason inherent in the circumstances
of eloquence. A noble theme does not unite with a sincere
and impassioned mind by casual chance, but they come
together naturally, by a process of fruition which is expressed
in the word *character*. The French have a phrase, 'grandeur
d'âme', which expresses this quality better still,[1] but a literal
translation, 'greatness of soul', will not serve our purpose very
well; 'soul' is an abused word, and because of the vagueness
of its meaning and the sentimentality of its emotional associations, is better avoided in scientific discussion.

Of true eloquence I shall give two examples, but to appreciate
one of the qualities of eloquence, namely its sustainment
throughout the duration of a theme, it would be necessary to
quote whole works, not dismembered fragments:

As those Images were limned in my minde (the morning Starre
now almost arising in the East) I found my thoughts in a mild
and quiet calme; and not long after, my Senses one by one forgetting their uses, began to give themselves over to rest, leaving me
in a still and peaceable sleepe; if sleepe it may be called, where
the Minde awaking is carried with free wings from out fleshlie
bondage? For heavy lids had not long covered their lights, when
mee thought, nay, sure I was, where I might discerne all in this
great *All*; the large compasse of the rolling Circles, the brightnesse
and continuall motion of those Rubies of the Night, which (by
their distance) heere below can not bee perceived; the silver
countenance of the wandring Moone, shining by anothers light,
the hanging of the Earth (as environed with a girdle of Christall)
the Sunne enthronized in the midst of the Planetes, eye of the
Heavens, Gemme of this precious Ring the World. But whilst
with wonder and amazement I gazed on those celestiall Splendors,

---

[1] I have particularly in mind the use of that phrase by Vauvenargues,
Introduction à la connaissance de l'esprit humain, XLIV.

and the beaming Lampes of that glorious Temple (like a poore
Countrieman brought from his solitarie Mountaines and Flockes,
to behold the magnificence of some great Citie) There was presented
to my sight a MAN, as in the spring of His yeares, with that selfe
same Grace, comelie feature, majesticke Looke which the late ———
was wont to have: on whom I had no sooner fixed mine eyes, when
(like one Planet-stroken) I become amazed: but Hee with a milde
demeanour, and voyce surpassing all humane sweetnesse appeared
(mee thought) to say,

What is it doth thus paine and perplexe thee? Is it the remembrance of Death, the last Period of wretchednesse, and entrie to
these happie places; the Lanterne which lighteneth men to see
the Misterie of the blessednesse of Spirites, and that Glorie which
transcendeth the Courtaine of things visible? Is thy Fortune
below on that darke Globe, (which scarce by the smalnesse of it
appeareth here) so great, that thou art heartbroken and dejected
to leave it? What if thou wert to leave behinde thee a ——— so
glorious in the eye of the World (yet but a mote of dust encircled
with a pond) as that of mine so loving ———, such great Hopes.
These had beene apparent occasions of lamenting, & but apparent?
Dost thou think thou leavest Life too soone? Death is best young;
things faire and excellent, are not of long indurance upon Earth.
Who liveth well, liveth long; Soules most beloved of their Maker
are soonest releeved from the bleeding cares of Life, & with almost
a sphericall swiftnesse wafted through the Surges of Humane
miseries. Opinion (that great Enchantresse and Peiser of things,
not as they are, but as they seeme) hath not in any thing more,
than in the conceit of Death abused Man: Who must not measure
himselfe, and esteeme his estate, after his earthlie being, which is
but as a dreame: For, though hee bee borne on the earth, hee is
not borne for the Earth, more than the Embryon for the mothers
wombe. It plaineth to bee releeved of its bands, and to come to
the light of this World, and Man waileth to bee loosed from the
Chaines with which hee is fettered in that Valley of vanities: it
nothing knoweth whither it is to goe, nor ought of the beauty of
the visible works of God, neither doth Man of the magnificence of
the intellectuall World above, unto which (as by a Mid-wife) hee
is directed by death. Fooles, which thinke that this faire and
admirable Frame, so variouslie disposed, so rightly marshalled,
so strongly maintained, enriched with so many excellencies, not
only for necessity, but for ornament and delight, was by that
supreme Wisedome brought forth, that all things in a circulary
course, should bee and not bee, arise and dissolve, and thus continue, (as if they were so many Shadowes careleslie cast out and
caused by the encountring of those superiour celestiall Bodies,
changing onelie their fashion and shape, or fantasticall Imageries,
or shades of faces into Christall). But more [fools] They, which

beleeve that Hee doth no other-wayes regard this his worke than as a Theater, raised for bloudy Sword-playeres, Wrastlers, Chasers of timorous and Combatters of terrible Beastes, delighting in the daily torments Sorrowes distresse and Miserie of Mankind. No, no, the Eternall Wisedome did make Man an excellent Creature, though hee faine would unmake himselfe, and returne unto nothing: and though hee seeke his felicity among the reasonlesse Wights, he hath fixed it above. Hee brought him into thei world as a Master to a sumptuous well-ordered and furnished Inn, a Prince to a populous and rich Empire, a Pilgrime and Spectator to a Stage full of delightfull Wonders and wonderfull Delightes. And as some Emperour or great Monarch, when hee hath raised any stately Citie, the worke being atchieved, is wont to set his Image in the midst of it, to bee admired and gazed upon: No otherwise did the Soveraigne of this World, the Fabricke of it perfected, place Man (a great Miracle) formed to his own Paterne, in the midst of this spacious and admirable Citie, by the divine splendor of his Reason to bee an Interpreter and Trunchman of his Creation, and admired and reverenced by all his other Creatures. God containeth all in Him, as the midst of all; inferiour things bee in Man more noblie than they exist, superiour things more meanely, celestiall thinges favour him, earthly thinges are vassaled unto him, hee is the knot and Band of both; neither is it possible but that both of them have peace with Man, if Man have peace with Him who made the Covenant betweene them and Him. Hee was made that hee might in the Glasse of the World behold the infinite Goodnesse, Power, Magnificence, and Glorie of his Maker, and beholding know, and knowing Love, and loving enjoy, and to hold the Earth of him as of his Lord Paramount, never ceasing to remember and praise Him. It exceedeth the compasse of Conceit, to thinke that Wisedome which made everie thing so orderlie in the parts, should make a confusion in the whole, and the chiefe Masterpiece; how bringing forth so many excellencies for Man, it should bring forth Man for basenesse and miserie. And no lesse strange were it, that so long life should be given to Trees, Beastes, and the Birds of the Aire, Creatures inferiour to Man, which have lesse use of it, and which can not judge of this goodlie Fabricke, and that it should bee denyed to Man: Unlesse there were another manner of living prepared for him, in a Place more noble and excellent.

WM. DRUMMOND OF HAWTHORNDEN,
A Cypresse Grove.

It was as if they had gathered there into a vast deafening chorus; I shall never forget how—speaking, that is, for my own sense— they filled those vast halls with the influence rather of some complicated sound, diffused and reverberant, than of such visibilities as one could directly deal with. To distinguish among

these, in the charged and coloured and confounding air, was
difficult—it discouraged and defied; which was doubtless why my
impression originally best entertained was that of those magnificent
parts of the great gallery simply not inviting us to distinguish.
They only arched over us in the wonder of their endless golden
riot and relief, figured and flourished in perpetual revolution,
breaking into great high-hung circles and symmetries of squandered
picture, opening into deep outward embrasures that threw off the
rest of monumental Paris somehow as a told story, a sort of wrought
effect or bold ambiguity for a vista, and yet held it there, at every
point, as a vast bright gage, even at moments a felt adventure, of
experience.   This comes to saying that in those beginnings I felt
myself most happily cross that bridge over to Style constituted by
the wondrous Galerie d'Apollon, drawn out for me as a long but
assured initiation, and seeming to form with its supreme coved
ceiling and inordinately shining parquet a prodigious tube or
tunnel through which I inhaled little by little, that is again and
again, a general sense of *glory*.   The glory meant ever so many
things at once, not only beauty and art and supreme design, but
history and fame and power, the world in fine raised to the richest
and noblest expression.   The world there was at the same time,
by an odd extension or intensification, the local present fact, to my
small imagination, of the Second Empire, which was (for my
notified consciousness) new and queer and perhaps even wrong,
but on the spot so amply radiant and elegant that it took to itself,
took under its protection with a splendour of insolence, the state
and ancientry of the whole scene, profiting thus, to one's dim
historic vision, confusedly though it might be, by the unparalleled
luxury and variety of its heritage.   But who shall count the sources
at which an intense young fancy (when a young fancy *is* intense)
capriciously, absurdly drinks?—so that the effect is, in twenty
connections, that of a love-philtre or fear-philtre which fixes for
the senses their supreme symbol of the fair or the strange.   The
Galerie d'Apollon became for years what I can only term a splendid
scene of things, even of the quite irrelevant or, as might be, almost
unworthy; and I recall to this hour, with the last vividness, what a
precious part it played for me, and exactly by that continuity of
honour, on my awaking, in a summer dawn many years later, to
the fortunate, the instantaneous recovery and capture of the most
appalling yet most admirable nightmare of my life.   The climax
of this extraordinary experience—which stands alone for me as a
dream-adventure founded in the deepest, quickest, clearest act
of cogitation and comparison, act indeed of life-saving energy, as
well as in unutterable fear—was the sudden pursuit, through an
open door, along a huge high saloon, of a just dimly-descried figure
that retreated in terror before my rush and dash (a glare of inspired
reaction from irresistible but shameful dread), out of the room I

had a moment before been desperately, and all the more abjectly defending by the push of my shoulder against hard pressure on lock and bar from the other side. The lucidity, not to say the sublimity, of the crisis had consisted of the great thought that I, in my appalled state, was probably still more appalling than the awful agent, creature or presence, whatever he was, whom I had guessed, in the suddenest wild start from my sleep, to be making for my place of rest. The triumph of my impulse, perceived in a flash as I acted on it by myself at a bound, forcing the door outward, was the grand thing, but the great point of the whole was the wonder of my final recognition. Routed, dismayed, the tables turned upon him by my so surpassing him for straight aggression and dire intention, my visitant was already but a diminished spot in the long perspective, the tremendous, glorious hall, as I say, over the far-gleaming floor of which, cleared for the occasion of its great line of priceless *vitrines* down the middle, he sped for *his* life, while a great storm of thunder and lightning played through the deep embrasures of high windows at the right. The lightning that revealed the retreat revealed also the wondrous place, and, by the same amazing play, my young imaginative life in it of long before, the sense of which, deep within me, had kept it whole, preserved it to this thrilling use; for what in the world were the deep embrasures and the so polished floor but those of the Galerie d'Apollon of my childhood? The 'scene of something' I had vaguely then felt it? Well I might, since it was to be the scene of that immense hallucination.

HENRY JAMES, *A Small Boy and Others*, pp. 360-4.[1]

These two examples of eloquence are extremely different in inspiration, but agree in their rhetorical characteristics—in their sustained periods and long rhythmical cadences, in their intense or lyrical phrases ('the silver countenance of the wandring Moone', 'a poore countrieman brought from his solitarie Mountaines and Flockes', 'the Courtaine of things visible', 'a sphericall swiftnesse', 'the charged and coloured and confounding air', 'high-hung circles and symmetries of squandered picture', 'a vast bright gage', 'the state and ancientry of the whole scene'), and in 'the general sense of *glory*' which each passage radiates. Eloquence is, indeed, closely related to glory, for one is the expression in deeds, as the other is in words, of the same animating principle of human conduct.

[1] Macmillan.

CHAPTER XIV

*

Unity

'ALL THE LAWS OF good writing', wrote Pater in his 'Essay on Style', 'aim at a unity or identity of the mind in all the processes by which the word is associated to its import. . . . To give the phrase, the sentence, the structural member, the entire composition, song, or essay, a similar unity with its subject and its self:—style is in the right way when it tends towards that.'

Such is the final aim of rhetoric—the balance and reconciliation as Coleridge put it, 'of a more than usual state of emotion with more than usual order; judgment ever awake and steady self-possession with enthusiasm and feeling profound or vehement'. But it was Gerard Manley Hopkins, in a letter to Coventry Patmore, who came closest to defining the quality in a prose style essential for such unity. He called it 'the strain of address':

. . . When I read your prose and when I read Newman's and some other modern writers' the same impression is borne in on me: no matter how beautiful the thought, nor, taken singly, with what happiness expressed, you do not know what *writing prose* is. At bottom what you do and what Cardinal Newman does is to think aloud, to think with pen to paper. In this process there are certain advantages; they may outweigh those of a perfect technic; but at any rate they exclude that; they exclude the belonging technic, the belonging rhetoric, the own proper eloquence of written prose. Each thought is told off singly and there follows a pause and this breaks the continuity, the *contentio*, the strain of address, which writing should usually have.

The beauty, the eloquence, of good prose cannot come wholly from the thought. With Burke it does and varies with the thought; when therefore the thought is sublime so does the style appear to be. But in fact Burke had no style properly so called: his style was colourlessly to transmit his thought. Still he was an orator in form and followed the common oratorical tradition, so that his writing has the strain of address I speak of above.

But Newman does not follow the common tradition—of writing. His tradition is that of cultured, the most highly educated, conversation; it is the flower of the best Oxford life. Perhaps this gives it a charm of unaffected and personal sincerity that nothing else could. Still he shirks the technic of written prose and shuns the tradition of written English. He seems to be thinking 'Gibbon is the last great master of traditional English prose; he is its perfection: I do not propose to emulate him; I begin all over again from the language of conversation, of common life'.

You too seem to me to be saying to yourself 'I am writing prose, not poetry; it is bad taste and a confusion of kinds to employ the style of poetry in prose: the style of prose is to shun the style of poetry and to express one's thoughts with point'. But the style of prose is a positive thing and not the absence of verse-forms and pointedly expressed thoughts are single hits and give no continuity of style.

Further Letters of Gerard Manley Hopkins. Oxford Univ. Press, 1938, p. 231.

There is a famous passage in the *Biographia Literaria* where Coleridge, speaking of the poet's 'images', remarks that these do not of themselves characterize the poet—'They become proofs of original genius only so far as they are modified by a predominant passion, or by associated thoughts or images awakened by that passion'. Coleridge had in mind the unity of a poetic composition, and he contends that such unity is imposed on the poet's expression only by virtue of a sustained mood or passion. What Coleridge had in mind *on an intense scale* for the composition of poetry, Hopkins wished to extend to the writing of prose. Adopting Coleridge's phrase, we might say that all the modes of rhetoric which we have been considering become proofs of original genius only so far as they are modified by a predominant passion in the writer. The sense of the quality of words; the use of appropriate epithets and images; the organization of the period, the paragraph and the plot; the arts of exposition and of narrative; all the gifts of thought and sensibility—these are only dry perfections unless they are moved by a spirit which is neither intelligence nor emotion, but the sustained power of reason. And by reason in this context I do not mean ratiocination or rationality, but, as I have said in another connection, 'the widest evidence of the senses, and of all processes and instincts

developed in the history of man. It is the sum total of awareness, ordained and ordered to some specific end or object of
attention'.[1] Such a quality in a writer is no innate instinct,
but a conscious achievement. It is more than character,
because it necessarily implies intelligence; and it is more than
personality, because it necessarily implies a realm of absolute
ideals. A life of reason is more than a life of self-development,
because it is also a life of self-devotion, of service to outer and
autocratic abstractions.

This is merely to say that a good style is not the making
of a great writer; and the corollary is, that a great writer is
always a good stylist. The greatest English prose writers
Swift, Milton, Taylor, Hooker, Berkeley, Shelley, are great
not only by virtue of their prose style, but also by virtue of
the profundity of their outlook on the world. And these are
not separable and distinct virtues, but two aspects of one
reality. The thought seems to mould and accentuate the
style, and the style reacts to mould and accentuate the thought.
It is one process of creation, one art, one aim.

In the last chapter I have defined true eloquence as determined by the dominance of some idea in the mind of the
writer, ordering the rhetoric to the single purpose of that idea.
If for 'idea' we substitute the word 'ideal' we have a definition
of the quality which I am concerned with now. Not merely
ideal, but a life of ideals, is perhaps a more accurate conception.
But even this is a dangerous phrase, for it must be further
desiderated that the ideals are intelligent—not sentimental,
or unreal. Sentimental ideals will, it is true, give rise to a
predominating passion of a sort. But there is a hierarchy in
everything, and the higher the concept the more difficult it
is to differentiate the subtle graduations of value. A certain
degree of passion is to be found in a writer like Walter Pater;
his style is everywhere definitely his own; it has character and
it has beauty, and we feel that such an outer unity must
spring from an inner unity. But how describe this inner
unity, in Pater's case? It is a subtle matter, and some critics
have doubted if anything more considerable than just a self-

---

[1] *Reason and Romanticism* (London, Faber and Gwyer, 1926), p. 27.

consuming passion for style, an educated taste, an abnormal
sensibility for the tonal value of words, could be deduced.
These qualities are not to be despised, but contrast them with
the qualities of another writer whose style is equally integral
and equally eloquent—I mean John Henry Newman. Newman's aim in writing was almost directly contrary to Pater's;
he tells us (*Letters*, II. 477, quoted by Canon Beeching in
Craik's *English Prose*, v. 444) that he has never written for
writing's sake, but that his one and single desire and aim had
been 'to do what is so difficult, viz. to explain clearly and
exactly my meaning; this has been the whole principle of all
my corrections and re-writings'. The eloquence that is
undeniably his, one of the most persuasive in English literature,
in the first instance owes little to conscious rhetoric or composition. It is a spirit, in his case definitely recognizable as the
religious spirit, which finds the modes of its eloquence inherent
in its moods. 'Newman's style being in its lowest terms an
effort after a clear and exact representation of his thought, it
follows that not a little of the fascination it exercises is the
influence of the writer's beautiful and subtle mind, which it
clothes in light and transparent vesture'.[1] In kind, it is the
eloquence of Vanzetti; but unlike Vanzetti's eloquence it is
not created by a stress of emotion, but is a sustained state, a
predominating passion—passion always, in this context,
implying control.

Newman is perhaps not a good example to take, except as a
contrast to Pater. Newman's passion is too subtle, and too
little understood. Swift is easier of comprehension, and
admirable for 'predominance'. I do not for a moment
pretend that his sardonic humour is a simple matter, or one
for vulgar explication. But whatever the diagnosis, its
symptoms are plain to be seen; and they are not to be explained
in the terms of rhetoric and composition. They depend on a
particular insight into the world, a particular view of life, a
predominating passion. We may not altogether like this
passion, since it strikes at the roots of all complacency and
satisfaction, but we cannot explain the style without it.

[1] Canon Beeching, *op. cit.* p. 444.

Henry James provides a still more illuminating example. He developed a very complex and a very personal style, a style which has encountered a good deal of shallow depreciation. But, once his mind was made up, the aim of Henry James was essentially the same as Newman's—to explain clearly and exactly his meaning, and not to bother about writing for writing's sake. Now the 'meaning' which Henry James was concerned to express was generally very complicated. It was concerned with life at its finest creative point— the point where moral judgments are formed. The deeper this penetrating mind delved into the psychological complexity of human motives the more involved his world became. But it was obviously the real world, the only world worth describing, once your course is set that way. Henry James went ahead, fearlessly, irretrievably, into regions where few are found who care to follow him. He was driven by a force far more powerful than 'writing for writing's sake', by what he himself would have called a sacred rage, by what Coleridge called a predominating passion.

The question to consider, in this final chapter, is to what extent this predominating passion that gives a style its unity, its strain of address, is a personal intuition ('judgment ever awake and steady self-possession'), to what extent a common tradition, the technical tradition of written English.

The ordinary use of the word 'tradition' implies a 'handing down' of something vital—a torch, lit in the remote past, whose light is the only light capable of guiding us in the particular darkness surrounding us at the moment of present existence. There is a good deal to be said for this conception: it implies continuity; it also implies activity. It is not, however, completely satisfactory, if only for the fact that it makes no provision for the athletes of the metaphor, who race from point to point with the burning brand. It assumes, so to speak, that a runner is miraculously there at the relay point, to seize the torch from the exhausted fore-runner. But such an assumption is a begging of the whole question:

. . . if the only form of tradition, of handing down, consisted in following the ways of the immediate generation before us in a blind or timid adherence to its successes, 'tradition' should positively be discouraged. We have seen many such simple currents soon lost in the sand; and novelty is better than repetition. Tradition is a matter of much wider significance. It cannot be inherited, and if you want it you must obtain it by great labour. It involves, in the first place, the historical sense . . . and the historical sense involves a perception, not only of the pastness of the past, but of its presence; the historical sense compels a man to write not merely with his own generation in his bones, but with a feeling that the whole of the literature of Europe from Homer and within it the whole of the literature of his own country has a simultaneous existence and composes a simultaneous order.[1]

In this passage, and more generally in the essay from which it is taken, Mr. Eliot has succeeded in showing how little tradition is a mere question of blind 'following', but is rather the presence in the writer of a particular kind of sensibility. It is a sensibility, not only to historical continuity, but also to historical wholeness, or integrity. To realize this age-long integrity is necessarily to feel the irrelevance of those idiosyncrasies upon which, as we saw in Chapter XII, the personal writer depends. It is only possible to come to this realization by a process of education. Through the interplay of sensibility and experience there arises this particular style which we describe as traditional; in a more general sense such interplay gives rise to the phenomenon of *Taste*.

A tradition in prose (as in poetic) style first takes shape when a body of critical opinion crystallizes around the idiomatic structure of a language. For some time influences—personal, imitative, even social and religious—have been moulding a language; a point occurs when suddenly it is realized that these influences have resulted in an appropriateness: in a fit relation of sound, sense and conversational ease. Such a moment came in English literature in the second half of the seventeenth century, and particularly in the person of Dryden, who has been commonly recognized as the starting point of the main traditional style in English. This is not to say that there were not writers before his time who were contributory to this tradition—for besides Tillotson, whom Dryden acknowledged, too generously, as his master, there is what I am

[1] T. S. Eliot, *The Sacred Wood* (1920), Methuen, pp. 44–5.

tempted to call the whole firmament of fixed stars—Bunyan, Milton, Taylor, Browne, Donne, Bacon, Hooker, the Bible translators, and Malory. Among these authors there are, indeed, visible relationships and even (as, for example, in the case of Bunyan and the English Bible) direct descents. But there is no corporate literary sense; most of our early writers are solitary writers; sometimes therefore idiosyncratic, like Sir Thomas Browne; but more often instructed by some conscious discipline. But by Dryden's time the corporate sense had been born; literature had become a profession, and something like professional pride was engendered. Dryden himself was the first writer to be wholly conscious of this sense, and it is a tribute to his real greatness that he himself became its first exemplar.

Let us now examine a series of fairly short but typical passages from those writers whom we may regard as constituting the English tradition, beginning with Dryden:

But to return from this digression to a farther account of my poem; I must crave leave to tell you, that as I have endeavoured to adorn it with noble thoughts, so much more to express those thoughts with elocution. The composition of all poems is, or ought to be, of wit; and wit in the poet, or *Wit writing* (if you will give me leave to use a school-distinction), is no other than the faculty of imagination in the writer, which, like a nimble spaniel, beats over and ranges through the field of memory, till it springs the quarry it hunted after; or, without metaphor, which searches over all the memory for the species or ideas of those things which it designs to represent. *Wit written* is that which is well defined, the happy result of thought, or product of imagination. But to proceed from wit, in the general notion of it, to the proper wit of an Heroic or Historical Poem, I judge it chiefly to consist in the delightful imagining of persons, actions, passions, or things. 'Tis not the jerk or sting of an epigram, nor the seeming contradiction of a poor antithesis (the delight of an ill-judging audience in a play of rhyme), nor the jingle of a more poor paronomasia; neither is it so much the morality of a grave sentence, affected by Lucan, but more sparingly used by Virgil; but it is some lively and apt description, dressed in such colours of speech, that it sets before your eyes the absent object, as perfectly, and more delightfully than nature. So then the first happiness of the poet's imagination is properly invention, or finding of the thought ; the second is fancy, or the variation, deriving, or moulding, of that thought, as the judgment

represents it proper to the subject; the third is elocution, or the art
of clothing and adorning that thought, so found and varied, in
apt, significant, and sounding words: the quickness of the imagination is seen in the invention, the fertility in the fancy, and the
accuracy in the expression. For the two first of these, Ovid is
famous amongst the poets; for the latter, Virgil. Ovid images
more often the movements and affections of the mind, either
combating between two contrary passions, or extremely discom-
posed by one. His words therefore are the least part of his care;
for he pictures nature in disorder, with which the study and choice
of words is inconsistent. This is the proper wit of dialogue or
discourse, and consequently of the Drama, where all that is said
is supposed to be the effect of sudden thought; which, though it
excludes not the quickness of wit in repartees, yet admits not a
too curious election of words, too frequent allusions, or use of
tropes, or, in fine, anything that shows remoteness of thought, or
labour in the writer. On the other side, Virgil speaks not so often
to us in the person of another, like Ovid, but in his own: he relates
almost all things as from himself, and thereby gains more liberty
than the other, to express his thoughts with all the graces of elocution, to write more figuratively, and to confess as well the labour
as the force of his imagination.

JOHN DRYDEN, *Preface to Annus Mirabilis.*

Nothing is more pleasant to the fancy, than to enlarge it-self by
degrees in its contemplation of the various proportions which its
several objects bear to each other, when it compares the body of
man to the bulk of the whole earth, the earth to the circle it
describes round the sun, that circle to the sphere of the fixt stars,
the sphere of the fixt stars to the circuit of the whole creation, the
whole creation it self to the infinite space that is every where
diffused about it; or when the imagination works downward, and
considers the bulk of a human body in respect of an animal, a
hundred times less than a mite, the particular limbs of such an
animal, the different springs which actuate the limbs, the spirits
which set these springs a going, and the proportionable minuteness
of these several parts, before they have arrived at their full growth
and perfection. But if, after all this, we take the least particle of
these animal spirits, and consider its capacity of being wrought
into a world, that shall contain within those narrow dimensions
a heaven and earth, stars and planets, and every different species
of living creatures, in the same analogy and proportion they bear
to each other in our own universe; such a speculation, by reason
of its nicety, appears ridiculous to those who have not turned their
thoughts that way, though at the same time it is founded on no
less than the evidence of a demonstration. Nay, we may yet
carry it farther, and discover in the smallest particle of this little

world a new and inexhausted fund of matter, capable of being spun
out into another universe.

JOSEPH ADDISON, *Spectator*, *No.* 420.

Rasselas went often to an assembly of learned men, who met
at stated times to unbend their minds, and compare their opinions.
Their manners were somewhat coarse, but their conversation was
instructive, and their disputations acute, though sometimes too
violent, and often continued till neither controvertist remembered
upon what question they began.   Some faults were almost general
among them: everyone was desirous to dictate to the rest, and
every one was pleased to hear the genius or knowledge of another
depreciated.

In this assembly Rasselas was relating his interview with the
hermit, and the wonder with which he heard him censure a course
of life which he had so deliberately chosen, and so laudably
followed.   The sentiments of the hearers were various.   Some were
of opinion, that the folly of his choice had been justly punished by
condemnation to perpetual perseverance.   One of the youngest
among them, with great vehemence, pronounced him a hypocrite.
Some talked of the right of society to the labour of individuals,
and considered retirement as a desertion of duty.   Others readily
allowed, that there was a time when the claims of the people were
satisfied, and when a man might properly sequester himself to
review his life, and purify his heart.

One who appeared more affected with the narrative than the
rest, thought it likely, that the hermit would in a few years, go
back to his retreat, and perhaps, if shame did not restrain, or death
intercept him, return once more from his retreat into the world :
'For the hope of happiness', said he, 'is so strongly impressed, that
the longest experience is not able to efface it.   Of the present state,
whatever it be, we feel, and are forced to confess, the misery; yet,
when the same state is again at a distance, imagination paints it
as desirable.   But the time will surely come, when desire will be
no longer our torment, and no man shall be wretched but by his
own fault.'

'This', said a philosopher, who had heard him with tokens of
great impatience, 'is the present condition of a wise man.   The
time is already come, when none are wretched but by their own
fault.   Nothing is more idle, than to inquire after happiness, which
nature has kindly placed within our reach.   The way to be happy
is to live according to nature, in obedience to that universal and
unalterable law with which every heart is originally impressed;
which is not written on it by precept, but engraven by destiny;
not instilled by education, but infused at our nativity.   He that
lives according to nature will suffer nothing from the delusions of
hope, or importunities of desire: he will receive and reject with

equability of temper; and act or suffer as the reason of things shall
alternately prescribe. Other men may amuse themselves with
subtle definitions, or intricate ratiocination. Let them learn to
be wise by easier means: let them observe the hind of the forest,
and the linnet of the grove: let them consider the life of animals,
whose motions are regulated by instinct; they obey their guide
and are happy. Let us therefore, at length, cease to dispute, and
learn to live; throw away the encumbrance of precepts, which they
who utter them with so much pride and pomp do not understand,
and carry with us this simple and intelligible maxim, That deviation
from nature is deviation from happiness.'

When he had spoken, he looked round him with a placid air,
and enjoyed the consciousness of his own beneficence. 'Sir', said
the prince, with great modesty, 'as I, like all the rest of mankind,
am desirous of felicity, my closest attention has been fixed upon
your discourse: I doubt not the truth of a position which a man so
learned has so confidently advanced. Let me only know what it is
to live according to nature.'

'When I find young men so humble and so docile', said the
philosopher, 'I can deny them no information which my studies
have enabled me to afford. To live according to nature, is to act
always with due regard to the fitness arising from the relations
and qualities of causes and effects; to concur with the great and
unchangeable scheme of universal felicity; to co-operate with the
general disposition and tendency of the present system of things.'

The prince soon found that this was one of the sages whom he
should understand less as he heard him longer. He therefore
bowed and was silent, and the philosopher, supposing him satisfied,
and the rest vanquished, rose up and departed with the air of a
man that had co-operated with the present system.

SAMUEL JOHNSON, *Rasselas.*

The renewal, or perhaps the improvement, of my English life
was embittered by the alteration of my own feelings. At the age
of twenty-one I was, in my proper station of a youth, delivered from
the yoke of education, and delighted with the comparative state
of liberty and affluence. My filial obedience was natural and easy;
and in the gay prospect of futurity, my ambition did not extend
beyond the enjoyment of my books, my leisure, and my patrimonial
estate, undisturbed by the cares of a family and the duties of a
profession. But in the militia I was armed with power; in my
travels, I was exempt from control; and as I approached, as I
gradually passed my thirtieth year, I began to feel the desire of
being master in my own house. The most gentle authority will
sometimes frown without reason, the most cheerful submission
will sometimes murmur without cause; and such is the law of our
imperfect nature, that we must either command or obey; that our

personal liberty is supported by the obsequiousness of our own
dependants. While so many of my acquaintance were married or
in parliament, or advancing with a rapid step in the various roads
of honour and fortune, I stood alone, immovable and insignificant;
for after the monthly meeting of 1770, I had even withdrawn myself
from the militia, by the resignation of an empty and barren com-
mission. My temper is not susceptible of envy, and the view of
successful merit has always excited my warmest applause. The
miseries of a vacant life were never known to a man whose hours
were insufficient for the inexhaustible pleasures of study. But I
lamented that at the proper age I had not embraced the lucrative
pursuits of the law or of trade, the chances of civil office or India
adventure, or even the fat slumbers of the church; and my repent-
ance became more lively as the loss of time was more irretrievable.
Experience showed me the use of grafting my private consequence
on the importance of a great professional body; the benefits of those
firm connexions which are cemented by hope and interest, by
gratitude and emulation, by the mutual exchange of services and
favours. From the emoluments of a profession I might have derived
an ample fortune, or a competent income, instead of being stinted
to the same narrow allowance, to be increased only by an event
which I sincerely deprecated. The progress and the knowledge
of our domestic disorders aggravated my anxiety, and I began to
apprehend that I might be left in my old age without the fruits
either of industry or inheritance.

EDWARD GIBBON, *Memoirs of my Life and Writings.*

If any man had a right to look down upon the lower accom-
plishments as beneath his attention, it was certainly Michel Angelo:
nor can it be thought strange, that such a mind should have
slighted or have been withheld from paying due attention to all
those graces and embellishments of art, which have diffused such
lustre over the works of other painters.

It must be acknowledged, however, that together with these,
which we wish he had more attended to, he has rejected all the
false, though specious ornaments, which disgrace the works of
even the most esteemed artists; and, I will venture to say, that
when those higher excellencies are more known and cultivated by
the artists and patrons of arts, his fame and credit will increase
with our increasing knowledge. His name will then be held in
the same veneration as it was in the enlightened age of Leo the
Tenth; and it is remarkable that the reputation of this truly great
man has been continually declining as the art itself has declined.
For I must remark to you, that it has long been much on the decline,
and that our only hope of its revival will consist in your being
thoroughly sensible of its deprivation and decay. It is to Michel
Angelo that we owe even the existence of Raffaelle; it is to him

Raffaelle owes the grandeur of his style. He was taught by him
to elevate his thoughts, and to conceive his subjects with dignity.
His genius, however, formed to blaze and to shine, might, like
fire in combustible matter, for ever have lain dormant, if it had
not caught a spark by its contact with Michel Angelo; and though
it never burst out with *his* extraordinary heat and vehemence,
yet it must be acknowledged to be a more pure, regular, and chaste
flame. Though our judgment must, upon the whole, decide in
favour of Raffaelle, yet he never takes such a firm hold and entire
possession of the mind as to make us desire nothing else, and to
feel nothing wanting. The effect of the capital works of Michel
Angelo perfectly corresponds to what Bouchardon said he felt from
reading Homer; his whole frame appeared to himself to be enlarged,
and all nature which surrounded him, diminished to atoms.

Sir Joshua Reynolds, The Fifth Discourse.

If an Age of Religion has thus everywhere, as I venture to
surmise, been preceded by an Age of Magic, it is natural that we
should enquire what causes have led mankind, or rather a portion
of them, to abandon magic as a principle of faith and practice
and to betake themselves to religion instead. When we reflect
upon the multitude, the variety, and the complexity of facts to be
explained, and the scantiness of our information regarding them,
we shall be ready to acknowledge that a full and satisfactory
solution of so profound a problem is hardly to be hoped for, and
that the most we can do in the present state of our knowledge is to
hazard a more or less plausible conjecture. With all due diffidence,
then, I would suggest that a tardy recognition of the inherent
falsehood and barrenness of magic set the more thoughtful part of
mankind to cast about for a truer theory of nature and a more
fruitful method of turning her resources to account. The shrewder
intelligences must in time have come to perceive that magical
ceremonies and incantations did not really effect the results which
they were designed to produce, and which the majority of their
simpler fellows still believed that they did actually produce. This
great discovery of the inefficacy of magic must have wrought a
radical though probably slow revolution in the minds of those
who had the sagacity to make it. The discovery amounted to this,
that men for the first time recognised their inability to manipulate
at pleasure certain natural forces which hitherto they had believed
to be completely within their control. It was a confession of human
ignorance and weakness. Man saw that he had taken for causes
what were no causes, and that all his efforts to work by means of
these imaginary causes had been vain. His painful toil had been
wasted, his curious ingenuity had been squandered to no purpose.
He had been pulling at strings to which nothing was attached;
he had been marching, as he thought, straight to the goal, while

in reality he had only been treading in a narrow circle. Not
that the effects which he had striven so hard to produce did not
continue to manifest themselves. They were still produced, but
not by him. The rain still fell on the thirsty ground: the sun still
pursued his daily, and the moon her nightly journey across the
sky: the silent procession of the seasons still moved in light and
shadow, in cloud and sunshine across the earth: men were still
born to labour and sorrow, and still, after a brief sojourn here, were
gathered to their fathers in the long home hereafter. All things
indeed went on as before, yet all seemed different to him from
whose eyes the old scales had fallen. For he could no longer cherish
the pleasing illusion that it was he who guided the earth and the
heaven in their courses, and that they would cease to perform their
great evolutions were he to take his feeble hand from the wheel.
In the death of his enemies and his friends he no longer saw a
proof of the resistless potency of his own or of hostile enchantments;
he now knew that friends and foes alike had succumbed to a force
stronger than any that he could wield, and in obedience to a destiny
which he was powerless to control.

SIR JAMES G. FRAZER, *The Golden Bough*, pp. 56–7,
Abridged Edition.[1]

It is impossible, in the course of these short extracts, to feel
the full flow of a traditional style. As we read an author, say
Dryden or Addison or Gibbon, a distinct knowledge of the
pattern of his style is formed in our mind. Between such
authors as I have quoted one can easily perceive a similarity
of pattern. It is not only a similarity, but also a development.
At each change of author the pattern, though formed of the
same elements, is given a slight turn, which we may ascribe
to the author's personality. But the author is conscious all
the time of a certain objective mould into which he is content
to fit as much of his expression as the mould will take. Here
and there a phrase slips over, such as 'yet admits not a too
curious election of words',—which is purely Dryden's, or 'to
unbend their minds, and compare their opinions', 'the
consciousness of his own beneficence', 'the air of a man that
had co-operated with the present system', which are purely
Johnson's. But these, and other phrases which could be
quoted from these authors, are phrases only. Tradition is
concerned more with the tone and temper of expression, and

[1] Macmillan.

so with the period rather than the phrase, with the paragraph rather than the period, and with the general *manner* of the whole rather than the conduct of the parts. It is embodied in a sense of personal decency rather than in a code of rhetoric; it is an ideal of character rather than a system of rules. But it is character which expresses itself consciously, as is implied in the word 'ideal'. It is not the 'humour' of Jonson, nor the 'charm' and 'personality' of the writers we have discussed in Chapter XII. It is, that is to say, a positive style, and when Francis Jeffrey criticized Swift it was from the point of view of this positiveness:

> Of his style, it has been usual to speak with great, and, we think, exaggerated praise. It is less mellow than Dryden's, less elegant than Pope's or Addison's, less noble than Lord Bolingbroke's, and utterly without the glow and loftiness which belonged to our earlier masters. It is radically a low and homely style, without grace and without affectation, and chiefly remarkable for a great choice and profusion of common words and expressions.

That is not altogether just to regard Swift's style from this point of view I have remarked in my Introduction, in relation to the hypothesis of Pure Prose (see p. xii). But Jeffrey, himself a follower of the tradition he is praising, is justified if we allow the force of that tradition. And its force is the force that comes of all disciplines, all dogma and all co-ordinate aims. Nothing, in the end, is so wearisome as idiosyncrasy and waywardness; the universal alone is stable, and a universal style is an impersonal style. Certain writers, like Swift, may get away with a technique of 'thinking aloud', but the quality of their mind assures the dignity of their style. Less talented writers will, like Gibbon or like Stevenson, set themselves a standard and sedulously ape it. Such dependence has serious defects. It leads to a mechanical structure, to timidity of phrasing (a timidity not inconsistent with an occasional kick over the traces) and rigidity of rhythm. It is apt to sacrifice fluidity to formality. It is obvious that a tradition which can control personality in the interests of uniformity can also mark the absence of personality by wearing the outer garments of such an uniformity. Given an easy command of words, it is not difficult to build them into a shoddy structure which in appearance at least is indistinguishable from real architecture. Nothing, in any art, is so easy to fake as the grand manner. Coleridge perceived this:

After the Revolution, the spirit of the nation became much more commercial than it had been before; a learned body, or clerisy, as such, gradually disappeared, and literature in general began to be addressed to the common miscellaneous public. That public had become accustomed to, and required, a strong stimulus; and to meet the requisitions of the public taste, a style was produced which by combining triteness of thought with singularity and excess of manner of expression, was calculated at once to soothe ignorance and to flatter vanity. The thought was carefully kept down to the immediate apprehension of the commonest understanding, and the dress was as anxiously arranged for the purpose of making the thought appear something very profound. The essence of this style consisted in a mock antithesis, that is, an opposition of mere sounds, in a rage for personification, the abstract made animate, far-fetched metaphors, strange phrases, metrical scraps, in every thing, in short, but genuine prose.

Lecture XIV.

The tradition we have described, that beginning with Dryden and still prevalent to-day, is only one tradition Other traditions are possible, though perhaps only by evolution. Here again the analogy of manners in society would seem to hold good. There is, after all, a difference of tone between Dryden and Sir Joshua Reynolds, but it is difficult to know how much of this difference should be ascribed to a difference in personality. Not everything, for merely a change in the face value (or 'purchasing power') of words is enough to effect a difference in tone, and therefore in tradition. But discounting these temporal changes we must still hazard this axiom: that in matters of style tradition is a good instrument but a bad machine. It is a discipline that needs to be informed by the originating forces of mental energy, clear vision, and fine sensibility.

APPENDIX

THE FOLLOWING ADDITIONAL passages of English prose have been selected for comparison and analysis.

1. THE GOLDEN LEGEND.

2. JOSEPH CONRAD
These two passages should be compared for their use of epithets—spareness in No. 1, superfluity in No. 2. Contrast the speed on the narrated action. Try re-writing No. 2, omitting as many epithets as possible.

3. HERMAN MELVILLE
For the analysis of use of epithets, present participles, and rhythm. Relation of paragraphing to the development of the action.

4. IZAAK WALTON

5. JOHN RUSKIN
Two passages for contrast in rhythm and the relation of rhythm to the structure of the paragraph. A metrical analysis of each passage may be made, and a comparison made of the specific metres employed by each writer.

6. WILLIAM FAULKNER
An extended example of the impressionistic style. Contrast its rhythmical structure with Nos. 4 and 5. Try re-writing with normal syntax and punctuation, and estimate the loss of impressionistic effect.

7. T. E. LAWRENCE
Analyse for all the common faults of pretentious writing, above all for literary clichés.

8. ELIZABETH BOWEN
A further example of the impressionistic style. Analyse for consistency of imagery and tone.

9. SACHEVERELL SITWELL
An example of 'the pathetic fallacy'—animation of the inanimate. Try to re-write in 'inanimate' prose and estimate the gain or loss of effect.

10. GEOFFREY GRIGSON
The quality of vividness due to 'the microscopic eye'.

1. THE GOLDEN LEGEND. From *The Life of St. Thomas of Canterbury*. Englished by William Caxton, 1483.

Then one of the knights smote him as he kneeled before the altar on the head. And one Sir Edward Grim, that was his crossier, put forth his arm with the cross to bear off the stroke, and the stroke smote the cross asunder and his arm almost off, wherefore he fled for fear, and so did all the monks, that were that time at compline. And then smote each at him, that they smote off a great piece of the skull of his head, that his brain fell on the pavement. And so they slew and martyred him, and were so cruel that one of them brake the point of his sword against the pavement. And thus this holy and blessed Archbishop S. Thomas suffered death in his own church for the right of all holy church. And when he was dead they stirred his brain, and after went into his chamber and took away his goods, and his horse out of his stable, and took away his bulls and his writings, and delivered them to Sir Robert Broke to bear into France to the king. And as they searched his chamber they found in his chest two shirts of hair made full of great knots, and then they said: Certainly he was a good man; and coming down into the churchyard they began to dread and fear that the ground would not have borne them, and were marvellously aghast, but they supposed that the earth would have swallowed them all quick. And then they knew that they had done amiss. And anon it was known all about how that he was martyred, and anon after they took his holy body, and unclothed him, and found bishop's clothing above, and the habit of a monk under. And next his flesh he wore hard hair, full of knots, which was his shirt. And his breech was of the same, and the knots sticked fast within the skin, and all his body full of worms; he suffered great pain.

2. JOSEPH CONRAD. From *An Outcast of the Islands*.[1]

From time to time he felt on his face the passing, warm touch of an immense breath coming from beyond the forest, like the short panting of an oppressed world. Then the heavy air round him, the air full of heat, odorous and sickly, was pierced by a sharp gust of wind, bringing with it the fresh, damp feel of the falling rain; and all the innumerable tree-tops of the forests before his eyes, swayed to the left and sprang back again in a tumultuous balancing of nodding branches and shuddering leaves. A light frown ran over the river, the clouds stirred slowly, changing their aspect but not their place, as if they had turned ponderously over; and when the sudden movement had died out in a quickened tremor of the slenderest twigs, there was a short period of formidable immobility above and below, during which the voice of the thunder was heard, speaking in a sustained, emphatic and vibrating roll,

[1] J. M. Dent and Sons, Ltd.

with violent louder bursts of crashing sound, like a wrathful and threatening discourse of an angry god. For a moment it died out, and then another gust of wind passed, driving before it a white mist which filled the space with a cloud of water-dust that hid suddenly from Willems the canoe, the forests, the river itself; that woke him up from his numbness in a forlorn shiver; that made him look round despairingly to see nothing but the whirling drift of rain spray before the freshening breeze, while through it the heavy big drops fell about him with sonorous and rapid beats upon the dry earth. He made a few hurried steps up the courtyard and was arrested by an immense sheet of water that fell all at once on him, fell sudden and overwhelming from the clouds, cutting his respiration, streaming over his head, clinging to him, running down his body, off his arms, off his legs. He stood gasping while the water beat him in a vertical downpour, drove on him slanting in squalls, and he felt the drops striking him from above, from everywhere; drops thick, pressed and dashing at him as if flung from all sides by a mob of infuriated hands. From under his feet a great vapour of broken water floated up, and he felt the ground become soft—melt under him—and saw the water spring out from the dry earth to meet the water that fell from the sombre heaven. An insane dread took possession of him, the dread of all that water around him, of the water that pressed him on every side, of the slanting water that drove across his face in wavering sheets which gleamed pale red with the flicker of lightning streaming through them, as if fire and water were falling together, monstrously mixed, upon the stunned earth; were falling continuous and mingled in a piercing hiss—a hiss, loud, prolonged, persistent and indestructible—that vanished in every burst of crashing and tearing noise amongst the invisible clouds: only to return and fill the waste of falling water with the sound of its distinct and passionless whisper.

He wanted to run away, but when he moved it was to slide about painfully and slowly upon that earth which had become mud so suddenly under his feet. He fought his way up the court-yard like a man pushing through a crowd, his head down, one shoulder forward, stopping often, and sometimes carried back a pace or two in the rush of water which his heart was not stout enough to face. Aissa followed him step by step, stopping when he stopped, recoiling with him, moving forward with him in his toilsome way up the slippery declivity of the courtyard, of that courtyard, from which everything seemed to have been swept away by the first rush of the mighty downpour. They could see nothing. The tree, the bushes, the house, and the fences—all had disappeared in the thickness of the falling rain; and they seemed to progress into an infinite space full only of deafening sound, of blinding fire, and of water falling vertical and heavy. Their hair stuck, streaming, to their heads; their clothing clung to them, beaten close to their bodies; water ran off them, off their heads over their shoulders, as they moved, patient, upright, slow and dark, in the gleam clear or fiery of the falling drops, under the roll of unceasing thunder which they seemed not to hear. And they appeared like two wandering ghosts of the drowned that, condemned to haunt the water for ever, had come up from the river to look at the world under a deluge.

On the left the tree seemed to step out to meet them, appearing vaguely, high, motionless and patient; with a rustling plaint of its innumerable leaves through which every drop of water tore its separate way with cruel haste. And then, to the right, the house surged up in the mist, very black, and clamorous with the patter of rain on its high-pitched roof—the quick, loud patter that rang sharp and distracting above the steady plash of the water running off the eaves. Down the plankway leading to the door flowed a thin and pellucid stream, and when Willems began his ascent it broke over his foot as if he were going up a steep ravine in the bed of a rapid and shallow torrent. Behind his heels two streaming smudges of mud stained for an instant the purity of the rushing water, and then he splashed his way up with a spurt and stood on the bamboo platform before the open door under the shelter of the overhanging eaves—under shelter at last!

3. HERMAN MELVILLE. From *Billy Budd, Foretopman.*

Now when the foretopman found himself closeted, as it were, in the cabin with the Captain and Claggart, he was surprised enough. But it was a surprise unaccompanied by apprehension or distrust. To an immature nature, essentially honest and humane, forewarning intimations of subtler danger from one's kind came tardily, if at all. The only thing that took shape in the young sailor's mind was this: 'Yes, the Captain, I have always thought, looks kindly upon me. I wonder if he's going to make me his coxswain. I should like that. And maybe now he is going to ask the Master-at-arms about me.'

'Shut the door there, sentry,' said the commander. 'Stand without and let nobody come in.—Now, Master-at-arms, tell this man to his face what you told of him to me;' and stood prepared to scrutinize the mutually confronting visages.

With the measured step and calm collected air of an asylum physician approaching in the public hall some patient beginning to show indications of a coming paroxysm, Claggart deliberately advanced within short range of Billy, and mesmerically looking him in the eye, briefly recapitulated the accusation.

Not at first did Billy take it in. When he did the rose-tan of his cheek looked struck as by white leprosy. He stood like one impaled and gagged. Meanwhile the accuser's eyes, removing not as yet from the blue, dilated ones, underwent a phenomenal change, their wonted rich violet colour blurring into a muddy purple.

Those lights of human intelligence losing human expression, gelidly protruding like the alien eyes of certain uncatalogued creatures of the deep.

The first mesmeric glance was one of surprised fascination; the last was the hungry lurch of the torpedo-fish.

'Speak, man!' said Captain Vere to the transfixed one, struck by his aspect even more than by Claggart's, 'Speak! defend yourself.' Which appeal caused by a strange, dumb gesturing and gurgling in Billy; amazement at such an accusation so suddenly sprung on inexperienced nonage; this, and it may be horror at the accuser, serving to bring out his lurking defect, and in this instance for the time intensifying it into a convulsed tongue-tie; while the intent head and entire form straining forward in an agony of ineffectual eagerness to obey the injunction to speak and defend himself, gave an expression to the fact like that of a condemned vestal priestess in the moment of her being buried alive, and in the first struggle against suffocation.

Though at the time Captain Vere was quite ignorant of Billy's liability to vocal impediment, he now immediately divined it, since vividly Billy's aspect recalled to him that of a bright young schoolmate of his whom he had seen struck by much the same startling impotence in the act of eagerly rising in the class to be foremost in response to a testing question put to it by the master. Going close up to the young sailor, and laying a soothing hand on his shoulder, he said. 'There is no hurry, my boy. Take your time, take your time.' Contrary to the effect intended, these words, so fatherly in tone, doubtless touching Billy's heart to the quick, prompted yet more violent efforts at utterance—efforts soon ending for the time in confirming the paralysis, and bringing to the face an expression which was as a crucifixion to behold. The next instant, quick as the flame from a discharged cannon at night his right arm shot out and Claggart dropped to the deck. Whether intentionally, or but owing to the young athlete's superior height, the blow had taken effect full upon the forehead, so shapely and intellectual-looking a feature in the Master-at-arms; so that the body fell over lengthwise, like a heavy plank tilted from erectness. A gasp or two and he lay motionless.

'Fated boy,' breathed Captain Vere in a tone so low as to be almost a whisper, 'what have you done! But here, help me.'

The twain raised the felled one from the loins up into a sitting position. The spare form flexibly acquiesced, but inertly. It was like handling a dead snake. They lowered it back. Regaining erectness, Captain Vere with one hand covering his face stood to all appearance as impassive as to the object at his feet. Was he absorbed in taking in all the bearings of the event, and what was best not only now at once to be done, but also in the sequel? Slowly he uncovered his face; forthwith the effect was as if the moon, emerging from eclipse, should reappear with quite another aspect than that which had gone into hiding. The father in him, manifested towards Billy thus far in the scene, was replaced by the military disciplinarian. In his official tone he bade the foretopman retire to a state-room aft, (pointing it out), and there remain till thence summoned. This order Billy in silence mechanically obeyed. Then, going to the cabin door where it opened on the quarter-deck, Captain Vere said to the sentry without, 'Tell somebody to send Albert here.' When the lad appeared his master so contrived it that he should not catch sight of the prone one. 'Albert,' he said to him, 'tell the surgeon I wish to see him. You need not come back till called.'

When the surgeon entered—a self-poised character of that grave sense and experience that hardly anything could take him aback—Captain Vere advanced to meet him, thus unconsciously interrupting his view of Claggart and interrupting the other's wonted ceremonious salutation, said, 'Nay, tell me how it is with yonder man,' directing his attention to the prostrate one.

The surgeon looked, and for all his self-command, somewhat started at the abrupt revelation. On Claggart's always pallid complexion, thick black blood was now oozing from mouth and ear. To the gazer's professional eyes it was unmistakably no living man that he saw.

4. IZAAK WALTON. From the *Life of Dr. John Donne*.

Thus variable, thus virtuous was the life; thus excellent, thus exemplary was the death of this memorable man.

He was buried in that place of St. Paul's Church which he had appointed for that use some years before his death and by which he passed daily to pay his public devotions to Almighty God (who was then served twice a day by a public form of prayer and praises in that place). But he was not buried privately, though he desired it; for, beside an unnumbered number of others, many persons of nobility and of eminency for learning, who did love and honor him in his life, did show it at his death by a voluntary and sad attendance of his body to the grave, where nothing was so remarkable as a public sorrow.

To which place of his burial some mournful friend repaired, and as Alexander the Great did to the grave of the famous Achilles, so they strewed his with an abundance of curious and costly flowers, which course they (who were never yet known) continued morning and evening for many days, not ceasing till the stones that were taken up in that church to give his body admission into the cold earth (now his bed of rest) were again by the mason's art so levelled and firmed as they had been formerly and his place of burial undistinguishable to common view.

The next day after his burial some unknown friend, some one of the many lovers and admirers of his virtue and learning, writ this epitaph with a coal on the wall, over his grave.

Reader! I am to let thee know,
Donne's body only lies below;
For, could the grave his soul comprise,
Earth would be richer than the skies.

Nor was this all the honor done to his reverend ashes; for as there be some persons that will not receive a reward for that for which God accounts himself a debtor, persons that dare trust God with their charity, and without a witness, so there was by some grateful unknown friend, that thought Dr. Donne's memory ought to be perpetuated, an hundred marks sent to his two faithful friends and executors towards the making of his monument. It was not for many years known by whom; but after the death of Dr. Fox, it was known that 'twas he that sent it; and he lived to see as lively a representation of his dead friend as marble can express, a statue indeed so like Dr. Donne that, as his friend, Sir Henry Wotton, hath expressed himself, it seems to breathe faintly; and posterity shall look upon it as a kind of artificial miracle.

He was of stature moderately tall, of a straight and equally-proportioned body, to which all his words and actions gave an inexpressible addition of comeliness.

The melancholy and pleasant humor were in him so contempered that each gave advantage to the other and made his company one of the delights of mankind.

His fancy was inimitably high, equalled only by his great wit; both being made useful by a commanding judgment.

His aspect was cheerful and such as gave a silent testimony of a clear-knowing soul and of a conscience at peace with itself.

His melting eye showed that he had a soft heart, full of noble compassion, of too brave a soul to offer injuries and too much a Christian not to pardon them in others.

He did much contemplate—especially after he entered into his sacred calling—the mercies of Almighty God, the immortality of the soul, and the joys of heaven, and would often say, in a kind of sacred ecstasy, 'Blessed be God that he is God only and divinely like himself.'

He was by nature highly passionate but more apt to reluct at the excesses of it. A great lover of the offices of humanity and of so merciful a spirit that he never beheld the miseries of mankind without pity and relief.

He was earnest and unwearied in the search of knowledge; with which his vigorous soul is now satisfied and employed in a continual praise of that God that first breathed it into his active body, that body which once was a temple of the Holy Ghost and is now become a small quantity of Christian dust.

But I shall see it reanimated.

5. JOHN RUSKIN. From *Modern Painters*.

Not long ago, I was slowly descending this very bit of carriage-road, the first turn after you leave Albano, not a little impeded by the worthy successors of the ancient prototypes of Veiento. It had been wild weather when I left Rome, and all across the Campagna the clouds were sweeping in sulphurous blue, with a clap of thunder or two, and breaking gleams of sun along the Claudian aqueduct lighting up the infinity of its arches like the bridge of chaos. But as I climbed the long slope of the Alban Mount, the storm swept finally to the north, and the noble outline of the domes of Albano, and graceful darkness of its ilex grove, rose against pure streaks of alternate blue and amber; the upper sky gradually flushing through the last fragments of rain-cloud in deep palpitating azure, half aether and half dew. The noonday sun came slanting down the rocky slopes of La Riccia, and their masses of entangled and tall foliage, whose autumnal tints were mixed with the wet verdure of a thousand evergreens, were penetrated with it as with rain. I cannot call it colour, it was conflagration. Purple, and crimson, and scarlet, like the curtains of God's tabernacle, the rejoicing trees sank into the valley in showers of light, every separate leaf quivering with buoyant and burning life; each, as it turned to reflect or to transmit the sunbeam, first a torch and then an emerald. Far up into the recesses of the valley, the green vistas arched like the hollows of mighty waves of some crystalline sea, with the arbutus flowers dashed along their flanks for foam, and silver flakes of orange spray tossed into the air around them, breaking over the grey walls of rock into a thousand separate stars, fading and kindling alternately as the weak wind lifted and let them fall. Every blade of grass burned like the golden floor of heaven, opening in sudden gleams as the foliage broke and closed above it, as sheet-lightning opens in a cloud at sunset: the motionless masses of dark rock—dark though flushed with scarlet lichen, casting their quiet shadows across its restless radiance, the fountain underneath them filling its marble hollow with blue mist and fitful sound; and over all, the multitudinous bars of amber and rose, the sacred clouds that have no darkness, and only exist to illumine, were seen in fathomless intervals between the solemn and orbed repose of the stone pines, passing to lose themselves in the last, white, blinding lustre of the measureless line where the Campagna melted into the blaze of the sea.

6. WILLIAM FAULKNER. From *Intruder in the Dust*.[1]

. . . Because he was free: in bed: in the cool familiar room in the cool familiar dark because he knew what he was going to do and he had forgotten after all to tell Aleck Sander to give Highboy the extra feed against tomorrow but in the morning would do just as well because he was going to sleep tonight because he had

1 Random House.

something about ten thousand times quicker than just sheep to count; in fact he was going to go to sleep so fast he probably wouldn't have time to count more than about ten of them: with rage, an almost unbearable excruciation of outrage and fury: any white man to shoot in the back but this one of all white men at all: youngest of a family of six brothers one of whom had already served a year in federal penitentiary for armed resistance as an army deserter and another term at the state penal farm for making whiskey, and a ramification of cousins and inlaws covering a whole corner of the county and whose total number probably even the old grandmothers and maiden aunts couldn't have stated offhand—a connection of brawlers and farmers and foxhunters and stock- and timber-traders who would not even be the last anywhere to let one of its number be killed by·anyone but only among the last since it in its turn was integrated and interlocked and intermarried with other brawlers and foxhunters and whiskey-makers not even into a simple clan or tribe but a race a species which before now had made their hill stronghold good against the county and federal government too, which did not even simply inhabit nor had merely corrupted but had translated and transmogrified that whole region of lonely pine hills dotted meagrely with small tilted farms and peripatetic sawmills and contraband whiskey-kettles where peace officers from town didn't even go unless they were sent for and strange white men didn't wander far from the highway after dark and no Negro at any time—where as a local wit said once the only stranger ever to enter with impunity was God and He only by daylight and on Sunday—into a synonym for independence and violence: an idea with physical boundaries like a quarantine for plague so that solitary unique and alone out of all the county it was known to the rest of the county by the number of its survey co-ordinate—Beat Four—as in the middle twenties people knew where Cicero Illinois was and who lived there and what they did who neither knew nor cared what state Chicago was in: and since this was not enough choosing the one moment when the one man white or black—Edmonds—out of all Yoknapatawpha County or Mississippi or America or the world too for that matter who would have had any inclination let alone power and ability (and here he had to laugh even though he was just about to go to sleep, remembering how he had even thought at first that if Edmonds had been at home it would have made any difference anywhere, remembering the face the angle of the hat the figure straddled baronial as a duke or a squire or a congressman before the fire hands clasped behind it and not even looking down at them but just commanding two nigger boys to pick up the coins and give them back to him, not even needing to remember his uncle reminding him ever since he had got big enough to understand the words that no man could come between another man and his destiny because even his uncle for all Harvard and Heidelberg

couldn't have pointed out the man with enough temerity and
delusion just to come between Lucas and merely what he wanted
to do) to try to stand between Lucas and the violent fate he had
courted was lying flat on his back in a New Orleans operating
room: yet that was what Lucas had had to pick, that time that
victim and that place: another Saturday afternoon and the same
store where he had already had trouble with a white man at least
once before: chose the first suitable convenient Saturday afternoon
and with an old single action Colt pistol of a calibre and type not
even made anymore which was exactly the sort of pistol Lucas
would own exactly as no other still alive man in the county owned
a gold toothpick lay in wait at the store—the one sure place where
sooner or later on Saturday afternoon that whole end of the county
would pass—until the victim appeared and shot him and nobody
knew why yet and as far as he had discovered that afternoon or
even when he finally left the square that night nobody had even
wondered yet since why didn't matter least of all to Lucas since
he had apparently he had been working for twenty or twentyfive
years with indefatigable and unflagging concentration toward this
one crowning moment; followed him into the woods about one
good spit from the store and shot him in the back within hearing
distance of the crowd around it and was still standing over the
body the fired pistol put neatly away into his hip pocket again when
the first ones reached the scene where he would without doubt
have been lynched immediately out of hand except for the same
Doyle Fraser who had saved him from the singletree seven years
ago and old Skipworth, the constable—a little driedup wizened
stonedeaf old man not much larger than a half-grown boy with a
big nickel-plated pistol loose in one coat pocket and in the other a
guttapercha eartrumpet on a rawhide thong around his neck like
a foxhorn, who on this occasion anyway revealed an almost
gratuitous hardihood and courage, getting Lucas (who made no
resistance whatever, merely watching this too with that same calm
detached not even scornful interest) out of the crowd and took
him to his home and chained him to the bedpost until the sheriff
could come and get him and bring him in to town and keep him
while the Gowries and Workitts and Ingrums and the rest of their
guests and connections could get Vinson buried and Sunday passed
and so be fresh and untrammelled for the new week and its duties
and believe it or not even the night passed, the tentative roosters
at false dawn then the interval then the loud fairy clangor of the
birds and through the east window he could see the trees against
gray light and then the sun itself high and furious above the trees
glaring at him and it was already late, this of course must happen
to him too: but then he was free and he would feel better after breakfast and he could always say he was going to Sunday school but then
he wouldn't have to say anything by going out the back, strolling:
across the back yard and into the lot and across it and through the

woods to the railroad to the depot and then back to the Square then he thought of a simpler way than that and then quit thinking about it at all, through the front hall and across the front gallery and down the walk to the street and it was here he would remember later having first noticed that he had seen no Negro except Paralee when she brought his breakfast; by ordinary at this hour on Sunday morning he would have seen on almost every gallery housemaids or cooks in their fresh Sunday aprons with brooms or perhaps talking from gallery to gallery across the contiguous yardspaces and the children too fresh and scrubbed for Sunday school with clutched palmsweaty nickels though perhaps it was a little too early for that or perhaps by mutual consent or even interdiction there would be no Sunday school today, only church and so at some mutual concorded moment say about halfpast eleven all the air over Yoknapatawpha County would reverberate soundlessly like heatshimmer with one concerted adjuration calm the hearts of these bereaved and angry men vengeance is mine saith the lord thou shalt not kill except that this was a little late too, they should have mentioned this to Lucas yesterday, past the jail the barred second storey window whose interstices on an ordinary Sunday would have been thick with dark hands and beyond them even a glint now and then of eyewhites in the shadows and the mellow voices calling and laughing down to the Negro girls and women passing or stopping along the street and this was when he realised that except for Paralee he had seen no Negro since yesterday afternoon though it would be tomorrow before he would learn that the ones who lived in the Hollow and Freedmantown hadn't come to work at all since Saturday night: nor on the Square either, not even in the barbershop where Sunday morning was the bootblack's best day shining shoes and brushing clothes and running errands and drawing baths for the bachelor truckdrivers and garage hands who lived in rented rooms and the young men and the ones not so young who worked hard all week in the poolhall and the sheriff really had finally got back to town and had even torn himself away from his Sunday to go for Lucas: listening: hearing the talk: a dozen of them who had hurried out to Fraser's store yesterday afternoon and returned empty-handed (and he gathered one car full had even gone back last night, yawning and lounging now and complaining of lack of sleep: and that to be added to Lucas' account too) and he had heard all this before too and had even thought of it himself before that;

7. T. E. LAWRENCE. From *Seven Pillars of Wisdom*.[1]

Some of the evil of my tale may have been inherent in our circumstances. For years we lived anyhow with one another in the naked desert, under the indifferent heaven. By day the hot

[1] Doubleday.

sun fermented us; and we were dizzied by the beating wind. At night we were stained by dew, and shamed into pettiness by the innumerable silences of stars. We were a self-centred army without parade or gesture, devoted to freedom, the second of man's creeds, a purpose so ravenous that it devoured all our strength, a hope so transcendent that our earlier ambitions faded in its glare.

As time went by our need to fight for the ideal increased to an unquestioning possession, riding with spur and rein over our doubts. Willy-nilly it became a faith. We had sold ourselves into its slavery, manacled ourselves together in its chain-gang, bowed ourselves to serve its holiness with all our good and ill content. The mentality of ordinary human slaves is terrible— they have lost the world—and we had surrendered, not body alone, but soul to the overmastering greed of victory. By our own act we were drained of morality, of volition, of responsibility, like dead leaves in the wind.

The everlasting battle stripped from us care of our own lives or of others. We had rope about our necks, and on our heads prices which showed that the enemy intended hideous tortures for us if we were caught. Each day some of us passed; and the living knew themselves just sentient puppets on God's stage: indeed, our taskmaster was merciless, merciless, so long as our bruised feet could stagger forward on the road. The weak envied those tired enough to die; for success looked so remote, and failure a near and certain, if sharp, release from toil. We lived always in the stretch or sag of nerves, either on the crest or in the trough of waves of feeling. This impotency was bitter to us, and made us live only for the seen horizon, reckless what spite we inflicted or endured, since physical sensation showed itself meanly transient. Gusts of cruelty, perversions, lusts ran lightly over the surface without troubling us; for the moral laws which had seemed to hedge about these silly accidents must be yet fainter words. We had learned that there were pangs too sharp, griefs too deep, ecstasies too high for our finite selves to register. When emotion reached this pitch the mind choked; and memory went white till the circumstances were humdrum once more.

Such exaltation of thought, while it let adrift the spirit, and gave it licence in strange airs, lost it the old patient rule over the body. The body was too coarse to feel the utmost of our sorrows and of our joys. Therefore, we abandoned it as rubbish: we left it below us to march forward, a breathing simulacrum, on its own unaided level, subject to influences from which in normal times our instincts would have shrunk. The men were young and sturdy; and hot flesh and blood unconsciously claimed a right in them and tormented their bellies with strange longings. Our privations and dangers fanned this virile heat, in a climate as racking as can be conceived. We had no shut places to be alone in, no thick clothes to hide our nature. Man in all things lived candidly with man.

8. ELIZABETH BOWEN. From *The Heat of the Day*.[1]

That Sunday, from six o'clock in the evening, it was a Viennese orchestra that played. The season was late for an outdoor concert; already leaves were drifting on to the grass stage—here and there one turned over, crepitating as though in the act of dying, and during the music some more fell.

The open-air theatre, shelving below the level of the surrounding lawns, was walled by thickets and a few high trees; along the top ran a wattle fence with gates. Now the two gates stood open. The rows of chairs down the slope, facing the orchestra, still only filled up slowly. From here, from where it was being played at the base of this muffled hollow, the music could not travel far through the park—but hints of it that did escape were disturbing: from the mound, from the rose gardens, from the walks round the lakes, people were being slowly drawn to the theatre by the sensation that they were missing something. Many of them paused in the gateways doubtfully—all they had left behind was in sunshine, while this hollow which was the source of music was found to be also the source of dusk. War had made them idolise day and summer; night and autumn were enemies. And, at the start of the concert, this tarnished bosky theatre, in which no plays had been acted for some time, held a feeling of sequestration, of emptiness the music had not had time to fill. It was not completely in shadow—here and there blades of sunset crossed it, firing branches through which they travelled, and lay along ranks of chairs and faces and hands. Gnats quivered; cigarette smoke dissolved. But the light was so low, so theatrical and so yellow that it was evident it would soon be gone. The incoming tide was evening. Glass-clear darkness, in which each leaf was defined, already formed in the thicket behind the orchestra and was the other element of the stage.

The Sunday had been brilliant, without a stain of cloud. Now, the burning turquoise sky of the afternoon began to gain in transparency as it lost colour: from above the trees round the theatre there stole away not only colour but time. Music—the waltzes, the marches, the gay overtures—now began to command this hourless place. The people lost their look of uncertainty. The heroic marches made them lift up their heads; recollections of opera moulded their faces into unconscious smiles, and during the waltzes women's eyes glittered with delicious tears about nothing. First note by note, drop by drop, then steadily, the music entered senses, nerves and fancies that had been parched. What first was a mirage strengthened into a universe, for the shabby Londoners and the exiled foreigners sitting in this worn glade in the middle of Regent's Park. This Sunday on which the sun set was the first Sunday of September 1942.

[1] Knopf.

Pairs of lovers, fatigued by their day alone with each other, were glad to enter this element not themselves: when their looks once more met, it was with refreshed love. Mothers tired by being mothers forgot their children as their children forgot them—one held her baby as though it had been a doll. Married couples who had sat down in apathetic closeness to one another could be seen to begin to draw a little apart, each recapturing some virginal inner dream. Such elderly people as had not been driven home by the disappearance of sun from the last chair fearlessly exposed their years to the dusk, in a lassitude they could have shown at no other time.

These were the English. As for the foreigners, some were so intimate with the music that you could feel them anticipate every note; some sat with eyes closed; others, as though aroused by some unbearable movement inside the breast, glanced behind them or quickly up at the sky. Incredulity, as when waking up from a deep sleep, appeared once or twice in faces. But in most of them, as they continued to sit and listen, stoicism only intensified.

A proportion of the listeners were solitary; and, of the solitary, those who came every Sunday, by habit, could be told from those who had come this Sunday by chance. Surprise at having stumbled upon the music was written on the faces of the first-timers. For many, chiefly, the concert was the solution of where to be: one felt eased by this place where something was going on. To be sitting packed among other people was better than walking about alone. At the last moment, this crowned the day with meaning. For there had been moments, heightening towards the end, when the Sunday's beauty—for those with no ambition to cherish, no friend to turn to, no love to contemplate—drove its lack of meaning into the heart.

9. SACHEVERELL SITWELL. From *Southern Baroque Art*, Part II, 'Les Indes Galantes'.[1]

The Spanish night is so deep and so pompous as quite to browbeat the noisier light of day. The buildings, which always look clear-cut and newly built, become, against the dark stress of evening, brilliantly crisp and more brittle than glass. A long line of white buildings will tower up to threaten you with its proud, wave-like bulwarks. At every corner, behind the dark trees that are deep, still areas of water, there will rise up another of those strutting waves out of the depth. In its turn it will draw up, holding itself to full height before it launches a leonine assault on your puny presence. Then it will hold itself back from you before the superior strength of the next glittering wave that you meet, as you walk through the brittle moonlight. In this way the slowest

[1] London (Duckworth and Co. Ltd.), 1924.

progress through a town will be running the gauntlet of a whole pack of hungry shadows.

Sometimes the light will be cut off for a moment as a stray cloud stands in front of the moon. This sudden darkness will enhance every effect of shadow and make the light seem more dazzling, still, when it comes back. One might imagine the rays of moonlight like a sharp-pointed sword as they pierce into every dark place and investigate its mysteries. Then, of a sudden, the moonlight dies and the Spanish captain trails his cloak along as if before a tired and dying bull. His arrival gives a new and unexpected turn to the atmosphere of the evening, and the shadows and the white squares of light, that are continually changing into each other's places, become so many pawns capturing each other on a huge chessboard. This is, indeed, a true parallel to the lives of those who are sleeping inside these palaces. It was a continual warfare between the wearers of glittering turbans and the cavaliers who wore helmets with glancing plumes that were a tribute, like steam to a train, of the speed and ferocity of their attack. This warfare lasted through many centuries, until the knights who wore turbans were driven out of their houses, which the richest among them had built in the manner of an artificial honeycomb, and the plumed horsemen were left to offer up their prayers of thanksgiving for victory. This they continued to do before altars on which they expended all the energy they had displayed in battle. There are many of such altars, still now in use, that rise sixty feet from the floor of the church almost to its roof, and are gilded and inlaid up all this height, like a parade breastplate by the most painstaking of armourers.

10. GEOFFREY GRIGSON. From *An English Farmhouse*.[1]

The ruin I have most watched, been most absorbed by, is the ruin of 'Bubbe's Tun', farmhouse and buildings alike; but there the quick pace of ruination was finally quickened by man. When I knew the farmhouse to begin with, some twelve years ago, it had been re-roofed with galvanised iron; and a farm-worker and his family lived there. The galvanised, anyway, was its warrant of execution. Then galvanised iron became scarce, and the farm-worker having left, the sheets were ripped away. First to feel the weather and feel it severely was, as it happened the brick portion added (like the brick portion at Ashton Farm) in the nineteenth century. The bricks were good, the construction was not so good; and whole sections of walling quickly slabbed to the ground. The nineteenth-century elm timbers had neither the bulk nor the durability of the timbers at the chalk end of the house. The panel doors did not last on their hinges like the older batten

[1] London (Max Parrish), 1948. By permission of the publishers and the author.

doors at the other end sturdily hung with band and hook. But pretty soon rain and frost began to devastate and tumble the chalk on to the overgrown flower-beds. The outside walls split and fell, the outer ends of the huge, still hard oak joists crashed with them, bringing the bedroom floors down on a slope. Pushed off, a climbing rose sprawled among the mess. Inside, the division walls were made in two ways in this older portion of the house. Some—presumably the older ones—were wattle-and-daub, once known in these parts as 'freething'; some were brick-nogging— bricks, that is to say, laid herring-bone-wise within timber frames. The daubed wattle-work in this house was not made, by the way, of hazel, the only wood mentioned for this purpose in book after book upon building construction, but of some species or other, so Kew determined for me, of willow—willow with the bark left on, still hard and sound under the plaster after three hundred years or more. Ducks-nest fireplaces of the early nineteenth century hung rustily and coldly in the bedroom walls, one filled with the sticks of a jackdaw's nest. Layers of wallpaper peeled off in the rain; but the bottom-most layer was never of a very old pattern. A few iron bedsteads had been left behind, and some old boots, and a tin chamber-pot. Last to fall—it is still there—will be the enormous, weighty, solid chimney stack. True, it is made of chalk, but its base is protected by the debris of the floors and the walls, and the brick cap and a side shaft of brick give some protection up above. The chalk, never exposed until now, has a naked, unnatural pallor. Grass seed has been taken by the wind to the upper steps of the chimney, but the grass dies and dries away quickly in the summer, though it keeps vivid below on the remains of the bedroom floor and the staircase, where its roots are moistened and away from the sun. Beams have broken off and their stumps jut out from the chalk. In the middle of the house, in the middle of its facade which looks over the plain, the oak panelling of one small room still clings to its wall; and on some of the beams rose-bay willow- herb has found decay enough to root in, and to mature. Perhaps within three or four years—perhaps sooner—the chimney stack will have crashed, and the whole ancient house will have become a mound—a nettle mound, with roses, laurel, balm, and soapwort and periwinkle on its fringes; and still, outliving the house, the two or three yew trees will continue at its south-west corner, between house, as it once was, and the ageing, decaying, blue-tit- frequented apple trees.

I have spoken of the pathos of two tags of telephone wire hanging from the chimney. Also, pathetically, on one of the last bits of chalk walling on the north-east of the house, is a fire-insurance sign, a rayed sun dated 1827, fixed there against a calamity which never happened, a premature death; a precaution curious to contemplate upon a ruinating scrap of a house.

CHRONOLOGICAL LIST OF
THE PRINCIPAL AUTHORS QUOTED

		PAGE
John Wycliffe	1320?–1384	100
Sir John Mandeville	14th century	99
Sir Thomas Malory	d. 1471	102
William Caxton	1422–1491	21, 196
Richard Hooker	1554?–1600	45
Francis Bacon	1561–1626	5
Thomas Dekker	1570?–1641?	168
John Donne	1573–1631	148
Ben Jonson	1573–1637	160
William Drummond	1585–1649	175
Izaak Walton	1593–1683	73, 200
Sir Thomas Browne	1605–1682	60
John Milton	1608–1674	62
Authorised Version of the Bible	1611	101, 138
Jeremy Taylor	1613–1667	6
1st Earl of Shaftesbury	1621–1683	115
John Bunyan	1626–1688	40, 104
John Dryden	1631–1700	186
Thomas Burnet	1635?–1715	19
Thomas Traherne	1636?–1674	149
Roger North	1653–1734	46
Daniel Defoe	1661?–1731	105
Jonathan Swift	1667–1745	24, 44, 169
Bernard de Mandeville	1670–1733	37
Joseph Addison	1672–1719	187
Lord Bolingbroke	1678–1751	44, 167
John ('Chevalier') Taylor	1703–1772	173
Henry Fielding	1707–1754	108
Samuel Johnson	1709–1784	40, 188
Laurence Sterne	1713–1768	57, 163, 167
Sir Joshua Reynolds	1723–1792	190
Oliver Goldsmith	1728–1774	67
Edmund Burke	1729–1797	35, 43
Edward Gibbon	1737–1794	189
William Blake	1757–1827	48
William Wordsworth	1770–1850	42
Samuel Taylor Coleridge	1772–1834	42, 48, 51, 75, 137, 194
Robert Southey	1774–1843	113, 129
Walter Savage Landor	1775–1864	47, 150
Jane Austen	1775–1817	109, 110
William Hazlitt	1778–1830	13, 28, 41, 136

		PAGE
Thomas de Quincey	1785–1859	147
Edward John Trelawny	1792–1881	116
Lord Macaulay	1800–1859	52, 72
George Borrow	1803–1881	118
Ralph Waldo Emerson	1803–1882	50, 72
Nathaniel Hawthorne	1804–1864	112
Emily Brontë	1818–1848	72, 111
Herman Melville	1819–1891	164, 198
John Ruskin	1819–1900	202
Sir Henry Maine	1822–1888	92
George Meredith	1828–1909	165
James Clerk Maxwell	1831–1879	30
William Morris	1834–1896	9
Walter Pater	1839–1894	21, 159
Charles M. Doughty	1843–1926	7, 34, 39, 48
Henry James	1843–1916	72, 73, 77, 177
Sir James G. Frazer	1854–1941	191
Joseph Conrad	1857–1924	196
Karl Pearson	1857–1936	54
Bart Kennedy	1861–1930	34
Sir William Bragg	1862–1942	26
George Santayana	b. 1863	30, 49
Rudyard Kipling	1865–1936	98
H. M. Tomlinson	b. 1874	60
G. K. Chesterton	1874–1936	171
Winston Churchill	b. 1874	171, 172
A. M. Remizov (translated)	b. 1877	132
James Joyce	1882–1941	34, 134
D. H. Lawrence	1885–1930	64, 140
T. E. Lawrence	1888–1935	205
T. S. Eliot	b. 1888	88, 184
Valentine Dobrée	b. 1894	32
Ludwig Wittgenstein		56
Sacheverell Sitwell	b. 1897	208
William Faulkner	b. 1897	155, 202
Elizabeth Bowen	b. 1899	207
Geoffrey Grigson	b. 1905	209

INDEX

Acts and Monuments, 104
actuality, 97
actualization, 31
Addison, Joseph, 67, 187, 192
adequate theme, 175
ad hoc eloquence, 174
Aesop and Rhodopé, 47
affectation, 12
Alice in Wonderland, 132
allegory, 107
alliteration, 7
Altar of the Dead, The, 72
Ancient Law, 91–6
Ancient Mariner, 48
Anglo-Saxon Poetry, 31
Annus Mirabilis, 186
antiquarianism, 9
antithesis, 40, 168
aphorism, 48
apostrophe, 168
Appeal from the New to the Old Whigs, 43
Aquinas, St. Thomas, 75
Arabia Deserta, 7, 34, 39, 47
arbitrariness, 126, 131, 134
Aristotle, xiv, 23, 84, 154 n
arrangement, 66–79
artificiality, 153, 154 n, 168–9
association, 7
Austen, Jane, 109–11
Authorized Version of the Bible, 101–4

background, 89
Bacon, Francis, 5, 67, 186
Bailly, Auguste, 156
balance, 44
Balzac, 78
Barnard, L. G., 16
Beckford, William, 134
Beeching, Canon, 183
beginning, 71
Berkeley, George, xiii
Bible in Spain, The, 117–24
Bible, 50, 102, 103, 107, 112, 138, 186
Billy Budd, Foretopman, 198
Biographia Literaria, 75–6, 126, 137, 181
biography, 113
Blake, William, 48
Bolingbroke, Lord, 40, 44, 167
Book of the Bear, The, 132
Borrow, George, 117–24
Bouchier, E. S., 23
Bowen, Elizabeth, 195, 207–8
Bragg, Sir William, 26–7
Brontë, Charlotte, 112
Brontë, Emily, 72, 111
Brown, S. J., 27
Browne, Sir Thomas, 60, 83, 186
Buber, Martin, 155 n
Bullen, Frank T., 17
Bunyan, John, xiii, 40, 104–5, 186
Burke, Edmund, 13, 37, 41, 43

Burnet, Thomas, 19
Byron, Lord, 52–4

Campbell, George, 50–1
Carlyle, Thomas, 23, 113
catalogue-subject, 43
Caxton, William, 20, 195, 196
Chapman, M. A., 27
character, 182, 193
Chesterton, G. K., 171
Child in the House, The, 21
Churchill, Winston, 172
clarity, 97, 114, 160
'classical', 138
clauses, arrangement of, 39
Cohen, Morris R., 26 n, 87 n
coherence, 76
Coleridge, S. T., 42, 48, 51, 75–6, 126,
    137–9, 181, 184, 194
colon and semicolon, 47
comparison, 25, 32
complexity, 184
conceits, 125
Concise Oxford Dictionary, 139
concreteness, 99, 109, 114, 152, 160
condensation, x
Confessions of an English Opium-Eater, 147
Congreve, William, 16
congruity, 8
conjunctions, 50–1
connectives, 51
Conrad, Joseph, 17 n, 49, 195, 196–8
control, 183
Convention of Cintra, The, 42
copula, 35
corporate sense, 186
Craik, Sir Henry, xiv, 183
Crystal Age, A, 133 n
currency, 8
Cypresse Grove, A, 175–7

decency, 193
declamation, 173
decoration, 143
Defoe, Daniel, xiii, 104–7, 112
Dekker, Thomas, 168
density, 143
De Quincey, T., 147, 152
Dickens, Charles, 78
directness, 111, 152
Dobrée, Bonamy, 71 n
Dobrée, Valentine, 32
Doctor, The, 129–31
Doctrine and Discipline of Divorce, The, 90
Dollard, John, 11
dominant idea, 171
Donne, John, 148, 152, 186
Dostoevsky, 78
Doughty, C. M., 7, 34, 39, 47
drama, 79
Dream of John Ball, The, 133

Drummond, William, 175
Dryden, John, 104, 185–6, 192–4
duration, 143

ease, 45, 166
Ecclesiastical Polity, 45, 75
economy of expression, 97, 109, 111, 143
Egoist, The, 165
egotism, 170
Egotism in German Philosophy, 29
elegance, 167–9
Eliot, George, 78
Eliot, T. S., 88, 184–5
eloquence, 167–79, 183
Emerson, R. W., 50, 67, 72
emotion, 143, 145–7, 152–3, 160, 180
emotional bias, 90
empathy, 155
end, 72
English Farmhouse, An, 98, 209
English Traits, 72
enthusiasm, 173
epic spirit, 98
epithets, 15–22; appropriate, 19;
    presumptuous, 16; unnecessary, 16–17
Erewhon, 133
essay, 66–74
euphony, 7
exposition, 26, 87–96
expression, 87
expressionism, 158–66
expressiveness, 3
extraversion, 85, 125

fable, 107
Fable of the Bees, The, 37
fairy tale, 127
false dramaticism, 34
false eloquence, 172–3
fancy, 125–35, 137
fantasy, 125–35
Faulkner, Wm., 112, 155–6, 195, 202–5
feeling, 85, 125
Fenollosa, Ernest, 22, 23 n, 32 n, 35
fiction, 77–9, 109, 112
Fielding, Henry, 78, 108
Finer, Grain, The, 73
Finnigan's Wake, 135
flatness, 13
Flaubert, G., 78
folk tale, 127
Foote, Samuel, 135 n
foreign idioms, 10, 49
formality, 193
Fowler, H. W., xiv, 59
Foxe, John, 104
Frazer, Sir James G., 191
Freeman, E. A., 113

gallicism, 10
gestalt, 60, 66
Gibbon, 40, 59, 113, 189, 192, 193
glory, 179

Golden Bough, The, 191
Golden Legend, The, 20, 196
Goldsmith, Oliver, 67–71
Grammar of Science, The, 54
Green Children, The, 127
Green, John Richard, 113
Greene, Graham, 108 n
Grigson, Geoffrey, 98, 195, 209–10
Grote, George, 113
Gulliver's Travels, 24
Gull's Hornbook, The, 168

Hardy, Thomas, 78
Harrison, Jane, 133
Hawthorne, Nathaniel, 112–13
Hazlitt, William, 13–14, 28–9, 41, 136–7
Heat of the Day, The, 207
Henley, Rev. S., 134
Herodotus, 83
hieroglyphical writers, 28
historical method, 91
history, 113
History of the Peninsular War, The, 113
Holy Dying, 6
Hooker, Richard, 45, 75, 182, 186
Hopkins, G. M., 146, 180–1
Hudson, W. H., xiii, 133 n
humours, 161–2, 193
hypallage, 168
hyperbole, 168

ideals, 182
idiom, 107, 112, 160
idiosyncrasy, 158
images, 181
Imaginary Conversations, 47, 150–4
imagination, 125–6, 135–45
immediacy, 153
impersonality 99, 193
impressionism, 145–57
impressions, 97, 145
individuality, 158
interest, xiii–xiv
introversion, 85, 125
Intruder in the Dust, 202
intuition, 85
invention, 136–44
inversion, 39
irony, 168, 169–70
isolation of words, 33

James, Henry, 29 n, 72, 73, 74 n, 77, 166,
    177–9, 184
jargon, 10–11
Jeffrey, Francis, 193
Jespersen, Otto, 5 n, 30, 33
Johnson, Samuel, 10, 24, 40–1, 188, 192
Jonson, Ben, 160–2
Joyce, James, 34, 78, 134, 156
Jung, C. G., 84–6, 125 n

Keightley, T., 127
Kennedy, Bart., 34

kennings, 30–1
Kingsley, Charles, 131
Kipling, Rudyard, 98
Koffka, K., 60

Lamb, Charles, 160
Landor, W. S., 47, 150–4
Langer, S. K., 79 n, 86
Last Days of Shelley and Byron, 116
Latinization, 10
Lawrence, D. H., 64, 140, 162 n
Lawrence, T. E., 195, 205–6
Life of Dr. John Donne, 200
Life of Nelson, 114
logic, 83–4, 87

Macaulay, 52, 72
Magic Garden, The, 8
Mahomet and Sergius, 150, 153–4
Maine, Sir Henry, 90–6
Malory, Sir Thomas, 102–3
Mandeville, Bernard de, 37–8
Mandeville, Sir John, 99–100
manner, 193
Many Inventions, 98
Matter and Motion, 30
Maxwell, J. Clerk, 30
mean subject, 171
mechanical structure, 193
Melville, Herman, 164–5, 195, 198–200
Meredith, George, 78, 165–6
metaphorical overtones, 22
metaphors, 23–32; dead, 16; decorative, 25; illuminative, 25; mixed, 29; run-away, 29
metonymy, 31
'microscopic eye', 98
Milton, John, 62–4, 90, 186
Mirrlees, Hope, 133
Modern Painters, 202
Montaigne, 13 n
Morris, William, 9
Morte d'Arthur, 102–3
Murry, John Middleton, 23

Napier, Sir W., 113
narrative, 26, 97–124
nationalism, 9
New English Dictionary, 3 n, 125
Newman, J. H., 183–4
News from Nowhere, 133
North, Roger, 46
novel, the, 77–9, 107

objectivity, 99, 127, 131–2
O'Faolain, Sean, 12 n, 74 n
Ogden, C. K., 87 n
onomatopœia, 3–6
oratory, 83
organic form, 77
ornateness, 104
Orwell, George, 10, 132, 133
Outcast of the Islands, 196

parable, 107
paragraph, 52–65, 193
paragraphing, rhythmical, 58; witty, 58
parallelism, 40–1
parody, 168
paronomasia, 168
Pater, Walter, 21–2, 159, 183
pathos, 146
pattern, 89, 192
Pearson, Karl, 54
Pepys, Samuel, 104 n
period, 42, 193
periphrase, 30
personality, 158, 182, 193
personification, 31–2
perspective, 143
persuasion, 158–9, 171
pertinacity, 171
phantasy, 125
Philosophy of Rhetoric, 50
Piaget, Jean, 33 n
'poetic' atmosphere, 34
Poetics, 23
poetry and prose, ix-xii, 138–9, 153
polite words, 13
Pound, Ezra, x
predominant passion, 181, 183
prose and poetry, ix-xii, 138–9, 153
psychic functions, 84–5
psychology, 90
punctuation, 45–7
'pure' prose, xii, 193

quaintness, 111 n
Querist, The, xiii

Rasselas, 188
rationalization, 90
reasoning, 87–90, 181–2
Reason in Society, 49–50
Remizov, A. M., 132
Renaissance, 104
Reflections on the Revolution in France, 35–7
Reformation in England, Of, 62–4
respiration, 45–6
Revival of Learning, 104
Reynolds, Sir Joshua, 190, 194
rhetoric, 83–6
rhythm, xi, 45–51, 58–65, 72, 146–7, 152–4, 166, 193
rhythmical notation, 47
Richards, I. A., 87 n
Richardson, Samuel, 78
riddles, 30–1,
rigidity of rhythm, 193
romance of words, 12
romantic, 138
Rousseau, J.-J., 160
Ruskin, John, 195, 202

Sack of Shakings, A, 17
Sacred Theory of the Earth, The, 19

Sacred Wood, The, 88, 92, 184
Sailor Tramp, A, 34
Saintsbury, George, 58–9, 107 n
Santayana, George, 29–30, 49–50
sardonic, 170
scientific prose, 26, 54
Sea and the Jungle, The, 60
Second World War, 172
Selborne, The Natural History of, 4
selection, 152
self-expression, 159
sensation, 85, 145, 146–7, 153
sensibility, 6, 159, 183, 185
sentence, 33–51; simple and complex, 35;
  compound, 38–9
sentimentality, 160
Sentimental Journey, A, 57–8
'serious' books, 54
Seven Pillars of Wisdom, 205
Sewell, Elizabeth, xi n
Shaftesbury, 1st Earl of, 115–16
Shakespeare, 35
shape, 60–1, 73–4
Shaw, G. B., xiii
short story, 73
simile, 25, 32
simple clause, 38
simplicity, 146
simulation, 5
sincerity, 90, 154, 171, 175
sing-song, 153
Siris, xiii
Sitwell, Sacheverell, 195, 208–10
skeleton structure, 75–6
Small Boy and Others, A, 177–9
Smith, Logan Pearsall, 5, 12 n
Smollett, Tobias, 78, 107
solidity, 54, 143
sophistication, 132, 133, 135
Sound and the Fury, The, 155–6
Southern Baroque Art, 208
Southey, Robert, xiii, 113–14, 128–31
Spectator, The, 187–8
speed, 97, 108–9, 111, 114
Spinoza, 75
Spirit of Patriotism, The, 44, 167
sprung rhythm, 146
Steele, Sir R., 67
Stendhal, 78
Sterne, Laurence, xiii, 57–8, 108, 163–4,
  166–8
Stevenson, R. L., 74 n, 160, 193
Stratton-Porter, Gene, 8
structure, 45, 73, 147, 153
style, xii, 89, 159, 183–4
suggestiveness, 5
Summa Theologica, 75
Sundering Flood, The, 9
surprise, 73
Swift, Jonathan, xiii, 24–6, 30, 44, 106–7,
  112, 169–70, 183, 193
symbols, 87
synecdoche, 31

taste, 183, 185
Taylor, Jeremy, 6, 182, 186
Taylor, John, 173
Thackerary, W. M., 78
thinking, 85
Thousand and One Nights, The, 134, 135
Tillotson, John, 185
Time Machine, The, 133
Times, The, 173–4
timidity of phrasing, 193
Tomlinson, H. M., 60
Tractatus Logico-Philosophicus, 56
tradition, 166, 184–92
Traherne, Thomas, 149, 153
tranquillity, 147
transformation, x
transitions, 50
transitive verbs, 35
travel, 113, 117
Trelawny, E. J., 116
Tristram Shandy, 163–4
Trollope, Anthony, 78
Twilight in Italy, 64–5
types, psychological, 84–5

Ulysses, 34, 134–5, 156
unctuousness, 174
unity, 180-94
unity of approach, 76
unity of argument, 54
Urn Burial, 60
Utopia, 133
utopias, 133

Vanzetti, 146, 152, 153, 183
Vathek, 134
Vauvenargues, 175 n
Vivante, Leone, x n, 12 n

Walton, Izaak, 73, 195, 200–1
Wardour Street English, 9
Water Babies, The, 131
Wavell, A. P., 57 n
Wells, H. G., 133
White, Gilbert, 4
Whitehead, A. N., 87 n
White Peacock, The, 140–3
Wimsatt, W. K., xvi, 40–1, 59
Wings of the Dove, The, 77
wit 167–71
Wittgenstein, L., 56
wonder, 134
Woolf, Virginia, 155
words, xi, 3–14
  „   quality of, 3
Wordsworth, William, 42, 147
World Crisis, The, 171–2
Wuthering Heights, 72, 111
Wycliffe, John, 100

Your Cuckoo Sings by Kind, 32